Credit and Faith

Credit and Faith

Philip Goodchild

ROWMAN &
LITTLEFIELD
INTERNATIONAL

London • New York

Published by Rowman & Littlefield International, Ltd.
6 Tinworth Street, London SE11 5AL
www.rowmaninternational.com

Rowman & Littlefield International, Ltd. is an affiliate of
Rowman & Littlefield
4501 Forbes Boulevard, Suite 200, Lanham, Maryland 20706, USA
With additional offices in Boulder, New York, Toronto (Canada), and London (UK)
www.rowman.com

British Library Cataloguing in Publication Information
A catalogue record for this book is available from the British Library

ISBN: HB 978-1-78661-423-0
ISBN: PB 978-1-78661-424-7

Library of Congress Cataloging-in-Publication Data Available

ISBN 9781786614230 (cloth : alk. paper)
ISBN 9781786614247 (paper : alk. paper)
ISBN 9781786614254 (electronic)

The paper used in this publication meets the minimum requirements of American National
Standard for Information Sciences Permanence of Paper for Printed Library Materials,
ANSI/NISO Z39.48-1992.

A human being has roots by virtue of his real, active and natural participation in the life of a community which preserves in living shape certain particular treasures of the past and certain particular expectations for the future.

—Simone Weil, *The Need for Roots*

Contents

Preface

A Lost Coin in Lieu of a Methodology

> Or what woman having ten silver coins, if she loses one of them, does not light a lamp, sweep the house, and search carefully until she finds it? When she has found it, she calls together her friends and neighbors, saying, 'Rejoice with me, for I have found the coin that I had lost'. (Luke 15.8–9)

Human understanding of life is deeply fragmented. It invariably evokes the feeling that if only we could add one last insight to our existing stock then we might possess an understanding of the whole. To think is to go in search of that final coin, the one that remains lost.

This is a book of lost coins. It is composed of a series of shorter or longer nuggets, each signifying something of value. Some of these have been borrowed, and yet, in the process, are lost to their owners: each nugget is turned to offer a different meaning from the one first received. Even so, it is hard to discern what is on offer here. One might ask, 'What is the point? What is at stake? What is the substance of this discussion'? And after nine attempts to come to the point, what matters still seems to elude capture. This is hardly surprising: what matters in any discussion is the bearing it has on other discussions. And unlike coins, the full value cannot be paid all at once.

We do not know what this woman's coins were for, and why the tenth was so necessary to complete the sum. Perhaps the coins had been set aside to pay wages or rent, to pay tithes or tax, to lend to someone in need, or to cancel out a set of debts. Perhaps the coins had been left with her for safe-keeping on trust. We do not know how this tenth coin, once passed on to another, will be used next, and where it will circulate thereafter; we do not know what difference its discovery would make to a wider economy, or what subsequent misfortunes may result from its loss. But when it comes to coins, it is this subsequent usage that matters far beyond collection in a group of ten. The point always lies elsewhere.

Each of the nuggets that compose this trilogy, if contracted to a single point or hypothesis, would itself take an entire book to establish – and then would still be subject to debate. In some cases, these books have already been written; in some cases, I have read them; in others, these books are yet to be written. Why borrow so much from others, rather than setting out straightforwardly and directly my own thought? Let me take a cue, if not a method, from the personalist philosopher John Macmurray:

> [T]here are few things which I can desire to do, and none which are of person-
> al significance, which do not depend upon the active co-operation of others.
> We need one another to be ourselves. This complete and unlimited dependence
> of each of us upon the others is the central and crucial fact of personal exis-
> tence. Individual independence is an illusion; and the independent individual,
> the isolated self, is a nonentity. In ourselves we are nothing; and when we turn
> our eyes inward in search of ourselves we find a vacuum. [1]

Or to take a further cue from the Buddhist philosopher Nagarjuna, any points I might make on their own are empty, like the city of celestial musicians, illusions, mirages, nets of hair, foams, bubbles, phantoms, dreams and wheels of firebrand. [2] One cannot hear the sound of one hand clapping; one cannot engage in meaningful conversation with a proposition. My concern is not to establish the points but to seek their wider significance. It is not the individual purchase of truth but the wider economy of value that is at issue here. I have sought to express real thinking as it is, in all its partiality and inconclusiveness, rather than pretending to construct a persuasive argument. Each discussion is kept brief – the aim is less to be convincing than to discern what might be at stake if the value of such coins were to be trusted and spent.

Yet if one looks more closely, one will see that my stock in trade is neither lost coins nor unfounded propositions but shifts in perspective. Each nugget is just long enough to enact a shift. Like Spinoza, I am a lens grinder; or perhaps each lens, whether drawn from scripture, history, philosophy, fiction or finance, is simply a parable – it sheds light on something else. Like a forest whose roots entangle and communicate beneath the soil, the thoughts represented here are surface effects of a deeper entanglement. The aim has been to practise a synthetic and redemptive philosophy, as proposed (if not practised) by Friedrich Nietzsche's character Zarathustra: 'I walk among men as among fragments of the future, that future which I scan. And it is all my art and aim, to compose into one and bring together what is fragment and riddle and dreadful chance'. [3] Perhaps this task is better exemplified by con-temporary British stand-up comedy: digression follows after digression, yet the punchline consists in an unexpected repetition of a phrase from a previ-

ous wayward digression, now with a new sense – as though one had redis-
covered a coin that had been lost. Or to shift the analogy once more, it is like
an old, slow computer that generates a pixelated image point by point, in an
apparently random order – perhaps it distributes points in order of colour
rather than in order of location. Only when the picture is close to completion
can one discern the image of the face. The subject matter of this trilogy is the
whole, the image, the face. Each coin, nugget or lens only has value to the
extent to which it contributes to the whole. And alas, the face cannot be
expressed in a single point. It is only when one can see the whole face that
one can read the meaning of this trilogy, and yet the meaning is present
throughout. It is only when one has already read the three volumes that one
can start again and see the links to the whole, bringing the image at last into
focus. And finally, one might find that instead of seeing the face, one is seen
by it. The face is a whole perspective, a way of seeing and living. It is not my
face; it is, I hope, the face of an angel, one who sees clearly where I can
barely see at all.

Introduction

The modern world has been characterised by a series of crises where the solutions to each one condition the inevitability of the next.[1] In response, philosophy has sought solutions either in what is eternally stable and unchanging or else in the ideals of universal emancipation. Where wonder at the order of life gave rise to a philosophy grounded in metaphysics, resistance to oppressive order gave rise to a philosophy grounded in liberty. In turn, disordered liberty gives rise to crisis. Perhaps philosophy has been slow to respond to a deepening sense of crisis: for crisis may give birth to a philosophy grounded in trust, credit and faith. In times of crisis, nothing is more needful than appropriate trust. Philosophy is concerned with trust, for truth is that which is to be trusted; likewise, the source of all human cooperation and wealth creation is trust. To develop such a philosophy, it is helpful to engage with economic and religious life.

The determining idea to be explored in this book is that problems of economic credit and religious faith meet and are indeed two sides of the same human experience. While such a hypothesis is not entirely new,[2] it does challenge the sharp distinction between the secular and the religious that has developed in the modern world.[3] The production and distribution of goods and services is a matter of human subjectivity in the form of preferences, commitments and credit, and so is regulated in practice by a comprehensive vision of life, including a vision of justice – an implicit theology. Human interiority, in turn, is manifested accurately not in statements of belief but in key decisions about the allocation of scarce time, commitments and resources, including whom we trust, with whom we enter into contractual relations, what we make and what we do – an implicit economy. Economics and theology, perhaps misguided and powerless without each other, may be conceived in and through each other. Theology gives grounds for trust, for

1

values, for commitments, for justice and for allocation, and so informs economic decisions in practice, whether one is aware of one's implicit theology
or not. Economics gives a theory of how the world works, of consequences,
of the responses of others, and so informs actual judgements of trust and
value, whether one recognizes this role or not. Theology needs the dose of
present reality provided by economics to gain pertinence and prevent thought
and desire from becoming lost in the short-circuit of imagination of an ideal
past or future, while economics needs the orientation provided by theology to
prevent the short-circuiting of the deeper meaning of life by superficial corre-
lations in the present. There is an economy to be disclosed within theology,
and a theology to be disclosed within economy.[4]

The common domain of economics and theology is the ordering and
orientation of trust, whether in the form of credit – taking the value, significance, response and reliability of things for granted – or in the form of faith,
trusting in the good intentions of others. In contemporary economic life, trust
and obligation are ordered around contract and debt. This is a matter of
shaping life by a future orientation: life is oriented towards finite and specific
acts of contractual fulfilment and debt settlement. As Søren Kierkegaard
once remarked, while life can only be understood backwards, it has to be
lived forwards.[5] This future orientation is simply a matter of offering credit
or faith – one lives by trusting, venturing and experimenting, spending oneself for what will come after. One may question how far the underlying
thought frameworks of mainstream economics and theology are capable of
addressing this future orientation. Theology opens up the possibility of a
living relation to the past: it saves the mind from complete conditioning by
the present age, enabling it to receive the legacy of the wisest of those who
have gone before. Reinterpretation and reappropriation of this legacy are the
acts that make a tradition live; yet the structure upon which interpretation
takes hold of the past is typically offered by a framing of thought by either
metaphysics, history or law. Economics, by contrast, is a social science that
seeks a living engagement with the present. Assessing, quantifying and modelling present evidence offers a framework for the construction of empirical
knowledge. Where theology endeavours to isolate what is good, economics
endeavours to isolate what is necessary. Where theology endeavours to orient
the soul towards the good, economics endeavours to orient decisions in accordance with the outcome of the responses of others. Dangers arise when
one simply asserts a reconciliation of the good and the necessary: whether by
suggesting that a particular theological understanding is necessary, and so
exposing it in all its historical contingency, or whether by suggesting that a
particular economic principle is good or brings welfare to all, so exposing all
the harm that is done in endeavouring to realise such a principle. There
appears to be a separation between the good and the necessary. Reconcilia-

tion, if it is to be achieved at all, may only come in the future: it is an object of credit and faith.

A key focus of this book, then, is the development of an orientation and framework for thinking that is adequate for this future orientation. As such, this is essentially a work of philosophy – an experimental and synthetic philosophy, irreducible to the analytic and critical philosophies which are dominant today.[6] It takes theological and economic discussions as materials through which to think things through. What is at stake is investment in and attention to an entire field, task and discipline in philosophy which has hitherto been largely neglected or overlooked. This new thinking, as Franz Rosenzweig indicated, 'needs another person and takes time seriously'.[7] Now, distinctions between the corporeal and the spiritual, the theoretical and the practical, or the experiential and the obligatory have structured Western thought since its inception. Even if confusions and contradictions are evaded by keeping these realms strictly separate, their very separation, as, for example, science and morality, points towards a future reunification where thought is applied to produce an outcome in experience. For life is at once both corporeal and spiritual. According to a purely instrumental paradigm of reason, science provides the means while morality provides the ends. Immanuel Kant adopted this distinction between means and ends for both his account of practical reason and his philosophy of religion, treating the fundamental religious delusion as a confusion between means and ends.[8] At the same time, however, Kant attributed the faith required to act morally in the hope that it would produce happiness in experience to the religion that supports morality.[9] Kant therefore pointed towards a distinctive field of *religious reason*, separate from theoretical and practical reason yet ensuring their reunification.[10] To think forwards, in the hope of reconciling the necessary with the good, is to think in terms of credit and faith; one may think of this as an art of living. Yet Kant immediately obscured this field again by means of his critique of judgement: he understood philosophy of religion in terms of purposiveness, the adaptation of means and ends. In such modern thought, the paradigm of orientation towards the future is understood primarily in terms of means and ends. This shorthand offers a distortion of temporal conduct since the imagined future, when it eventually arrives, is never an end – at the very least, time continues onwards, and the actual version of the imagined future event has its own past and future, its own relations to other beings, and its own problems to be solved. The philosophy of religion, which can be understood as a philosophy of credit and faith, is entirely falsified when reduced to the instrumental paradigm of means and ends.[11]

The task for this inquiry is to explore the conceptions, transformations and orientations of thinking that might structure a renewed philosophy of religion. It is less a matter of defining and mastering credit and faith, as though using words as a means to an end, than a matter of thinking that offers credit and expresses faith. As such, it is an inquiry which has to discover its concepts and principles as it proceeds. Nevertheless, since this inquiry is neither geared towards knowledge, as an instance of theoretical reason, nor geared towards action, as an instance of practical reason, nor geared towards judgement, as an instance of aesthetic or speculative reason, its gearing may be somewhat unfamiliar to modern readers. It may therefore be helpful to offer some preliminary orientation to guide readers' expectations, a few points to which to return when inevitable misunderstandings occur. For if what follows appears more like a workbook than a polished presentation of a thesis, more like a set of unfinished notes and experiments, this is not only because life and thought do not have any neat terminus apart from the accidental occurrence of death, but also because such raw thought is more thought-provoking: by offering less to be asserted or denied, it offers more to think through and participate in. As Jean-Jacques Rousseau once put it, 'The honest man is an athlete, who loves to wrestle stark naked; he scorns all those vile trappings, which prevent the exertion of his strength, and were, for the most part, invented only to conceal some deformity'.[12] Deformities may abound: that my readers may come to trust my thoughts is a far less creditable goal than that my readers may come to trust living thoughts of their own.

1. A philosophy of credit and faith does not become trustworthy itself by making claims about knowledge or about moral obligations; often these prove to be partial. Instead, it is necessary to write from the perspective of being-in-the-world: from a finite and partial perspective, situated before other persons by whom one is affected and whom one seeks to affect in turn. Likewise, one is situated in a physical environment, enabled by a physiology within the context of determinate institutions, networks, social obligations, history, language, grammar and previous allocations of trust, both known and unknown. Far from pointing towards a transcendent or universal perspective as a condition for trust, acceptance of finitude and partiality is a first condition for being sufficiently grounded in concrete reality for others to risk their weight, like stepping onto deep ice on a frozen lake instead of seeking to navigate across it merely by the orientation of the stars. A temporary provocation or resting place for thought is the best service to be offered.

2. Another condition for trustworthiness is that thought must become flesh and blood: one can only become trustworthy if one takes a risk by appropriating and embodying one's discoveries in one's own way of thinking. Instead of recommending one's insights for inclusion in the library of finally established truth, as though all our endeavours were directed towards a future civilisation based on perfect knowl-

edge, it is far less significant to point out one's insights than it is to live from them, and think differently in and through them, producing irreversible changes.

3. The task has been helpfully characterised by Hannah Arendt:

> What I propose in the following is a reconsideration of the human condition from the vantage point of our newest experiences and most recent fears. This, obviously, is a matter of thought, and thoughtlessness – the heedless recklessness or hopeless confusion or complacent repetition of 'truths' which have become trivial and empty – seems to me among the outstanding characteristics of our time. What I propose, therefore, is very simple: it is nothing more than to think what we are doing.[13]

Such thoughtfulness is contrasted with the 'thoughtlessness' which may not lack knowledge or moral precepts, but, even so, has little comprehension of its being-in-the-world. In this regard, by way of contrast, it is helpful to note Arendt's account of thoughtless ideology insofar as it generated totalitarian regimes:

> Ideologies are never concerned with the miracle of being. They are historical, concerned with becoming and perishing, with the rise of fall of cultures, even if they try to explain history by some 'law of nature'. The word 'race' in racism does not signify any genuine curiosity about the human races as a field for scientific explanation, but is the 'idea' by which the movement of history is explained as one consistent process. . . . Ideologies always assume that one idea is sufficient to explain everything in the development from the premise, and that no experience can teach anything because everything is comprehended in this consistent process of logical deduction. The danger in exchanging the necessary insecurity of philosophical thought for the total explanation of an ideology and its worldview is not even so much the risk of falling for some usually vulgar, always uncritical assumption as of exchanging the freedom inherent in man's capacity to think for the strait jacket of logic with which man can force himself almost as violently as he is forced by some outside power.[14]

Thinking, on this account, is a matter of distrusting explanations for the contingencies of human history – and not merely those explanations grounded on those pseudo-sciences of race, class conflict, or competitive selection which became dominant political ideologies in the twentieth century, but also much of what passes for explanation in contemporary economics, theology and philosophy. Reality itself arises from a conjunction of heterogeneous causes rather than the outworking of a few fundamental principles. Thoughtfulness draws attention to dimensions of experience which are easily overlooked.

4. Since thinking involves speech, and being expresses itself in appearance, it belongs, contra Arendt, within what she terms the political world. Instead of the contemplation of eternal truth, thinking becomes a temporal event undertaken before others and for the sake of others.[15] It is a unique initiative within a network of already existing relationships: unlike thoughtless repetition, it makes a difference. In this respect, every act of thinking is unique in its relation to a plurality of persons. Where Arendt saw the power to promise and forgive as the human capacities which could maintain the world of distinctively personal relationships against their own tendencies to decay, the initiative of thinking itself may be considered as a forging of relationship, manifest in acts of creation, redemption and judgement.

5. The material appropriated for consideration here is neither a matter of theories, propositions or values, but the events of thinking offered by others.[16] The 'unit' of thought – in the sense of that upon which one temporarily focuses attention – is an episode of thinking embodied in a quotation or narrative. The task is not to agree or disagree with any opinion which is proposed, but to appropriate the ideas of others, to participate in the elaboration of meaning and significance which such episodes make possible, and to transform their significance (which in effect offers a new episode of thought) by means of repeating such thoughts within new contexts and juxtapositions. A series of inversions, suspensions, repetitions and conjunctions transform one episode into another with a quite different significance: these new episodes are expressed once more in discussions and narratives.

6. The criterion for selection of any episode included here is its capacity to offer the possibility for 'thinking otherwise'. The opinions and arguments of those with whom I agree have often been edited out; there is no aspiration here to produce a rounded perspective. Nevertheless, difference from existing presuppositions and practices of thought or mere originality should not be taken as criteria of value. The greatest thinkers are not the most outlandish, those who stand out most from the crowd, but those who have the most to offer. To write something unheard of by any of those who have written before, yet a commonplace to those who follow after, may be one criterion of success. Yet the greatest thinkers of all are those who are most to be trusted – they restore thinking to being, bring to light what matters, direct attention to what needs to be counted and offer an art of living which distributes credit and attracts faith. Far from attracting public acclamation, they vanish as forgotten mediators between thought and reality. In this respect, no one can possibly assess the significance of such work: it vanishes before their very eyes. Yet work of any significance can only be generated by living out the virtues of faith, hope and love.

In this project, a fresh examination of theology, as a discipline that seeks meaning in terms of intention, and economics, as a discipline that seeks necessity in terms of social causation, may extract from each a dimension in interaction with the other. Following Rosenzweig, 'Theological problems must be translated into human terms, and human problems brought into the pale of theology'.[17] When theology becomes a discourse on how to manage the household of thought, and economics becomes a discourse that evokes trust in institutions, then their concerns and interactions will reveal a more complex relation between thinking and being than is found in either theoretical or practical reasoning alone. The philosophy of credit and faith offers fresh orientation and substance to the philosophy of religion, an understanding which may in turn enrich economic, political and religious life.

The core conceptual framework to be established and utilised in what follows can be stated most concisely thus:

a. That *goods of appropriation*, things that can be mine only if they are not yours (the object of economics; what Locke included under property as the basis for rights), may be distinguished from *goods of participation*, things that can only be mine if they are also yours (the object of a tradition of ethical and political thought deriving from Aristotle), and further distinguished from *goods of offering*, things that can only be mine if I offer them in turn (such as time, attention and care, a loose development of existential realities described by Heidegger). Credit and faith are best understood in terms of the latter and distinguished from the former two.

b. That an economic style of thinking, concerned with managing attention and evaluation, may proceed through three operations of thought which are rooted in the Christian theological virtues:

- A *suspension* of established principles of judgement in expectation that the final grounds of judgement are not yet accessible to the human mind (linked to hope);
- An *inversion* of priorities, so that what starts to appear as of defining importance is found among that which had formerly been set aside as of little value (linked to faith);
- A *synthesis* of perspectives as a method of creation and repetition, such that one concern is viewed in the light of another, while that other is viewed in the light of the first (linked to love).

BRIEF OUTLINE OF THE THREE VOLUMES

All religions involve an ordering of time and attention, care and evaluation, and trust and cooperation. As such, religions have throughout history offered an unspoken bond which makes collective life possible. In the contemporary world, much of this ordering role is now enacted in and through economic life. Beyond the dimension of the market, concerned with the exchange and distribution of goods and services which may be paid for and appropriated, and beyond the dimension of democratic capitalism as a political system, concerned with participation in collective life through establishing and ensuring rights and laws, there is also a further dimension to economic life: credit and debt. Credit and debt are the way in which time and attention, care and evaluation, and trust and cooperation are ordered – most successfully, when they are taken for granted. Likewise, religious faith enacts such ordering of the same dimension of human existence when it enables much to be taken for granted. In both cases, taking matters for granted can be understood as establishing a 'mindset', a way of thinking embodied in a mode of existence. In spite of their apparently different areas of concern, often conceived as the respective needs of body and soul, economic credit and religious faith have frequently collided insofar as they involve different orderings of the same dimension of life.

In this volume, an exploration of the 'economic' dimension of Christianity is proposed: it concerns the distribution of time and attention, care and evaluation, and trust and cooperation. This dimension of the religion, while intimately connected to elaborations of doctrine and history, metaphysics and law, liturgy and community, experience and spiritual practice, is not entirely brought to light in theological studies around such headings. Moreover, our exploration is neither theoretical, exploring either the varieties or true essence of the Christian mindset, nor practical, exploring what ought to be a Christian mindset. For Christianity also consists in an ascesis – a distinctive way of transforming mindsets. Of course, there are many varieties of Christianity, and what has been chosen for our focus is determined in part by the situatedness of the author, in part because of the origins of Christianity in borrowing notions from economic life, and in part because of the long cohabitation of Anglican Christianity with a form of economic life based on distinctive property ownership which was to expand out of England to become a globalising economic system. Nevertheless, our focus is not the history of this particular relation of religion and economy, nor its role in constituting the lineaments of a global order, but on a certain distinctively Christian ascesis as a way of continually transforming mindsets. The philosophy of credit and faith can start from a philosophical appropriation of a certain heritage of Christianity.

In Part I: Gospel and Economy: Theological Roots, the inquiry starts with the problem that much of the initial presentation of Christian teaching was articulated in terms of economic life yet offers little guidance for household management nor little explicit statement of theological doctrine. Its main objective is to draw on Synoptic, Pauline and Johannine writings to develop the core conceptual framework summarised above.

In Part II: Value and Debt: Philosophical Roots, the inquiry can then turn to an explicit formulation of its philosophical task interpreted within this core conceptual framework. The task for philosophical thinking is outlined in a double formulation: (1) to discover the way of thinking or truth by which thinking may conform to being; (2) to redeem thinking by removing the 'log in the eye', now understood in terms of debt, as that which constrains the adoption of perspectives. It articulates a philosophy of attention and evaluation, drawn from Jules Lagneau and Simone Weil, as a synthesis of idealism and materialism and as a solution to the Kantian problem of freedom and necessity. Once the three dimensions of existence are understood in terms of appropriation, participation and offering, then key errors arise when these are confused. Matters should be understood according to their appropriate categories. Estrangement can be understood as a confusion of objects of appropriation and participation (articulated in terms of a critical reading of the early Marx). Sacrifice can be understood as a confusion of goods of offering and goods of appropriation (articulated in terms of a critical reading of Nietzsche's genealogy of promise and debt). Such errors, partially identified by Marx and Nietzsche, have crucial significance for how one thinks about the relation between religious and economic life.

In Part III: Credit and Creation: Economic Roots, the task is to chart the passage of credit from its initial expression as trust within interpersonal relations, such as those of the household formalised by Christian teaching, to impersonal structures and dynamics which extend investment beyond the household. Through capital, banking and money, credit has expanded to become the impersonal institutional basis of a potentially global economic order. The creative power of investing with value (credit), illustrated in terms of the kenotic Anglican theology of W. H. Vanstone, is handed over to be conceived purely in terms of debt in economic life. Engaging in passing with medieval debates about usury, the discussion charts the emergence of early theories of capital and banking through a consideration of credit, drawing on some neglected historical figures. It culminates in an exploration of how the Financial Revolution in England was able to conceal the credit economy which was its foundation and foster the pursuit of self-interest as the apparent means to the common good. The stage is then set for the modern world to imagine the economy in independence of theology. Nevertheless, the very basis of modern economic life is an ordering of credit, one which operates by concealing its inherently theological structure.

Given these preparations, the Conclusion endeavours to renarrate the principal themes of the book in a new light: the reframing of philosophy of religion, the elaboration of a Christian mindset and the emergence of a capitalist machine.

The second volume, *Economic Theology*, can then turn to the neglected theological constitution of the current economic era. Trust, as the basis for human cooperation, has not been replaced; it has simply been ordered and concealed by the habits of thinking and financial practices which it makes possible. When economic life is misrecognised as 'free market capitalism' rather than as a distinctive ordering of the creative power of investing value (based around credit and debt), there is a divorce between thinking and being. While the focus of the volume is a critical account of contemporary economic life and thought, exploring its own incoherence and unsustainability, this choice is again a matter of the historical situatedness of the author. The underlying agenda is philosophical: it is about how a mindset establishes and ossifies itself, attracting credit, in and through the very crises and contingencies it provokes in its failure to conform thinking to being. The effects of grounding economic theory and practice by thinking in terms of money and markets will be explored in the form of exploitation, disequilibrium economics, and attempts at rectification through finance. Within this mindset, thinking the miracle of being is displaced in favour of a thoughtless appropriation, substitution and anticipation.

The third volume, *Metaphysics of Trust*, has the task of finding a more accurate way of conforming thinking to being within the framework of appropriation, participation and offering that had previously been set out in this volume. The aim is to develop a way of ordering credit and faith which is profoundly different from those achieved through money, banking and finance. If one of the roots of the dominant mindset is a conception and practice of appropriation as enclosure, then a rethinking of appropriation in terms of household life may enable a more faithful way of receiving what has been offered to us by the past, by others and by the environment. If one of the roots of the dominant mindset is a conception and practice of participation in terms of sovereign political power, then a rethinking of political participation in terms of trust in justice may enable a more effective collaboration in collective life. If one of the roots of the dominant mindset is a conception of offering in terms of capital and credit as automatic machines producing their own self-fulfiling outcomes, then a rethinking of credit in terms of the necessity of grace may offer some escape from the self-reinforcing ossification of dominant mindsets. This third volume aims to deepen a rather tentative and speculative Christian philosophy – one which, though highly distinctive, offers itself, through the vanishing of its own conscious identity, for appropriation by others of any religious faith or none.

I

Gospel and Economy:
Theological Roots

Chapter One

Through the Eye of a Needle

Again I tell you, it is easier for a camel to go through the eye of a needle than
for someone who is rich to enter the kingdom of God. (Matt. 19.24)

For the largest animal to pass through the smallest aperture is a physical
exemplification of a contradiction: no two solid objects can be at the same
place at the same time. The law of noncontradiction applies whether one
considers solid objects or discretely defined facts. It sets limits to what can be
thought and achieved. As for the salvation of the rich, we are informed that it
is a matter of faith, 'For mortals it is impossible, but for God all things are
possible' (Matt. 19.26). The question of salvation does not concern static,
solid objects nor discrete facts: it concerns transformation. For a rich man to
enter the kingdom of God may require some transformation, whether in
regard to property, becoming poor, or in regards to perspective, becoming
humble in spirit. Perhaps a transformed perspective reveals the rich man to
be already poor, or perhaps some spiritual transformation is required which is
beyond the power of mere mortals. In any case, words of salvation are words
of transformation, not assertions about temporal or eternal facts. A word that
enacts creation, redemption or judgement has a different logic from a word
that asserts what is the case: it may be less a matter of knowledge or action
than of faith directed by attention and evaluation. Likewise, a word which
produces the reality it presupposes, as in rituals, promises, property rights,
debts, money, markets and derivatives, also has a distinctive logic. The
wealth of the rich man is a product of words, words that are given credit. The
task before us is to discern something of these logics as they govern credit
and faith. In both theology and economics, then, facts and contradictions
offer weak grounds for trust. Perhaps one might extend a measure of trust to
Martin Heidegger's claim: 'Thinking does not begin until we have come to

know that the reason that has been extolled for centuries is the most stubborn adversary of thinking'.[1]

Theology may be concerned with the power of such words of transformation. The task is not merely to bear witness to transformations from the perspective of a third party. Only when words that create, redeem and judge have been spoken has theology taken place. It is necessary to utter such words in order to receive them: knowing God is a matter of being merciful as the Heavenly Father is merciful and being forgiven debts as one forgives the debts of others. For perhaps a true theology does not speak a word about God but speaks divine words. And it may be easier for a camel to pass through the eye of a needle than for a philosopher to speak such transformative words.

What, then, needs to be transformed? Let us lend a little credit to the notion that it is necessary to start thinking economically to receive any return. It is remarkable that the first presentation of the Christian gospel is economic, expressed largely in terms drawn from household or estate management.[2] Jesus spoke of the management of inheritances, estates, vineyards, fields, labourers, seed, sheep, lamps, coins, debts and slaves.[3] The gospel narratives record a series of meals, while Jesus himself proffered stories of lavish banquets. Jesus's teachings are concerned with needs, offerings, forgiveness and care. It is equally remarkable that one gains little sense of how to manage a household from these parables and principles.[4] Hence one might suppose that their true subject matter is theology rather than economics. Yet it is most remarkable that these economic analogies so often fail to express a credible theology – a key case will be considered directly. In sum, Jesus's economic teaching creates an impasse in respect of both economic practices and theological truths. A reader can only proceed here through a transformation of understanding. Such a transformation can come by experimenting in and with trust.

Let us take, as an example, the parable offered to explain why Peter should forgive his brother seventy-seven times: the parable of the unmerciful servant. It is a parable about debt collection, slavery, prison and torture, describing a king far removed in character from the holy God of prophetic vision, the sacred God of temple sacrifice, the redeeming God of Exodus, the just God of Deuteronomy, the intimate God of the Psalms, the gentle Father of Jesus's other teaching, and the transcendent thought of Plato and Aristotle. Instead, the material is drawn from the more familiar and worldly setting of an oppressive, conquering power who extorts tribute. For the character of such masters we need only turn to the words of a debtor in the parable of the talents: 'Master, I knew that you were a harsh man, reaping where you do not sow, and gathering where you do not scatter seed; so I was afraid' (Matt. 25.24–25) – a good description of usury as well as extortion. Such a lord does not proceed through careful estate management but merely pronounces words – words which create debts of tribute, which forgive debts, and which authorise punishment.

Our parable runs thus:

> For this reason the kingdom of heaven may be compared to a king who wished to settle accounts with his slaves. When he began the reckoning, one who owed him ten thousand talents was brought to him, and as he could not pay, his lord ordered him to be sold, together with his wife and children and all his possessions, and payment to be made. So the slave fell on his knees before him, saying, 'Have patience with me, and I will pay you everything'. And out of pity for him, the lord of that slave released him and forgave him the debt. But that same slave, as he went out, came upon one of his fellow slaves who owed him one hundred denarii; and seizing him by the throat, he said, 'Pay what you owe'. Then his fellow slave fell down and pleaded with him, 'Have patience with me, and I will pay you'. But he refused; then he went and threw him into prison until he would pay the debt. When his fellow slaves saw what had happened, they were greatly distressed, and they went and reported to their lord all that had taken place. Then his lord summoned him and said to him, 'You wicked slave! I forgave you all that debt because you pleaded with me. Should you not have had mercy on your fellow slave, as I had mercy on you'? And in anger his lord handed him over to be tortured until he would pay his entire debt. So my heavenly Father will also do to every one of you, if you do not forgive your brother or sister from your heart. (Matt. 18.23–35)

Whatever the sincerity of the first servant's pleading, the master grants him credit. Confusion arises when the servant seeks to make true his own words, fulfilling his promise to repay the debt by ensuring his income from others, rather than living out of the credit granted by his master's words. The servant fails to grasp how the situation has been transformed; he lacks faith in his own forgiveness. What principles can be extracted here? The first servant, whose debt amounts to the produce of a large estate or small region, simply repeats in relation to his own debtor the initial action threatened by the king to him; after all, he will only be in a position to pay future tributes and debts if he is successful in collecting his own. By contrast, it would seem that the king's act of mercy shows a greater concern for absolute submission and gratitude from his subjects than material income. Yet the servant confirms his absolute submission by becoming more rigorous in his own debt collection. The surprising twist in the narrative comes when the first servant is informed, rather too late, that he should have imitated his master in respect of mercy, not cruelty; his fate, as a result, is to be subjected to more severe cruelty.

The analogy fails because this changeable king offers a very poor model for God. First the king seeks to settle accounts, as though this is an exchange relation between equals, and yet the amount demanded is impossible. Then the king threatens to recover part of his losses by selling the servant, wife and

children into slavery, before forgiving the debt so as to intensify the obligation felt by the servant. Yet any credit granted to the servant is quickly
withdrawn, for at the end, the debt is reinstated, with repayment sought
through torture – which, although it might move such associates as the servant has to endeavour to alleviate his condition, it renders the servant himself
powerless to negotiate their aid. This may not be an effective way to recover
the debt; moreover, the unforgiving servant is not forgiven seventy-seven
times. His initial lack of faith in his own forgiveness has proved justified; the
master demonstrates what happens when forgiveness is merely occasional
and not repeated.

The brutality of this parable is designed to seize the listeners' attention:
the settlement of accounts for each servant is an irreversible event that gives
shape and meaning to their past and future lives. Their debts are matters of
torture and slavery, life and death. The listeners' sympathy is elicited by the
judgements made by the fellow servants who are shocked at the dissonance
between the first servant's severity and his own prior forgiveness. By the
effect of contrast, attention is implicitly drawn to an immanent principle of
justice that is violated here: 'do as you would be done by', or love your
neighbour as yourself. A multitude of preachers have subsequently urged
that, should one desire to be forgiven for one's own faults, then one should
likewise forgive others. This may seem fine as a universal maxim to guide
conduct until, of course, it is broken. Our unforgiving servant is not forgiven
either by the king or by his fellow servants; neither is the unforgiving brother
nor sister forgiven by the heavenly Father. This immanent principle of justice
works only as an ideal; once deployed as a principle for judging others or
indeed the self, it is suspended by its very usage in the act of judgement. To
judge those who are unforgiving is for oneself to become unforgiving.

This puzzling parable is one of several that initiate the Christian tradition
by positing an intimate yet problematic relation between theology and economics. Any straightforward understanding of this relation through analogy,
however, is blocked from the outset. It may be easier for a camel to pass
through the eye of a needle than for a person laden with theological or
economic presuppositions to enter into an understanding of divine truth,
should any be on offer here. So much the better; one can only proceed on
faith. What can this mean? The difference in hermeneutic approach is this:
where, in the normal course of events, attention is attracted or distracted from
without, faith enacts its own ordering of attention from within. To listen with
faith is to listen not merely to the explicit content which is given, but to listen
with a second ear to a silent voice which gives another layer of meaning, a
layer which constitutes the very being and hearing of the listener. To listen
with faith is to receive and live from the stock of credit one has been given.
As Jesus explained his use of parables to his disciples, 'To you has been
given the secret of the kingdom of God, but for those outside, everything

comes in parables; in order that "they may indeed look, but not perceive, and may indeed listen, but not understand; so that they may not turn again and be forgiven"' (Mark 4.11–12, citing Isaiah 6.9–10). Let us not be too distracted by this appeal to secrecy, 'For nothing is hidden that will not be disclosed, nor is anything secret that will not become known and come to light. *Then pay attention to how you listen*' (Luke 8.17–18a).

Instead of asking from the parable a principle of judgement, let us ask instead for operations for directing attention – then it may speak to faith. The parable enacts certain transformations. The first surprising move is the suspension of accounts: the king does not settle the debt but forgives it altogether. Perhaps the servant errs because he does not fully accept this forgiveness but remains in terror. Attention is directed away from the debt itself, whether its quantity or the possibilities for its repayment, towards the relation between the king and servant. In a second move, the status of the servant is inverted: from being a debtor to being a creditor and again to being a debtor. Attention is directed from the large debt to the small debt and back again from the small debt to the large one. In terms of attention, the first shall be last and the last shall be first. In the third place, attention is directed towards a certain 'like-for-like':[5] the demand that the servant should forgive others as he has been forgiven, and the judgement that the servant should himself be treated as he treated his fellow servant. The three operations upon attention, here, are suspension, inversion and repetition. Perhaps this is what it means to think in faith. As we shall see, these are the acts of judgement, redemption and creation which are involved in issuing credit.[6]

The key theological question to raise here, then, is whether suspension, inversion and repetition may be used to pass through the eye of a needle and make that which had been secret known. The question is whether an analogy which is blocked at an explicit level may become fruitful for understanding when it passes through these formal procedures of suspension, inversion and repetition. The analogy which will focus our attention is that between the theological and economic dimensions of existence: credit and faith are at once theological and economic. The focus of this study is neither the interpretation of parables nor early Christian teachings on wealth, but how understanding credit and faith may illuminate our troubled times.

Chapter Two

Economy in the New Testament

Let us turn, then, to the significance of economy in the New Testament for the problem of finding an orientation in thought – after first situating its innovations in a given context. Economic concerns, for the ancient Greeks, were primarily matters of household or estate management; trade was merely one element of household responsibilities. Aristotle effectively treated humanity as an economic or household animal.[1] Of course, he named humanity as a 'political animal',[2] since the whole is prior to the part in at least two respects: the community is the condition for the existence and survival of the household, and the good household is ordered towards the good of the community. Yet direct participation in politics was the sole preserve of the master of the household, while all humanity, including women, children and slaves, would participate in household life. The ordering of a household might be shared between its master and matron, but the matron, excluded from the life of political action and the life of the mind, could excel in a one-dimensional, economic life with its own happiness and virtues. As Xenophon had made clear in his treatise on household management, economics (*oikonomikos*) was understood as a theoretical and practical knowledge by which one could increase the totality of one's property, understood as the things which are useful for life.[3] Nevertheless, the purpose of generating wealth was to enable the participation of the master of the household in politics and philosophy. Wealth, when subordinate to virtue, was created in order to be given, so that a master could demonstrate his benevolence towards his friends, allowing them leisure time. 'Economic justice', in Aristotle's sense, was the subordination of economic concerns to political and philosophical ones, ordering the household towards political action and the life of the mind: it was justice between master and matron.[4] Justice consisted in the hierarchical ordering of the three spheres: the life of the mind was the ultimate human fulfilment, supported by the life of political activity, itself made possible by household life. Any rebalancing of this order was regarded as unjust and unnatural. For while the pursuit of gain in household life, especially as facilitated by money and retail trade, had no intrinsic limits, Aristotle explained that those preoccupied with such a pursuit were concerned with living only, not with living well.[5] The good life was the pursuit of virtue, friendship, leisure and free thought.

The New Testament may present us with an opportunity to rethink the relations between these three spheres. For Aristotle's hierarchy is expressed through the logic of mastery involved in distinguishing means and ends. This logic of mastery remains with us today. Whereas, in the case of ancient Greece, slaves were treated as instruments of production and women as instruments of reproduction, in the modern economy the environment and those without property may be treated as mere means for the ends of consumption, profit and the repayment of debt. Furthermore, this logic of mastery remains implicit in critical thought which seeks the ends beyond the means. For those who take this classical ordering of the three spheres of life as a model, the primary problem of our contemporary era is how the economic sphere, with its pursuit of unlimited gain, has come to predominate over the public sphere of political action and the philosophical sphere of the life of the mind. This condition is sometimes called 'neoliberalism' insofar as it prioritises economic liberty over political liberty and freedom of thought. For Hannah Arendt, and those who follow her, such an inversion leads to a diminution of the good life.[6] Even Simone Weil, building on Aristotle and Kant, insisted that the fundamental folly that causes human oppression throughout history is the inversion of means and ends found in the pursuit of power or money for their own sake.[7] There are some who explain the dominance of economic and religious imperatives in the modern world over political or philosophical ones as an outcome of the Christian tradition. On this account, it is Christianity, with its emphasis upon household life and divine economy, which has subordinated politics and philosophy. Some, in the wake of Max Weber and Michel Foucault, even attribute the origins of contemporary neoliberalism to the adoption of distinctively Christian modes of governance throughout modern institutions. For Christian thought has given priority, first in its theology and then in its practice, to the notion of 'economy' and the pursuit of gain.[8]

Now the classical ordering of spheres of life described by Aristotle and Xenophon need not be taken as normative. For this model overlooks the crucial role in all previous human societies of religion and piety for the grounding, enabling and ordering of trust, attention and obligation. It is the democratic polis, ordering trust through persuasion, and the modern economy, ordering trust through banking and state regulation, that stand out as exceptions here. Moreover, religion has always been deeply involved in economy: trust and obligation are manifest above all in what one does with one's resources, while piety is manifest in what one does with one's time such as in sacrifice, tithe, prayer and meditation. These belong to the contingent, historical and interpersonal dimensions of life, with their changeable bonds and dependencies. Credit and faith, rather than the selection and achievement of ends, are the operative powers in such a world. The logic of mastery, involving means and ends, offers little purchase here. It has always been difficult to gain a rational understanding of the world of change, dependency, fortune, custom and grace, and modern science offers little better prospect of understanding the accidental and coincidental than Aristotelian reason. Prudence, when it cannot simply follow custom and experience, has consisted for the most part in managing the changeable by the eternal, whether by metaphysical ordering or political ordering, whether by legal subjugation or prophetic interpretation, or whether by mathematical modelling or by statistical classification. Perhaps none of these strategies for prudence fully captures the temporal and interpersonal experience of life. None offer an adequate understanding of the meaning of existence. To appeal to a now unfashionable contrast, the Hebraic thinking of relationships is not the Hellenistic thought of substance. Leaving fashion aside, what is at stake is an entirely different mode of power and orientation in thought. Our task is to seek out the possibilities afforded for philosophy and politics by credit and faith.

The economic world of the New Testament was not the economic world of classical Athens. Assimilation into the Roman Empire had turned Judea and Galilee into effective tax farms or private estates, a patchwork of households where the pursuit of unlimited production was the primary objective.[9] The discourse of the New Testament is comparable to that of women and slaves, those lacking opportunity to engage in political agency according to philosophical principle – there are no politicians or philosophers here.[10] Imperial relations of patronage, including private bonds of debts and dependencies, are more in evidence than market relations of exchange between freeholders of land. Empire was constructed for the unlimited pursuit of gain. The basic economic units were often households or estates in which the master was largely absent – a situation resonating in widely divergent ways with the theology of Judaism, the history of colonisation, and corporations having public ownership. In this context, the primary sense of *oikonomos* in the New Testament is that of a household manager or steward;[11] it is this sense that will be our initial concern. Such a role is commissioned, entrusted or appointed: the steward can be prudent and faithful, and so entrusted with full authority (Luke 12.42), or wasteful or dishonest, and so called to give an account (Luke 16.2). The role was clearly an institutionalised and readily recognisable one, with regal, municipal and private types;[12] it was pivotal in the Roman Empire, condensing in microcosm its relations of power. It was situated between others: there are servants, slaves, land and resources to be managed, and there is a master to whom one is accountable.

To understand the meaning of 'economy' in the New Testament more precisely requires some brief textual analysis of its usage in Paul's writings – where, due to the fraught nature of what is at stake, some technical digression is necessary. It would seem that only one of these relations, that of obligation and accountability, is foregrounded in the metaphorical usage of *oikonomos* for the apostolic commission in the undisputed epistles of Paul, where the role is explicitly separated from any sense of contractual exchange, employment or reward: 'If I proclaim the gospel, this gives me no ground for boasting, for an obligation is laid on me, and woe to me if I do not proclaim the gospel! For if I do this of my own will, I have a reward; but if not of my own will, I am entrusted with a commission (*oikonomian*)' (1 Cor. 9.16–17). For all Paul's 'freedom in Christ', he was not a master who set his own ends. Paul wrote of his role as a slave to Christ, one who made himself a slave to all (1 Cor. 9.19). But this latter is clearly an overstatement: while he might serve all with the gospel, he is accountable solely to the Lord: 'But with me it is a very small thing that I should be judged in any human court' (1 Cor 4.3). Paul also believed that personal accountability to the Lord extends to all others, and this commission extends as far as their secret thoughts. 'Therefore do not pronounce judgement before the time, before the Lord comes, who will bring to light the things now hidden in darkness and will disclose the purposes of the heart. Then each one will receive commendation from God' (1 Cor. 4.5). Apostolic accountability is also clearly in the foreground in the crucial opening remarks of this passage: 'Think of us in this way, as servants of Christ and stewards (*oikonomous*) of God's mysteries. Moreover, it is required of stewards (*oikonomois*) that they be found trustworthy' (1 Cor. 4.1–2).[13]

Setting aside this main emphasis on commission and accountability, then, the metaphor of steward for Paul's appointed role begs the question: Who are the servants and what are the resources for which Paul is responsible? The obvious answer might be the Corinthian congregation itself, and this seems consistent with the way Paul thought.[14] Yet the phrasing 'stewards of God's mysteries' opens up a fateful ambiguity about the sense of 'economy': Is Paul a steward appointed in and through and by God's mysteries (in line with the manner of his calling and his heavenly visions), or are God's mysteries themselves the resources at Paul's disposal?[15] Is Paul just a servant of the gospel or also its manager, distributing the blessings of divine grace? Is the gospel a command or a gift?[16] Does Paul steward souls or the gospel itself? Or is this a false alternative grounded in a false conception of the power involved in divine grace? This matter will only be resolved once we have illuminated the power involved in divine credit or forgiveness.

When it comes to the usage of *oikonomos* in the Pauline epistles where the question of direct authorship is more doubtful, this ambiguity is expanded. On the one hand, the emphasis on commission is intensified: 'For surely you have already heard of the commission (*oikonomian*) of God's grace that was given me for you, and how the mystery was made known to me by revelation' (Eph. 3.2–3). Paul is appointed in and through the act of revelation of the mystery of the gospel; he is a servant of the gospel (Eph 3.7). On the other hand, his task is to understand the mystery of Christ, now made known through the Spirit, and 'to make everyone see what is the plan (*oikonomia*) of the mystery hidden for ages in God' (Eph. 3.9). In this variant usage of the word, it would seem that God has become the steward, the household manager, and the divine household is nothing but creation and the course of history, 'a plan (*oikonomian*) for the fullness of time' (Eph. 1.10). According to the standard translations, the word is used for both commission and plan.[17] The difficulty with extending the metaphor so far is that God cannot be an 'economist' or steward: even if masters do occasionally indulge in a little household planning, God is neither appointed nor accountable.[18] This problem arises when one identifies by association the commission with the plan itself. The two are kept strictly separate, even when associated, in the somewhat derivative Colossian epistle: 'I became its [i.e., the church's] servant according to God's commission (*oikonomian*) that was given to me for you, to make the word of God fully known, the mystery that has been hidden throughout the ages and generations but has now been revealed to his saints' (Col. 1.25–26). It is all too easy to identify the commission with a plan or mystery. These ambiguities remain in place in the role of the bishop or overseer as God's steward (Titus 1.7).

These passages are amongst the many sources for Eucharistic theologies of God as given resource as well as theologies of the mystery of salvation history. Appealing respectively to the primacy of metaphysical understanding or the primacy of political will, such theologies are grounded in metaphor and expressed through metaphor; the power they have is the power of metaphor. Even if one distils the metaphor into analogy, such that the divine economy is designated as the original of which any earthly economy is a mere copy, one's grasp of the divine original and its earthly image are little enhanced but postponed for eschatological consummation. Theology is 'seeing though a mirror in a riddle' (1 Cor. 13.12). While metaphor may help a little with vision, such understanding comes at the cost of compulsion: a responsibility for handling resources is far less significant than a divine commission for which one is accountable. Paul wrote of the gospel as the revelation of a mystery of extraordinary power that has grasped him. Less of this potency remains in the theological management of the resources of metaphor. After all, Paul's message of the gospel came 'not in word only, but also in power and in the Holy Spirit and with full conviction' (1 Thess. 1.5).

Where Paul writes of a commission, with all the force and obligation this implies, subsequent theologians write merely of a plan.[19] Where Paul may have seen himself as steward of the divine power of salvation, theologians have become stewards of metaphors. The truth of such understandings of the gospel is not at issue here; its manifest power to save is more questionable. What metaphorical thought lacks is *necessity*: an active power to transform by the renewing of minds (Rom. 12.2).[20]

A thought of such power would have quite some philosophical significance. Could there be a sense of necessity in thought which is broader than mere logical necessity: one which, as in economic life, is concerned with meeting what is needful? Might there be a sense of the 'gospel' in thought which is a power of appointing and commissioning: one which, as in religious commitment, leaves the thinker not strictly as a master of the household of their thought, accepting or rejecting opinions by an arbitrary decision, but as an appointed steward, accountable to the primary insight?[21] Is faith a fidelity to a truth rather than a decision to accept an opinion? Do we play host to our thoughts or are our minds simply guests in ideas? May we be shaken out of our conventions and preconceptions only when truth behaves as a discourteous host or an impertinent guest? Indeed, is there an alternative path to Christian theological reflection that does not start from the presupposition that the gospel is a gift or resource to be handled or a mystery to be disclosed?

If we briefly recall the first proclamation of the Christian gospel in the message of Jesus, the more literal sense of *oikonomia* as household management is entirely in evidence. A characteristic feature of Jesus's teaching is the substitution of economic terminology such as debt for religious terminology such as law. This striking anomaly often escapes comment. Jesus did not teach after the manner of the scribes and the Pharisees, hardly speaking of how to interpret the law correctly. Early Christianity embodied its own teaching through its *koinonia*, its sharing of resources.[22] Yet the use of parables suggests that to take early Christian attitudes towards wealth as determinative of the full meaning of the gospel would be to miss the point. Similarly, Jesus seems to have had little to say to anything the modern world would include under 'economics'. Although the issues of taxation and coinage are frequently raised, market exchange for the sake of money is only a concern for Judas Iscariot. Overall, in Jesus's teaching, household management seems to be a far more prominent concern than ritual purity, temple sacrifice, political government, philosophical principle or mythological mystery. Nevertheless, the plain sense of household management is suspended, leaving us at a loss as to how to proceed.

Paul may offer us a clue. He discusses the spiritual life by writing extensively about the body. For example, if we return to Paul's statement of his commission we find an explicit answer to our question of what resources

Paul was called to administer: his self, life and person – '*I have made myself a slave to all*'. Paul's various becomings – as a Jew, as one under the law, as one outside the law, as weak, that he might win each of these – may seem insincere but may also be the condition for communication of an otherwise inexpressible truth. 'I have become all things to all people, so that I might by all means save some' (1 Cor. 9.22). In this context, the apostolic sense of *oikonomia* or household management becomes explicitly related to the philosophical virtue of *enkrateia*, self-control, the final entry in Paul's list of fruits of the Spirit (Gal. 5.23). For Paul extends his own commission to others to imitate his approach to the Christian life:

> Do you not know that in a race the runners all compete, but only one receives the prize? Run in such a way that you may win it. Athletes exercise self-control (*enkrateia*) in all things; they do it to receive a perishable wreath, but we an imperishable one. So I do not run aimlessly, nor do I box as though beating the air; but I punish my body and enslave it, so that after proclaiming to others I myself should not be disqualified. (1 Cor. 9.24–27)

Paul's own body was his primary resource as a tool for communication; the body is the temple of the Holy Spirit (1 Cor. 6.9). *Enkrateia*, for Paul as for the Stoics, involves controlling the passions – Paul even recommends remaining unmarried (1 Cor. 7.8–9). The body is meant for the Lord, and the Lord for the body (1 Cor. 6.13). Those who sin with the body – and Paul offers a long list, from sexual sins, through idolatry and drunkenness to robbery – will not inherit the kingdom of God (1 Cor. 6-9–10). Nevertheless, according to Paul's gospel, human accountability as stewards is the basis for divine judgement when 'God, through Jesus Christ, will judge the secret thoughts of all' (Rom. 2.16). Body and thought are inseparable. Sinning with the body may even be a way of manifesting secret thoughts, thoughts perhaps secret even to oneself. The Christian steward is ultimately a steward of their own thoughts, but these thoughts are expressed through bodies.

These preparatory considerations may help to situate our field of study. On the one hand, credit and faith are enacted through material relations of consumption, exchange and almsgiving. Any claims to possess a faith which does not manifest itself in material practice may be suspected of hypocrisy and self-deception. On the other hand, credit and faith are ways of managing one's expectations, oneself, and one's life. They include dimensions of *oikonomia* and *enkrateia*. Self-control, or management of one's secret thoughts through one's bodily practices, lies at the heart of both religious and economic life. Such considerations also suggest a philosophical method: it is how one handles a body of thought which communicates more than the content itself. There is a practical embedding and communication of thought in situations, institutions and episodic narratives. Philosophy may be pursued outside of concepts by adopting and transforming perspectives on features of daily life.

Now, in some ways, early Christianity inherited the philosophical conception of life as an ascesis, a work on oneself and through oneself: 'If any want to become my followers, let them deny themselves and take up their cross and follow me. For those who want to save their life will lose it, and those who lose their life for my sake, and for the sake of the gospel, will save it' (Mark 8.34–35).[23] Redemptive sacrifice, in early Christianity, was less a matter of legal observance or temple ritual than of almsgiving to those in need, distributing the substance of one's life.[24] This is the message of the story of the rich, young ruler who was dismayed by this call to sacrifice, provoking the judgement: 'It is easier for a camel to go through the eye of a needle than for someone who is rich to enter the kingdom of God' (Mark 10.25). It is also the message of the corresponding story of Zacchaeus, whose restitution of wealth provokes the judgement, 'Today salvation has come to this house' (Luke 19.9). This ascesis is articulated in economic terms of gain, profit, forfeit and return: 'For what will it profit them to gain the whole world and forfeit their life? Indeed, what can they give in return for their life'? (Mark 8.36–37) This ascesis is a matter of *oikonomia* and *enkrateia*, management of one's thoughts through a management of one's resources.

It is such ascetic practices that give primacy to the economic over the political sphere. These are the grounds for thinking that Christianity itself may be responsible for the elevating the primacy of economic and instrumental rationalities, concerned purely with measures and means, over political and ethical rationalities concerned with the free adoption of ends. If the Christian heritage has replaced rulers with ministers, then the contemporary world is ruled by the mentality of servants lacking any true purpose or direction. Such is the implication of Max Weber's notorious and questionable thesis that the 'Protestant ethic' lies at the basis of capitalism: accumulation is necessary but without purpose.[25] Many accounts of contemporary economic life extend this heritage further still: we have seen the emergence of a new mode of ascesis even within a consumer society – the task of becoming an entrepreneur of oneself.[26] Even the recent turn to philosophy as a spiritual practice, under the influence of Pierre Hadot, may be accused of being one more manifestation of an ascetic ideal which betrays noble self-affirmation through legislating one's own values in favour of a focus on the means for the acquisition of received virtues.

The discussion which follows is based on the suspicion that any return to Greek mastery over ends is as partial as any celebration of service and means. Participation in the active life of a community has no more ontological primacy than appropriating the means for the satisfaction of preferences and needs. Commissioning itself remains as a stubborn ontological residue. Indeed, it is a distinctively theological perspective, such as that found in the

New Testament, which still has potential to revolutionise the entire tradition of Western thought, ancient and modern. Far from establishing the primacy of household life, the foundation of Christianity in the teachings of Jesus and Paul makes use of economic content to communicate a properly 'spiritual' message: a word of creation, redemption and judgement. How the theological meaning of commissioning can be expounded in ontological terms is a most delicate matter, to be approached indirectly. Our task, in what follows, will be to extract certain categories and questions which might facilitate a fresh engagement with philosophical and economic life. Let us continue, therefore, with a story of the undermining of proper household management and hospitality. The emphasis, here, lies neither on the mastery and magnanimity of Simon the Pharisee nor on the self-abasement and service of the uninvited prostitute, but rather on the transformative effect of pronouncing forgiveness.

Chapter Three

Impertinent Guests

One of the Pharisees asked Jesus to eat with him, and he went into the Pharisee's house and took his place at the table. And a woman in the city, who was a sinner, having learned that he was eating in the Pharisee's house, brought an alabaster jar of ointment. She stood behind him at his feet, weeping, and began to bathe his feet with her tears and to dry them with her hair. Then she continued kissing his feet and anointing them with the ointment. Now when the Pharisee who had invited him saw it, he said to himself, 'If this man were a prophet, he would have known who and what kind of woman this is who is touching him – and that she is a sinner'. Jesus spoke up and said to him, 'Simon, I have something to say to you'. 'Teacher', he replied, 'speak'. 'A certain creditor had two debtors; one owed five hundred denarii, and the other fifty. When they could not pay, he canceled the debts for both of them. Now which of them will love him more'? Simon answered, 'I suppose the one for whom he canceled the greater debt'. And Jesus said to him, 'You have judged rightly'. Then turning toward the woman, he said to Simon, 'Do you see this woman? I entered your house; you gave me no water for my feet, but she has bathed my feet with her tears and dried them with her hair. You gave me no kiss, but from the time I came in she has not stopped kissing my feet. You did not anoint my head with oil, but she has anointed my feet with ointment. Therefore, I tell you, her sins, which were many, have been forgiven; hence she has shown great love. But the one to whom little is forgiven, loves little'. Then he said to her, 'Your sins are forgiven'. But those who were at table with him began to say among themselves, 'Who is this who even forgives sins'? And he said to the woman, 'Your faith has saved you; go in peace'. (Luke 7.36–50)

THE LAWS OF HOSPITALITY

What stands out in this narrative is the disruption of household management and the laws of hospitality: it is the impertinence of the guests. No motive for

29

Simon's generous offer of hospitality is offered. What interest might Simon have had in this wandering miracle worker and his band of hangers-on? To meet a stranger with extravagant hospitality is one way of defusing any potential threat that they might offer; it is also a way of demonstrating one's status through one's means and resources. Since there is no question of Jesus returning the favour and inviting Simon back to dinner, we are in the realm of unequal exchange, with all its ambiguities: as host, Simon seizes the role of patron, leaving Jesus as client, obliged to offer favours and service to his benefactor.[1] But Simon runs the risk that his hospitality will be interpreted as tribute or service to one of superior rank, like that of the women who were later to provide for Jesus out of their own resources (Luke 8.3). In this game of competitive hospitality, to generously and courteously host a formal meal yet be outdone by a woman of rude manners and doubtful character bearing an alabaster jar would be a costly disappointment, to say the least. It has been noted that the setting resembles the literary genre of a symposium, with guests reclining on a couch on one arm, their feet pointing away from the table.[2] The appearance of an uninvited woman in such a male gathering, especially with a reputation as a 'sinner', is already a sufficient cause for scandal.[3] Who knows what personal crisis had evoked her presence and her tears? Nothing is said of any prior acquaintance with Jesus. At any rate, with no reputation to lose, an extreme desperation had moved her to throw aside all convention, appear uninvited at a formal gathering, and stake a considerable portion of her disposable wealth on the opportunities afforded by this one encounter. Nothing is explicitly said of her penitence; much is said of her self-abasement. One cannot mistake the erotic tenor of the application of tears, hair and oil to Jesus's feet – this is the hospitality of the massage parlour performed in house of a Pharisee. Yet such a usage of hair is a pornographic performance taken to an extreme of degradation. Who knows to what kinds of humiliations workers like her were obliged to submit in a highly patriarchal society, where abuse of women might be purchased as much for a sense of power as a sense of pleasure, and tears might be a frequent occurrence? For her to outdo all such abasement in a performance of tears, hair and kisses bespeaks a desperate plea for recognition.

Recognition is precisely what Simon the Pharisee offers – he sees the effrontery of her presence, the inappropriateness of her behaviour, the impurity of her touching, the calculation behind her performance, all evidence that justifies the woman's reputation as a sinner. But what interests him here is Jesus: Simon speaks to himself of Jesus's acquiescence in the scandal, Jesus's own apparent lack of recognition, Jesus's self-indulgence and enjoyment of this bizarrely lavish attention. To accept such ministrations in public was perhaps as shocking then as it would be now, albeit for rather different reasons. Jesus's apparent lack of purity, decency, integrity, courtesy, insight and self-control are all summed up in the thought that if this man were a prophet, he would have understood the significance of this scandal. All this will subsequently be evoked by Jesus's reputation as a friend of tax collectors and sinners.

The dramatic irony of Luke's narrative hinges on this: Jesus, as a true prophet, has recognised something in both Simon and the woman that Simon has not. But if the woman's behaviour was outrageous, Jesus's behaviour was more so: his words provoke a far greater disquiet among the onlookers. Jesus will place Simon and the woman in comparison, as if they could be considered as notional equals. The Jewish legal and social framework employed to delineate their relative statuses is replaced by a purely monetary framework in the parable. In the first place, the parable implicitly compares their positive gestures of hospitality with the service of gratitude offered in response to release from a debt. As such, it ignores the social ambiguities and complexities these gestures contain just as it displaces the significance of the legal customs these employ or transgress. This radical simplification of obligation to a single monetary scale, allowing direct comparison, situates the debtors as relative equals. Furthermore, while the contract one forms with a moneylender may be an agreement between social equals, this moneylender only reestablishes the relation as a hierarchical one of obligation by cancelling the unpayable debt. For ever after, the forgiven debtor will feel obliged to offer service. The parable seems to replace legal obligation with primordial debt. As Bonaventure put it in his commentary on this passage: 'For everything we have we owe to God except the debt we incur because of sin [which Christ, of course, has paid for us] . . . we are obliged to the disposition of love . . . the one who sinned more has the greater obligation'.[4] Yet what seems most natural to Bonaventure, that any debt of sin owed to God should be enacted through service to Christ, is what seems most scandalous to Simon and his company. For God to be a judge who forgives sins of varying gravity just as a moneylender forgives debts of varying magnitude is one thing; but for the subsequent gratitude to be shown to Jesus is quite another. Does Jesus claim to be the creditor who subjects Simon and the woman by announcing their forgiveness? In contrasting the hospitality offered by Simon and the woman, Jesus seems to expect from Simon more than a host is obliged to offer: water for the feet, a kiss and anointing the head with oil – gestures of true welcome and friendship. Even if these had been offered, the woman had far surpassed them. Jesus insults his host by suggesting that a far superior standard of hospitality was owing, one actually provided by this sinful woman. If Jesus traps Simon into silence by introducing a debt of which Simon has never conceived, Simon is perhaps dumbfounded more by the impertinent behaviour of his guest than he is bemused by this rather unrabbinic argumentation. Finally, Jesus confirms the comparison of the moneylender in the parable with himself by actually announcing the forgiveness of sins. It is hardly surprising that tradition should identify the woman as

Mary Magdalene, ever after offering service to Christ and providing for him
out of her own means. As we see in the Zacchaeus story, Jesus lived off the
takings of tax collectors and prostitutes, the profits of exploitation and crime.
The juxtaposition of his outlandish claim to authority with his outrageous
associations is enough for the associates of Simon the Pharisee to place him
beyond the pale.

FORGIVENESS OF DEBT

In this story we observe the shocking consequences of the Christian replacement of a Jewish legal framework, where obligations are differentiated, qual-
ified and specified, with an economic framework, where obligations are conceived as debts. Debts, which are to be paid in the form of money, are
quantified, comparable and transferable: Jesus gave his life 'as a ransom for
many' (Mark 10.45). While it might make no sense in terms of justice that
another should be punished in my place – to regard the punishment of the
innocent as the dispensation of justice is more typical of Pilate than Paul[5] – it
can make perfect economic sense that another might pay my debt. Yet such
purely economic redemption is not yet social liberation. The act of redemption seems to place the redeemed in bondage; this transfer of debt effectively
renders it infinite. As Paul declares, 'You are not your own. For you were
bought with a price' (1 Cor. 6.19–20). The Christian is then called to emulate
the sinful woman in self-abasement and a life offered in service – as an old
story told by Ludwig Feuerbach and Friedrich Nietzsche runs. On this account, Christianity is conceived as a machine of enslavement or apparatus of
capture: mutual bonds and social obligations are first formalised in law, with
a primary obligation to be shown to the law itself; transgressions, however
minor, are subsequently reconceived in economic terms as debts, with sacrifices as payments; finally, the forgiveness of sins achieved by the one perfect
sacrifice sufficient to pay all debts inaugurates a new situation of unstruc-
tured and unlimited obligation to God. For many, both within and beyond the
faith, Christians live as slaves, under an infinite reprieve, as those who
should have died and now belong to their saviour.

   This is not the fate of the woman in the story itself. Moreover, the parable
is not presented as an analogy for the universal human condition before God
but is explicitly addressed to Simon. 'Simon', says Jesus, 'I have something
to say to you'. A tendency to compare relative statuses, primarily those of
Jesus and Simon, is that which Jesus discerns in Simon's heart, and it is this
tendency that Jesus turns against him. That any comparison between Simon
and the woman is quite unthinkable is perhaps the reason why Jesus introduces it: the comparison inverts, and therefore mocks, any display of power
based on ability to provide hospitality. After all, the woman has been far

more hospitable than Simon ever could. A competitive concern with status is a barrier to genuine relationship. By contrast, lavish self-abasement does at least open up receptivity to the other. The economic parable is introduced to destroy legal and social distinctions, erasing all records of debts (Col 2.14). Christianity acts like capitalism: 'all that is solid melts into air'.[6]

Jesus's courtesy to the woman is enacted by naming her behaviour as 'showing great love', and her self-abasement as 'faith', the loyalty shown to a patron. One can assume a lack of prior contact, for Simon, at least, takes them to be perfect strangers, the only opportunity for this personal encounter to occur was a public setting. This demonstrates that her display cannot arise from established intimacy. Whatever motivations led to this bizarre act, they cannot include 'great love'; instead, she offers a performance of 'great love', a display enacted for a stranger as if it were love – this is, after all, her profession. It is more likely that Jesus discerns her desperation, and surmises something of the circumstances of her life as 'a woman in the city who was a sinner'. Clearly, she looks to Jesus to offer her salvation from the life of abuse, exploitation and exclusion that she lives. There is no need to take Jesus's enjoyment of her ministrations as anything more than ironic. Indeed, the story concludes with him dismissing her: 'go in peace'. No further services are required. Far from being newly enslaved to Jesus, she is released. The declaration 'Your sins are forgiven' indicates that Jesus, unlike Simon, will not hold them against her, and invites others to think likewise. While such a declaration was insufficient to change the attitudes of those who were at the table, it may have opened the door to participation amongst Jesus's own company – and in this respect she may have truly received salvation from her former life that very day. Ultimate authority is not claimed by Jesus for himself, but attributed to his gospel of the forgiveness of sins – the abolition of judgements and debts – as the basis of changing lives and restoring community.

Jesus gives the woman *credit*. While her show of great love is effectively an empty promise endeavouring to institute a debt, Jesus's announcement has a transformative effect that enables her to love. As such, he offers her the substance with which to pay her self-imposed debt of love and loyalty. Rare are the occasions when such an offer of credit has such a transformative effect, but this is one such. The forgiveness of sins at once creates the opportunity for her love, redeems her from an unpaid obligation, and makes a judgement about this possibility of transformation through faith in forgiveness.

Such a gospel has a certain antitheoretical and therefore antitheological character, as the tensions between Jesus and his deeply religious contemporaries demonstrate: qualitative distinctions, whether grounded in law or in nature, are suspended in favour of the higher calling to love. In reformulating the gospel as epitomised by the crucified Christ, Paul appreciated this: 'a stumbling block to Jews and foolishness to Gentiles, but to those who are the called, both Jews and Greeks, Christ the power of God and the wisdom of God' (1 Cor. 1.23–24). At the same time, such a gospel also has a certain antieconomic character, teaching redistribution of wealth, payment without return and the forgiveness of debts. Quantitative estimates of obligation as debts are also abolished. In focussing the gospel on the love commandment, Paul also appreciated this: 'Owe no one anything, except to love one another' (Rom. 13.8). In the fields of both theology and economics, this gospel of forgiveness is an impertinent guest.

Nevertheless, at first sight such a gospel may not seem very promising: on the one hand, suspension of the bases of meaning through which daily life is conducted, whether religious or economic, threatens an apocalyptic destruction of the meaningful world just as Jesus explicitly threatened destruction of the sacred temple. Lacking qualitative and quantitative distinction, we would fall into the proverbial dark night in which all cows are black.[7] On the other hand, reducing all speech to direct personal address evacuates all mediation and context through which relationship may be built. But far from the gospel record abolishing differentiation and mediation, its message is proclaimed in and through differentiation and mediation. The characteristic gestures of philosophy, establishing differences, and economics, handling resources, are the vital components of its thought.

THREE GESTURES OF THOUGHT

Our problem lies in discerning how a few words addressed to Simon the Pharisee some two thousand years ago may have a wider pertinence without extracting a general principle or message. Better to write as an ingratiating prostitute, with tears and hair and oil, than as a learned Pharisee, with a command of traditions of interpretation. Above all, what has to be laid aside is a certain theoretical attitude, the notion that a common mind can be established between author and reader by laying out a common message or meaning for contemplation, consideration, debate and judgement. Whether grounded in public evidence or hidden mystery, in science or revelation, a theory falls short of an active practice of thinking. The solution lies in *oikonomia* and *enkrateia* – perhaps Jesus demonstrates a practice of hospitality, the management of the household of thought, which is capable of welcoming even us as guests. It is Jesus's characteristic ways of thinking, as demonstrated in this story, that we have the opportunity to appropriate and repeat for ourselves. This would be an elaboration of a 'Christian philosophy', one not grounded directly in dogmatics – for what is Christian dogmatics, after all, but a witness to the significance of the thinking of Jesus and his power to transform relationships? – but in the gospel record itself. It would also be one that makes its appeal to all, as Paul did, regardless of creed.

Let us confine ourselves to three characteristic gestures of thought. In the first place, Jesus enacted an eschatological *suspension* of the existing order: in announcing the forgiveness of sins to the woman, all the former criteria by which judgements can be made, all concerns with purity and righteousness, were set aside. All the customs by which Jesus might have conducted himself as a guest are abrogated. Jesus has an insight that is so compelling that all other thoughts are arrested. The economic imagery here is one of absolute expenditure: the revelation of the kingdom of God is compared to a treasure in a field which someone found and hid, and then sold all that he had to buy that field; likewise it is compared to a merchant in search of fine pearls who sold all that he had to buy the one pearl of great price (Matt. 13.44–46). Jesus made such a sacrifice in abandoning the expected conduct of a guest. The eschatological insight has absolute value and absolute authority: Jesus will refer to it as the 'kingdom of God'. It is expressed, in our story, in a single formulation: 'Your sins are forgiven'. While those at table heard this as a claim to authority, as though Jesus were claiming the right to offer or with-hold forgiveness, there is an alternative reading: that the rule of God is manifest only in mercy, that supreme power consists in the act of forgiving sins. In this alternative reading, the content of Jesus's proclamation is not his personal authority but the forgiveness of sins itself – it is to this gospel that he owed an absolute loyalty, even as far as death. Like Paul, he was commissioned by the insight or gospel itself. In ways yet to be established, nothing is going to be quite the same again. Nevertheless, this suspension of judgement remains a judgement.

In the second place, Jesus typically enacts a *chiasmic inversion*: the last shall be first and the first shall be last. The hospitality of the woman who was a sinner has a far greater claim on Jesus's attention than that of Simon – he receives the woman more warmly and courteously than Simon. Relative social status is inverted. Of course, this is not a principle that meets any Kantian test of universalizability: a repetition of the inversion would lead to Simon being restored to the position of respect, and the woman returned to being outcast.[8] Chiasmic inversion may only be invoked in a relevant context, such as in the parable of the Pharisee and the tax collector, where the prayer of penitence outweighs the prayer of gratitude: 'for all who exalt themselves will be humbled, but all who humble themselves will be exalted' (Luke 18.14). Jesus's typical objection to the Pharisees, however question-able its historical and psychological grounds, was that they substitute outer appearance for inner purity: 'there is nothing outside a person that by going in can defile, but the things that come out are what defile' (Mark 7.15). In the Sermon on the Mount, Jesus attempted to apply Pharisaic *enkrateia* to the inner life: sins, such as adultery, are committed in the heart (Matt. 5.28; cp.

the list of things that come out of the human heart that defile in Mark 7.21–22). Something of the Hellenistic conception of the soul or inner life as cause may be in evidence here; but there is no need to extend this to a full-blown dualism between soul and body.[9] The penitent tax collector prayed with location, posture and beating his breast (Luke 18.13); the prostitute entreated Jesus with tears, hair and oil. In chiasmic inversion, what is least noticeable of all – an expressed thought arising from the heart – is elevated to the highest status, while what is most apparent, conduct in line with public principles, customs and laws, is degraded to the lowest. It is therefore neither law, purity nor hierarchy as such that are directly challenged here, but a certain kind of self-management. Jesus's use of chiasmic inversion restores attention to what really matters, such as fidelity to relationship, above custom and tradition (Mark 7.12–13). Those who see what matters, who see their need to build or restore relationship, even if tax collectors and sinners, are those who will be exalted. This transformation of values enacts redemption.

In the third place, Jesus characteristically taught in parables. In this case, Simon is invited to see his situation in a different light, or through a different lens. Parables are lenses, tools of perception. Religious obligation is reformulated here as gratitude consequent upon forgiveness of a debt. While such economic imagery might be distant from the martial and legal imagery prevalent in scriptural accounts of salvation, the parable would not work unless it illuminated some existing aspect of Jewish theology – specifically, that the divine initiative to show mercy is prior to any human response. The parable bears witness to some aspect of the situation of critical significance, yet one whose importance may easily be overlooked: mercy, not purity, is the condition for closeness to God, as the previous-discussed parable of forgiven debtors, that of the unmerciful servant, indicates (Matt. 18.23–34). Simon is upbraided for his lack of mercy. Yet a parable remains a parable; it is not a theory. To apply it literally, as though the divine act of salvation should be understood primarily as forgiveness of a debt, rather than as expiation of guilt or redemption from bondage, is to miss its nature as a parable. In this respect, the parable does not stand above the situation as a transcendent idea, rule or criterion by which the situation may be judged. On the contrary, the situation has a bearing on the meaning of the parable itself. When Jesus asks which of the debtors will love the creditor more, he introduces a concern that is very rare in consideration of credits and debts – the gratitude that follows debt forgiveness is treated as far more significant than the original contract. The norms of economic relation manifested in the parable cannot remain unaffected by its new context in practices of hospitality aimed at establishing relationships. Debt and exchange, here, have no independence from personal relationships of loyalty. Far from the parable manifesting a transcendent truth, it builds an immanent alliance between one frame of thinking and living and another. The creative use of parables is sufficient to *crystallise* new relations and understandings that had not previously existed.

CONCLUSION

What concerns us here, most immediately, is neither an idea nor a logic but an economics of thought. It is a matter of allocating due credit to each thought, giving it the attention, weight and significance that it deserves. In this story, Jesus offered three economic gestures in the household management of thought: eschatological suspension, which abandons any unlimited quest for purity or righteousness in favour of a single insight that has absolute appeal; chiasmic inversion, which restores what intrinsically matters after extrinsic signs have been substituted for it; crystalline engagement through parables, which establishes relations between what had been taken as abstract, transcendent or disengaged. Such are the bases for a Christian philosophy and for a Christianity played in a minor key. While a distribution of thought has no intrinsic compulsion by itself, these particular gestures can gain significance from that which they accomplish: to unleash the force of governing insight, to restore attention to that which matters, to build transformative relations in thought – this would be a practice worthy of the name 'philosophy'. The power of such gestures may be clarified a little further by examining their place in the thought of Paul.

Chapter Four

The Economy of Salvation

> Even though our outer nature is wasting away, our inner nature is being re-
> newed day by day. For this slight momentary affliction is preparing us for an
> eternal weight of glory beyond all measure, because we look not at what can
> be seen but at what cannot be seen; for what can be seen is temporary, but
> what cannot be seen is eternal. (2 Cor. 4.16–18)

Paul followed Jesus in speaking of salvation in the economic terms of an
exchange. In this instance, the outer nature is expended, the inner renewed;
momentary affliction is the labour that prepares eternal glory; the sight of
what is seen is abandoned in favour of what is not seen. Nevertheless, this is
an unequal exchange: the eternal weight is 'beyond all measure'; it cannot be
seen; it is not to be found in the everyday household of thought. This conception of salvation presents us with an acute problem. How did Paul look at
what cannot be seen? How can Paul speak of 'things that are not to be told,
that no mortal is permitted to repeat'? (2 Cor. 12.4) How might such a
nonvision renew one's inner nature day by day? How might one appropriate
eternal truth within a temporal life?

This, baldly stated, is the fundamental problem of an eschatological
thought: If truth is only disclosed in its ultimate form at the end, what access
can one have to truth here and now? Where can one look for the presence, or
at least the anticipation, of truth? The answer, for Paul, was Christ. Yet this
relation to Christ is not the contemplation of a common meaning, not simply
a theoretical 'look'; it is rather a matter of mutual indwelling or hospitality:
Paul refers repeatedly to 'Christ in us', or 'being in Christ'. It is hard to know
what is inner and what is outer here, who is guest and who is host. In either
case, Paul is concerned with household management, with economy, with
welcoming and being welcomed. To live by hope, faith and love is to dwell
in Christ insofar as this particular hope, faith and love are those of Christ; but

it is also for the distinctive hope, faith and love found in Christ to live in the
believer. Salvation, in Paul, is less a theory than an economy: the 'inner
nature' is nourished and renewed through having the 'mind of Christ', a
practice of managing one's own thought: 'let the same mind be in you that
was in Christ Jesus' (Phil. 2.5).

Of course, there are no independent grounds for supposing that a practice
anticipates the ultimate truth any more than a theory. Paul is emphatic that
only the mind of Christ has eschatological significance (Phil. 2.9–10). What
kind of insight from the mind of Jesus has so overpowered Paul that he
believes that God has attributed ultimate cosmic significance to it? For Paul
is convinced that the message of the gospel 'came not in word only, but also
in power and in the Holy Spirit and with full conviction' (1 Thess. 1.5).

In eschatology, involving the resurrection of the dead, Paul is dealing
with a direct but partial anticipation of the divine:

> But each in his own order: Christ the first fruits, then at his coming those who
> belong to Christ. Then comes the end, when he hands over the kingdom to God
> the Father, after he has destroyed every ruler and every authority and power.
> For he must reign until he has put all enemies under his feet. . . . When all
> things are subjected to him, then the Son himself will also be subjected to the
> one who put all things in subjection under him, so that God may be all in all. (1
> Cor. 15.23–25, 28)

True judgement comes at the end: it is grounded in the spirit rather than
the flesh, the new creation rather than the old, the resurrection rather than this
life, the unseen rather than the seen. Paul announces a radical discontinuity
with the present order of things: no amount of historical-critical scholarship,
situating Paul's gospel in relation to Jewish prophecy, Hellenistic wisdom or
Roman power, will be capable of articulating this discontinuity – the ultimate
criteria lie elsewhere.[1] Paul sees himself as in Christ, not as one under ritual,
natural or political law. Nevertheless, Paul believes the discontinuity can be
overcome: when Christians walk by faith and not by sight, live by hope and
not by power, and order their lives by love and not by law, then, in their very
weakness and insufficiency, they already live 'in Christ', in the eschatological life of the Spirit. Moreover, this extraordinary power is actually effective
in and through weakness:

> As servants of God we have commended ourselves in every way: through
> great endurance, in afflictions, hardships, calamities, beatings, imprisonments,
> riots, labors, sleepless nights, hunger; by purity, knowledge, patience, kind-
> ness, holiness of spirit, genuine love, truthful speech, and the power of God;
> with the weapons of righteousness for the right hand and for the left; in honor
> and dishonour, in ill repute and good repute. We are treated as impostors, and
> yet are true; as unknown, and yet are well known; as dying, and see – we are
> alive; as punished, and yet not killed; as sorrowful, yet always rejoicing; as

poor, yet making many rich; as having nothing, and yet possessing everything. (2 Cor. 6.4–10)

Paul's eschatological thought therefore announces an ultimate truth, a criterion for all judgement, which is at once transcendent, embodied and effective. There are no worldly criteria by which one could assess the truth of such an eschatological gospel – there is nothing convincing here, whether based on public evidence or inner grounds. Yet for Paul, entertaining such a thought enacts a transformative and saving power: 'For the message about the cross is foolishness to those who are perishing, but to us who are being saved it is the power of God' (1 Cor. 1.18).

Undoubtedly, Paul placed the highest emphasis on the death and resurrection of Jesus Christ. If there is a lens through which eschatological truth may be seen, it is the cross itself. If Paul embodies his gospel in a parable, that parable is simply this death and resurrection. According to some interpretations, Paul largely ignored the teachings of the historical Jesus in favour of proclaiming the message of the crucified Christ. Yet it is also the case that Paul placed an immense emphasis on the 'mind of Christ',[2] and such a claim would be in bad faith if Paul had no interest in what Jesus taught directly, just as every proclamation of Jesus as Lord which takes little interest in Jesus's own life and teaching is wilful self-deception. There is an obvious solution: while Paul rarely repeated the content of Jesus's teaching,[3] he was deeply imbued in its economy of thought. Eschatological suspension, chiasmic inversion and mutual exchange are apparent throughout Paul's writing. Indeed, it is in these terms that Paul interprets the hope, faith and love present in Christ's death and resurrection. Paul's management of his own thinking enriches the practice of this Christian philosophy. Let us therefore take each element in turn.

HOPE

Eschatology suspends the normal ordering of life:

> I mean, brothers and sisters, that the appointed time has grown short; from now on, let even those who have wives be as though they had none, and those who mourn as though they are not mourning, and those who rejoice as though they were not rejoicing, and those who buy as though they had no possessions, and those who deal with the world as though they had no dealings with it. For the present form of this world is passing away. (1 Cor. 7.29–31)

Living in the world 'as if not' involves a suspension of judgement: the eternal weight of glory renders momentary sufferings insignificant. Hope is presented here not simply in the general sense of an expectation of a marvellous experience, but in the highly specific sense of an economy of disinvestment from attachments. Yet what is suspended is not the business of everyday life itself, with its marriage, mourning, rejoicing, owning and dealing, but a certain kind of mind, a set of judgements, a way of measuring and investing. Hope, as found in Christ, is an economic practice in the household of thought. It is a hope for righteousness; it is also a hope for mercy.

Hope, then, involves an eschatological suspension of judgement. There is a somewhat complex passage in the Epistle to the Romans where Paul alluded to Jesus's teaching against judgement from the Sermon on the Mount: 'Do not judge, so that you may not be judged. For with the judgement that you make you will be judged, and the measure you give will be the measure that you get' (Matt. 7.1–2). While Jesus has made the characteristic shift from a legal to an economic paradigm here, linking judgement to measure, Paul's own thinking illuminates Roman and Jewish law and power by seeing them in and through each other. After denouncing the achievements of pagan morality under Roman justice (Rom. 1.18–32), Paul enacts an astonishing change of direction in his argument:

> Therefore you have no excuse, whoever you are, when you judge others; for in passing judgment on another you condemn yourself, because you, the judge, are doing the very same things. You say, 'We know that God's judgment on those who do such things is in accordance with truth'. Do you imagine, whoever you are, that when you judge those who do such things and yet you do them yourself, you will escape the judgment of God? Or do you despise the riches of his kindness and forbearance and patience? Do you not realize that God's kindness is meant to lead you to repentance? But by your hard and impenitent heart you are storing up wrath for yourself on the day of wrath, when God's righteous judgment will be revealed. (Rom. 2.1–5)

Previously, Paul had been denouncing all that corrupts human relationship in the pagan world: 'Full of envy, murder, strife, deceit, craftiness, they are gossips, slanderers, God-haters, insolent, haughty, boastful, inventors of evil, rebellious towards parents; foolish, faithless, heartless, ruthless' (Rom. 1.29–31). No doubt slanderers as well as moralists would be quick to employ judgements such as these, pursuing their vindictive accusations in a way that is 'foolish, faithless, heartless, ruthless'. What is surprising is that Paul, after an extended bout of moralising on his own account, seems to slander the moralists themselves, accusing them, when they judge, of doing the very same thing about which they judge. In what sense can moral judgement be compared to 'every kind of wickedness, evil, covetousness, malice' (Rom. 1.29)?

Judgement, of course, can arise from malice or enact malice. One only has to consider the judgement of Simon the Pharisee on the woman of the city who was a sinner. Alternatively, the basis of *Pax Romana* was judgement exercised through force. The rhetoric of Roman rule was justified by a combination of force, fortune and virtue: those who were conquered and enslaved were judged as weak, despised by the gods and lacking in military virtues – deserving of their fate. To appeal to divine judgement as though it were evident here and now is to divinise the principles through which judgement is enacted. In this respect, those who judge are like the pagan sinners in that 'they exchanged the truth about God for a lie and worshiped and served the creature rather than the Creator' (Rom. 1.25). By contrast, God's own judgement is postponed in kindness and forbearance. There is an important philosophical point implicit here. For if God were to enact judgement in the here and now, there would be no difference between moral and natural law, no freedom to do good or evil, and no opportunity for penitence. Ultimately, God would be a brute and inexorable fact of nature – as brutal and inexorable as Roman rule. There would be nothing to respect and worship in such a present and immediate God, just as there is nothing to respect and worship in the laws of nature. There would be no scope for hope, faith or love. Perhaps most significantly, in this world without morality and religion, practical adaptation to realise objectives would be the only prudent course of action: God would determine all outcomes, but not necessarily all objectives. Divine judgement could be reduced from an end to a means. God could be used for individual purposes just as nature is so used. There would be no opportunity for internalising divine character to manifest hope, faith and love to enrich human relationships. So, in a somewhat paradoxical way, to bring the judgement of God forwards amounts to divinising one's own judgements and denying God altogether.

Paul, therefore, will have to speak of a righteousness apart from the law. Paul's theology is strictly eschatological: in order for divine judgement to transcend the order of this world, it must be postponed or delayed. Yet Paul still believes in a coming judgement. Divine judgement itself must be suspended in order to be divine; the divine is constituted as such through mercy. Likewise, the faithful Christian must also suspend judgement in mercy. Eschatology requires suspension – the present order, with all its criteria of truth and judgement, is passing away. But suspension requires eschatology – judgement will come in the end, but in accordance with truly divine criteria. So for those 'who are self-seeking and who obey not the truth but wickedness, there will be wrath and fury', while for those who 'by patiently doing good seek for glory and honour and immortality, he will give eternal life' (Rom. 2.7–8). Faith, enacted through deeds, seeking the true manifestation of God, is what brings justification. Paul's innovation is to suggest that people will be judged on their 'secret thoughts' (Rom. 2.16). The evidence on which divine judgement is to be made, as well as the ultimate criteria, are by no means publicly evident before the end.

Paul therefore offers a striking paradox: the law is only fulfiled through its own suspension. The precise nature of this fulfilment, and the subtle and precise nature of the final judgement, are things 'not seen'; they are only an object of hope. To offer an explanation would amount to claiming to offer an account of the mind of God. Paul does not offer any such explanation. He does, however, claim a unique privilege for the spiritual:

> Those who are unspiritual do not receive the gifts of God's Spirit, for they are foolishness to them, and they are unable to understand them because they are spiritually discerned. Those who are spiritual discern all things, and they are themselves subject to no one else's scrutiny. 'For who has known the mind of the Lord, so as to instruct him'? But we have the mind of Christ. (1 Cor. 2.14–16)

To be spiritual, for Paul, is a matter of having the 'mind of Christ'.

FAITH

Paul introduces the 'mind of Christ' through the chiasmic inversion of the Philippian hymn: 'Who, though he was in the form of God, . . . humbled himself . . . Therefore God has highly exalted him' (Phil. 2.6, 8, 9). For Paul, Jesus's death and resurrection enact the gospel saying, 'For those who want to save their life will lose it, and those who lose their life for my sake, and for the sake of the gospel, will save it' (Mark 8.35). Paul shares in the 'mind of Christ' to the extent that his entire account of his ministry is a commentary on this saying. For Paul has discovered the pearl of great price, and so articulates the chiasmic inversion in economic terms: 'I regard everything as loss because of the surpassing value of knowing Jesus Christ my Lord' (Phil. 3.8). Participation in Christ is participation in this economic inversion: 'For his sake I have suffered the loss of all things, and I regard them as rubbish, in order that I may gain Christ and be found in him. . . . I want to know Christ and the power of his resurrection and the sharing of his sufferings by becoming like him in his death, if somehow I may attain the resurrection from the dead' (Phil. 3.8–9, 10–11).

As a result of this insight, Paul understands eschatological judgement itself in terms of chiasmic inversion: 'God chose what is low and despised in the world, things that are not, to reduce to nothing things that are' (1 Cor. 1.28). The point is not that God elevates the lowly insofar as they are lowly, but that the things of God, the 'secret thoughts' such as faith, are found amongst the things that are rarely noticed: they are not announced by signs or by wisdom. The Christian participates in the mind of Christ to the extent that the Christian also notices that which Christ notices as being of ultimate account. The eschatological life of the Spirit is manifest in an economy of attention: 'For those who live according to the flesh set their minds on the things of the flesh, but those who live according to the Spirit set their minds on the things of the Spirit' (Rom. 8.5).

How does Paul flesh out this distinction? If Paul wrote so extensively of circumcision, of meat offered to idols, of the observation of special days, and of 'works of the law' – these being primarily concerned with the interrelated matters of temple sacrifice and ritual purity – it was to suspend a concern with such things 'of the flesh'. Paul's communities practised what must have appeared to the ancient world as a form of atheism. Partly as a result of Paul's influence, it is difficult for the modern world to comprehend the significance of sacrifice and ritual for social, political and economic life in the ancient world. Rites relating to home and family, to agricultural and commercial productivity, to military success and the order of the state, were the basis for trust, cooperation and authority. By contrast, Paul offered a rationalisation of worship, an ordering of attention to be enacted through the practice of daily life:

> I appeal to you therefore, brothers and sisters, by the mercies of God, to present your bodies as a living sacrifice, holy and acceptable to God, which is your spiritual (*logiken*) worship. Do not be conformed to this age, but be transformed by the renewing of your minds, so that you may discern what is the will of God – what is good and acceptable and perfect. (Rom. 12.1–2)

Just as Jesus taught against a concern for relative status, 'For all who exalt themselves will be humbled, and those who humble themselves will be exalted' (Luke 14.11), Paul also rejects the ritual formalisation of relative status – in his case on the economic grounds of the division of labour: 'For as in one body we have many members, and not all the members have the same function, so we, who are many, are one body in Christ, and individually we are members of one another' (Rom. 12.4–5). For Paul, to give attention to the things of the Spirit is to appeal to ethics as opposed to ritual as the basis for trust, cooperation and authority. By 'rational worship', Paul means enacting his parenesis:

> Let love be genuine; hate what is evil, hold fast to what is good; love one another with mutual affection; outdo one another in showing honor. Do not lag in zeal, be ardent in spirit, serve the Lord. Rejoice in hope, be patient in suffering, persevere in prayer. Contribute to the needs of the saints; extend hospitality to strangers. Bless those who persecute you; bless and do not curse them. Rejoice with those who rejoice, weep with those who weep. Live in harmony with one another; do not be haughty, but associate with the lowly; do not claim to be wiser than you are. (Rom. 12.9–16)

These are the kinds of matters to which Paul advises directing attention. To live in this way is to live by faith, for there is little evidence that such small matters will make a difference in the world or will be accounted highly in God's sight. These are not the obvious matters around which legislation can be formulated; they are not 'works of the law'. Faith, far from being opposed to ethics understood as 'works of the law', is enacted only in commitment to this kind of ethical life. For the 'works of the law' concern ritual and public conduct, but faith concerns the enactment of 'secret thoughts'.

LOVE

Paul's criterion in identifying which 'secret thoughts' count as virtues is, of course, love, 'for the one who loves another has fulfilled the law' (Rom. 13.8). Love, for Paul, is the grace that establishes relationship. He explains such relationship in economic terms by means of a chiasmic inversion: 'For you know the grace of our Lord Jesus Christ, that though he was rich, yet for your sakes he became poor, so that by his poverty you might become rich' (2 Cor. 8.9). Of course, if Jesus had simply been a rich person who became poor, there would have been no grace in that; the countless individuals who have suffered a reversal of fortune have not by this means brought about a transformation of the world. In Paul's thought, Jesus remains rich in a certain sense, even in his poverty, in order to make others rich. What is distinctive, here, is a certain economy of salvation: Jesus manifests his riches only in and through his poverty; he enriches others only through his poverty. The meaning is this: love, that which is most spiritual, is manifested primarily through the body. Paradigmatically, just as Jesus taught in parables, offering a particular embodiment of an idea or message, so Paul regards the death and resurrection of Christ as the particular embodiment of the love of God.

It would seem that Paul was familiar with some version of the saying that has been placed at the apex of the theology of the Fourth Gospel: 'Very truly, I tell you, unless a grain of wheat falls into the earth to the ground and dies, it remains just a single grain; but if it dies, it bears much fruit. Those who love their life lose it, and those who hate their life in this world will keep it for eternal life' (John 12.24–25). This is, once more, an economic image, offering the criterion of 'bearing much fruit'. Paul alludes to this saying in his account of the resurrection, refusing an interpretation of it in purely literal or earthly terms: 'Fool! What you sow does not come to life unless it dies. And as for what you sow, you do not sow the body that is to be, but a bare seed, perhaps of wheat or some other grain. But God gives it a body as he has chosen, and to each kind of seed its own kind of body. . . . There are both heavenly bodies and earthly bodies, but the glory of the heavenly is one thing, and that of the earthly is another' (1 Cor. 15.36–38, 40). The life one leads is conducted in and through the physical body, as though life itself were a matter of writing out the secret thoughts of one's soul. Then, 'in a moment, in the twinkling of an eye' (1 Cor. 15.52), there is a sudden transformation, a change of perspective, in which such secret thoughts become manifest and judged. 'So it is with the resurrection of the dead. What is sown is perishable, what is raised is imperishable. It is sown in dishonour, it is raised in glory. It is sown in weakness, it is raised in power. It is sown a physical body, it is raised a spiritual body' (1 Cor. 15.42–44). Now if such transformations are interpreted in purely individual terms, then we miss out on the way in which Paul invokes them to describe the establishing of relation through mutual understanding. For Paul, it is not the earthly body or some heavenly copy of it that is eternal: only the relational virtues of faith, hope and love abide (1 Cor. 13.13). The relation of love is the core of understanding: 'Now I know only in part; then I will know fully, even as I have been fully known' (1 Cor. 13.12). The body is used to disclose a kind of implicate order of love.

Paul explains this understanding as the true wealth: 'God . . . has shone in our hearts to give the light of the knowledge of the glory of God in the face of Jesus Christ' (2 Cor. 4.6). Yet it is a wealth that is only possessed insofar as it is passed on, manifested through the body to others:

> But we have this treasure in clay jars, so that it may be made clear that this extraordinary power belongs to God and does not come from us. We are afflicted in every way, but not crushed; perplexed, but not driven to despair; persecuted, but not forsaken; struck down, but not destroyed; always carrying in the body the death of Jesus, so that the life of Jesus may be also be made visible in our bodies. For while we live, we are always being given up to death for Jesus' sake, so that the life of Jesus may be made visible in our mortal flesh. So death is at work in us, but life in you. (2 Cor. 4.7–12)

This is how the body manifests secret thoughts. In Paul's apostolic ministry, the three economic gestures of eschatological suspension, chiasmic inversion and mutual exchange become the basis for establishing relationship. His ministry enacts the appeal of 'be reconciled to God' (2 Cor. 5.20) through being reconciled to Christ – in other words, to adopt the perspective that counts hope, faith and love as of ultimate significance. To live in this way is to manifest hope, faith and love – and so to offer these to others in order to establish relationship. Love is an offering that achieves reconciliation. It is this precise manifestation of hope, faith and love that is the life of Christ, so that Paul can declare: 'I have been crucified with Christ; and it is no longer I who live, but it is Christ who lives in me. And the life I now live in the flesh I live by faith in the Son of God, who loved me and gave himself for me' (Gal. 2.19–20).

CONCLUSION

Much of Paul's discussion and terminology is foreign to the teachings of Jesus as recorded in the Synoptic traditions. Nevertheless, it is by juxtaposing these heterogeneous bodies of thought that a common element, apparently insignificant and often overlooked, comes to the fore: both teach a spiritual practice that consists in an economics of thought or an ordering of attention. Both employ the resources of eschatological suspension, chiasmic inversion and mutual expression or relation. Both offer these distinctive ways of delineating the life of hope, faith and love. Both also seem utterly compelled by the absolute significance of this vision.

What must be emphasised here is that an elucidation of this economics of thought has no compelling power in and of itself. If such a philosophy is eschatological, then there is nothing within this world by which it might be judged or approved. If Jesus or Paul encountered the compelling force of the gospel through their understanding of the forgiveness of sins or the death and resurrection of Christ, that force is only available for those 'in Christ'. What is required, therefore, is not a matter of further conceptual precision, as though a better understanding of the form of hope, faith and love would enable us to be infused with their force, but a 'body', a household where resources need to be managed, a specific domain of application. Such ideas do not come to life by their mere presentation. It is rather a matter of experimentation, to think and to live in this way. It is a matter of conducting an inquiry in the spirit of hope, faith and love. There is no question of convincing opponents, of appealing to any force of reason, tradition, authority or even sacrifice to compel agreement. Yet if, in this experimentation, the spirit of hope, faith and love itself comes to life, in spite of the weakness and inadequacies of the thinker, then something fruitful will have been accomplished. To proceed with this inquiry into the economics of the gospel, therefore, we have a more urgent need than greater hermeneutical precision concerning the sources and form of this economics of thought. We need an appropriate body of application. What kind of thinking can be enriched by such an economy? It is time, at last, to return to early Christian teachings on wealth to clarify a distinctly Christian understanding of credit.

Chapter Five

Credit or Grace

If you love those who love you, what credit [*charis*, grace] is that to you? For even sinners love those who love them. If you do good to those who do good to you, what credit is that to you? For even sinners do the same. If you lend to those from whom you hope to receive, what credit is that to you? Even sinners lend to sinners, to receive as much again. But love your enemies, do good, expecting nothing in return. Your reward [*misthos*, wage] will be great, and you will be children of the Most High; for he is kind to the ungrateful and the wicked. Be merciful, just as your Father is merciful. (Luke 6.32–36)

Jesus's economic formulation of his gospel stands out for its utter unworldliness. The basis of human relations in reciprocity is granted no credit. Jesus repeatedly recommends the expenditure of scarce resources. One who lends without return is far from equilibrium. While he employs the terminology of estate management, its literal meaning and application is suspended: one learns nothing from his teaching about how to run a household, let alone about distribution and circulation in a wider economy. What, then, is the true subject matter, the conception of wealth articulated here?

The economic terminology here alludes to a celestial economy: by expecting nothing in return, one receives a heavenly wage.[1] It is presented as though one may enter into an economic transaction with God: by spending all, risking one's life, or staking everything, one fulfils the approved conditions and qualifies for a reward that outweighs all others. If understood according to an exchangist logic of sacrifice, then one seeks to bargain with God, reducing divine grace to human obligation. Even if Christian thought has often interpreted the celestial economy in this way,[2] one should perhaps hesitate to do so. For God becomes bound by his promises: everyone who asks receives. 'Is there anyone among you who, if your child asks for a fish, will give a snake instead of a fish? Or if the child asks for an egg, will give a scorpion'? (Luke 11.11–12). It would seem that God is reduced to a benign father whose main responsibility is the fulfilment of children's wishes, as if God's life and activity were reduced to the correlate of human need. Instead of people being raised to 'children of the Most High', God is degraded to being father of the most lowly. The problem, here, is that the most basic human needs seem to determine the character of God. If human acts of almsgiving are treated as an imitation of divine mercy and initiative in granting the charitable gift of salvation, then divine mercy in turn is understood under the paradigm of human almsgiving. This economic formulation of the gospel would appear to confound theology as much as it suspends economics.

Such obvious contradictions suggest that it may be possible to understand these matters on a different level.[3] A different formulation of the contradiction may assist us here, such as that offered in the first Johannine epistle. For this author speaks both against the love of worldly goods and for the fulfilment of human needs. On the one hand, the unworldliness of Christian life is stated most emphatically:

> Do not love the world or the things of the world. The love of the Father is not in those who love the world; for all that is in the world – the desire of the flesh, the desire of the eyes, the pride in riches – comes not from the Father but from the world. And the world and its desires are passing away, but those who do the will of God live for ever. (1 John 2.15–17)

What seems to be emphasised here is that a child's love for bread, fish or eggs is part of the world that is passing away; it is not the basis for eternal life. On the other hand, love is manifested by administration of the world's goods. 'We know love by this, that he laid down his life for us – and we ought to lay down our lives for one another. How does God's love abide in anyone who has the world's goods and sees a brother or sister in need and yet refuses to help'? (1 John 3.16–17) On this occasion, the need of the brother or sister is not condemned as 'the desire of the flesh, the desire of the eyes, the pride in riches', even if it is a need that can only be met by the world's goods. Such need forms the context in which love may be shown.

The simplest solution to this apparent contradiction is to suppose that what is denounced is not the things themselves but a certain subjective attitude: not the needs of the flesh, but the desire; not the pleasures of the eyes, but their desire; not the riches, but the pride in them.[4] On this reading, worldliness consists in a subjective attitude, a love of temporal things, which may be overcome by a greater love for eternal things. Is it sufficient to seek first the kingdom of God, so that the things of this world can be given to you with a clear conscience? The problem with this reading is that the love for eternal things remains a temporal love; one does not overcome the world so easily. There is a danger of self-deception and hypocrisy: one claims to love the things of the world as the gifts of God and loves them with a clear conscience; but God is invoked here merely to pacify the conscience – one 'loves God' so that one's behaviour can conform to that of the world, so that one can love the things of the world with a clear conscience. The Johannine author is rigorous in exposing such self-deception: 'Those who say, "I love God", and hate their brothers or sisters are liars; for those who do not love a brother or sister whom they have not seen, cannot love God whom they have not seen' (1 John 4.20). All imagination of God, all religious ideology, is judged by the standard of love for others. Subjective attitudes alone are insufficient; what distinguishes the children of God from the children of the devil is doing what is right (1 John 3.10). The Johannine distinction is not between two subjective attitudes, the love of God and the desires of the flesh, but between differing sources for both attitudes and deeds: while the whole world lies under the power of the evil one (1 John 5.19), 'everyone who loves is born of God and knows God' (1 John 4.7). By contrast to subjective attitudes, human need becomes a criterion for judging the authenticity of love: 'By this you know the Spirit of God: every spirit that confesses that Jesus Christ has come in the flesh is from God' (1 John 4.2). Christian thought is concerned with life in the flesh rather than with supposedly transcendent things. 'No one has ever seen God; if we love one another, God lives in us' (1 John 4.12). For this epistle speaks only of 'what we have heard, what we have seen with our eyes, what we have looked at and touched with our hands, concerning the word of life' (1 John 1.1). The authenticity of Christian love may be judged by its economic consequences.

The Johannine author therefore states the problem in an acute form: on the one hand, the love that comes from God does not consist in love of the world or the things of the world; on the other hand, this love is manifest in the flesh in the way it offers the world's goods to those in need. This problem can only be resolved by finding the appropriate way to draw distinctions between the earthly and the heavenly, darkness and light, the devil and God, distinctions which themselves must be articulated in terms 'of the flesh'. As if in indication of the direction in which one may seek an answer, the Johannine account of what is in the world – the desire of the flesh, the desire of the eyes, the pride of riches – recalls an important threefold formula from the Sermon on the Mount, and it is this latter passage that will offer the basis for our complex navigation between the gospel and economy:

> Do not store up for yourselves treasures on earth, where moth and rust consume and thieves break in and steal; but store up for yourselves treasures in heaven, where neither moth nor rust consumes and where thieves do not break in and steal. For where your treasure is, there will your heart be also.

> The eye is the lamp of the body. So, if your eye is healthy, your whole body will be full of light; but if your eye is unhealthy, your whole body will be full of darkness. If then the light in you is darkness, how great is the darkness!
>
> No one can serve two masters; for a slave will either hate the one and love the other, or be devoted to the one and despise the other. You cannot serve God and wealth.
>
> Therefore I tell you, do not worry about your life, what you will eat or what you will drink, or about your body, what you will wear. Is not life more than food, and the body more than clothing? (Matt. 6.19–25)

These sayings may be considered the source of the Johannine threefold condemnation of worldliness. The most salient characteristic of treasures on earth is that they are passing away; they correspond to the Johannine 'things of the world'. The light of the body corresponds to the desire of the eyes, while the service of wealth to the pride in riches. This threefold formula then leads to a most unworldly conclusion: do not worry about what you will eat, drink or wear. This need not be understood as a denial of the needs of the flesh or even of concern for them. What is crucial, here, is that life is more than food and the body more than clothing. In this 'more than', the entire conception of an incarnational notion of transcendence is at stake. Just as the body is a far more complex and rich entity than the two-dimensional clothing which conceals its appearance, and just as life is far more living than the dead food that gives it sustenance, so also is love far more profound than the needs that it meets or the gifts which it offers. The threefold formula can then be reinterpreted as spelling out some relevant dimensions of this 'more than', this transcendence that belongs to life and the body. These are the dimensions of credit.

INVESTMENT

The first saying concerns 'storing up treasure', whether through labour or investment. Now food and drink, clothing and ornament, are temporary: moth and rust consume them. Such temporary things are contrasted with 'treasures in heaven', things having the character of perpetuity or inviolability. Yet a second salient characteristic of earthly goods is that they can be stolen: what can be mine can also be yours, but only on the condition that I have it no longer. Earthly goods are *objects of appropriation*: they are mine only insofar as they are not yours. We cannot consume the same items of food and drink;[5] we cannot wear the same clothes and ornaments at the same time. Anything that can be appropriated is a scarce resource: food, possessions, land, property and assets, for example. Yet there are also scarce social resources, such as honours, privileges, patronage, status, recognition, sporting victories, competitive prizes, admiration and affection from family or lovers.[6] There are even scarce economic resources, such as employment opportunities, investments or supply contracts. Each of these meets human needs; they may be considered as the 'world's goods'. Jesus's saying points out that life is more than the things which can be consumed or appropriated; life is more than simple need. Moreover, a long tradition of Christian reflection has associated an overriding concern with such goods with selfishness, leading to rivalry and conflict.[7] Whether one elevates natural need or social recognition, the 'desire of the flesh' or the 'desire of the eyes', attention to these only offers a life of conflict and subjection to natural or social necessity. There are alternative objects of investment.

ATTENTION

How may we think of that which cannot be consumed or appropriated? A different kind of looking is required. The second saying inverts the optics of classical physics: we normally regard the eye as the destination rather than the source of light. From the earthly point of view, the eye can only see what the lamp illuminates; in Jesus's saying, the eye sees what it illuminates or notices. In what sense can we understand the eye as the 'lamp of the body'? The primary contrast is between a 'body full of darkness' and a 'body full of light'. But this 'body' is not the object of perception – an ultrasound image of the inside of a womb or bladder is not at stake here. Instead, this 'body' is in some sense the lived, managed and disciplined body, the body which determines where one looks: it is life regarded as a household, a way of being and dwelling, the ordering of experience according to light or darkness. This, in turn, enables vision. Human experience depends upon the health of the 'eye', the ordering and distribution of attention. In this respect, Jesus seems to be relating health to subjectivity, to intention and attention. In the Sermon on the Mount, Jesus seems to construct a philosophy of subjectivity without the use of concepts – one that has, of course, contributed to the development of modern philosophies of subjectivity.

There is much in modern philosophy that might help to illuminate the significance of the distinction proposed here between vision and property. One rather pertinent example will suffice. Adam Smith constructed his moral philosophy upon the basis of the subjective capacity for sympathy, and therefore offered a basis for understanding how intention might exceed need. It is worth quoting his inquiry into the fundamental grounds of economic motives:

> For to what purpose is all the toil and bustle of this world? What is the end of avarice and ambition, of the pursuit of wealth, of power, and pre-eminence? Is it to supply the necessities of nature? The wages of the meanest labourer can supply them. . . . From whence, then, arises that emulation which runs through

all the different ranks of men, and what are the advantages which we propose by that great purpose of life which we call bettering our condition? *To be observed, to be attended to, to be taken notice of with sympathy, complacency and approbation, are all the advantages which we can propose to derive from it. It is the vanity, not the ease, or the pleasure, which interests us.* [8]

The question of whether Smith is correct in identifying vanity as the dominant economic motive is not our immediate concern. Smith is observing that beyond the necessities of nature there is also a desire for social recognition: the eye counts for more than the body. To be seen, even by oneself, with approbation and sympathy, is suggested to be the principal form of satisfaction.[9] It is precisely this short-circuit between deed and satisfaction that Jesus had sought to break: 'But when you give alms, do not let your left hand know what your right hand is doing, so that your alms may be done in secret; and your Father who sees in secret will reward you' (Matt. 6.3–4). Smith's account of vanity, then, may help us to develop the Johannine conception of worldliness. For wealth, power, and preeminence are relative; they are competitive goods, or goods of appropriation. The approbation of others is scarce. Moreover, wealth, power and preeminence, here, function as signs: the world notices them. But what is at the root of this interest in wealth, power and preeminence that attracts attention from others? What does the world seek in wealth, power and preeminence? Smith's answer is sympathy and approbation. In other words, the acquisition of wealth, power and status is a *sign* that one might deserve sympathy and approbation. Wealth is a sign of possible virtue; virtue is a cause for admiration; and being admired is desirable because it leads to sympathy and recognition. On this account, neither wealth, power and status nor virtue are valued in and of themselves, but only for the sake of attracting attention. The path to virtue and its true recognition has been short-circuited. The capacity to love what is truly loveable has been replaced by the need to be loved. As for those whose virtues are not such as to bring wealth, power or status, they are simply not noticed: the world does not count their virtues as worthy of attention, for it counts as virtue only what attracts attention. In the Johannine account, the world constructs itself from a short-circuit of attention: 'They are from the world; therefore what they say is from the world, and the world listens to them' (1 John 4.5). At no point is true light or virtue able to illuminate this theatre of attention. If the light in you is darkness, how great is that darkness?[10]

There is, however, another way of directing attention which escapes the short-circuit of vanity, for life does not solely consist in competitive goods. There are also cooperative or public goods, things that can only be mine insofar as they are also yours.[11] There is much in the physical environment that cannot be easily appropriated: fresh air, precipitation, nonhuman organisms that live, reproduce and die according to their own nature. There are also many human institutions that operate by participation, whether or not anyone claims ownership of them and with it a dividend: schools, hospitals, universities and prisons, but also roads, communications, markets and governments. Even money only exists insofar as its value is collectively recognised. Daily life is constructed from a series of goods of participation, things that exist only insofar as they are shared, including cultures, languages, laws, families, contracts and freedom. There is a long tradition of moral philosophy, influenced by Aristotle, which regards virtue as that which makes collective life possible. To be virtuous, on this account, is to enrich the health of collective life. As the influential twentieth-century Anglican theologian, William Temple, explained cooperative goods at the end of his Gifford Lectures:

> Enjoyment of them by one prompts rather than hinders a similar enjoyment of them on the part of others. The scholar does not exhaust the stock of knowledge so that others must be ignorant that he may know; the poet does not suck the beauty from the sunset; the loyal friend or disciple does not make love more difficult for his fellows. These goods are multiplied by being possessed. [12]

To have an eye for the health of participatory goods is therefore to illuminate others. Moreover, this capacity to notice the wealth of participatory goods enriches the sight of the entire social body: if your eye is healthy, your whole body will be full of light.

DEVOTION

Jesus does not seem to have spoken directly about such participatory goods, or the moral or political visions that are based on them, unlike Paul and the Johannine author. His economic vocabulary did not lend itself to these essentially moral and political concerns. Instead, Jesus spoke of service more than participation, the economics of household or estate life more than the government of free citizens. [13] Such is the case with the saying on God and wealth. In line with this, Temple extended his discussion of the vision of cooperative goods beyond its Augustinian formulation into the domain of worship:

> The man who would see Truth must yield his mind to the facts; the man who would enjoy Beauty must surrender his soul to its spell; the man who would love must give his very self, for that is what love is. At every point therefore the aspiration towards these forms of good requires a denial of self, and in the measure of attainment passes over into worship, of which the meaning is total self-giving and self-submission to the Object of worship. This, then, it seems, is man's true good – to worship. [14]

One does not have to adopt the implicit epistemology, aesthetics or ethics at work here to notice the characteristic inversion: the mind that seeks to master truth, beauty or love does so by becoming a servant. It is precisely this kind of inversion that is enacted in the third element of our passage from the Sermon on the Mount: instead of wealth being the universal servant, the means by which one accomplishes whatever one wishes, Jesus treats wealth as a master, a rival to God. The fundamental conception of 'sin' here is a matter of misplaced devotion – to take a limited and temporary means, such as wealth, as an absolute end. The one who would do anything for money is essentially one who worships it; the one who would give anything for God, even life itself, is one who worships God. Jesus links worship with absolute expenditure.

Jesus's threefold formula therefore illuminates three aspects of life insofar as it exceeds meeting simple needs: life consists in 'storing up treasure', a temporal process of investment, whether actively through work or subjectively through placing one's heart; furthermore, life consists in directing attention, whether to illuminate the whole 'body' or to leave aspects of life in darkness; finally, life consists in service, in expenditure, in lending oneself without return. Here, perhaps, we have reached the heart of Jesus's formulation of the gospel in economic terms: life consists in credit – in investment, attention and expenditure. This is the aspect of the gospel that amounts to an 'economy of thinking'.

In this respect, Christian thought can be subsumed under an economic paradigm: it concerns the management of scarce resources, for thought, attention and life are scarce. Yet at the same time, economic life may be subsumed under a religious paradigm, for work, investment, attention and expenditure are treated as aspects of 'worship'. What separates worship, here, from mere investment, is the absence of any return. For life is absolute expenditure; one does not receive any return upon life itself. Life itself, here, does not belong to the 'world'; it does not consist in the abundance of one's possessions (Luke 12.15). Yet neither does it consist straightforwardly in home nor community, in dwelling and participation, without a prior renunciation (Luke 18.29–30). Even if life is spent on giving a life to others, that life does not return to the one who spent it. There is no reciprocity in life itself. Life itself, then, is worship. *Investment, attention and devotion are goods of offering: they can be mine only insofar as I give them.*[15] Any attempt to spend the scarce resource of life by seeking above all to preserve it is doomed to failure. 'For those who want to save their life will lose it, and those who lose their life . . . will save it. For what will it profit them to gain the whole world and forfeit their life'? (Mark 8.35)

Christian thought exceeds a purely economic subsumption under the immanent framework of the management of the household of thought because it is articulated in relation to creation and eschatology. The *oikonomos* is not simply a manager, but also a steward, appointed and accountable. At last, we can explore the philosophical significance of Paul's commission. In Christian thought, the individual does not own their life, body or time because these are not goods of appropriation.[16] One does not determine the conditions of one's own birth or life; one only attains to responsibility by inhabiting the given bonds, such as those to parents, society, culture and environment, that preexist one's own choices. Nearly everything that shapes the character and possibilities of life is provided by others. Yet even these prior bonds and conditions are subordinate to God: heaven and earth will pass away. If there is one respect in which divine omnipotence is directly manifest in natural law it is this: time passes. Prior to time being an object of individual expenditure, it is given and taken. This law of the passage of time is unconditional, infinite and inexorable. The Christian does not own their time; the Christian is appointed to their time. The life that one manages or spends is the life that one has been given. One only receives that time in managing and spending it.[17] The Christian is an appointed steward whose very life consists in receiving and granting investment, attention and devotion. Life is receiving credit by giving it.

FAITH IN FORGIVENESS

In addition to life insofar as it is given and life insofar as it is spent, there is also a third aspect: life insofar as it is judged. The *oikonomos* is accountable. What matters most, in the economic management of life, is not the goods of appropriation nor the goods of participation, but the judgement, the *credit* or grace that is received. Of course, all the images for this eternal life are taken from temporal life: it is described as a blessing, reward or wage, or else as participation in a celebratory feast. Yet what is truly radical in Jesus's account of divine judgement is his emphasis on forgiveness: What might this tell us about the nature of the credit that is received and the response of faith?

There is one more contradiction which will illuminate the nature of credit and faith. On the one hand, Jesus seems to make divine forgiveness conditional on offering forgiveness to others: 'forgive us our debts, as we also have forgiven our debtors' (Matt. 6.12). On the other hand, the divine initiative of announcing forgiveness is the condition for showing great love, as in the case of the woman with the alabaster jar (Luke 7.47). It is difficult to know which is the cause and which is the consequence here: whether divine forgiveness is the source of human forgiveness, or human forgiveness is the condition for divine forgiveness. But this is to miss the point: forgiveness itself is beyond means and ends; the gospel involves an eschatological suspension of the earthly laws of causality. It is not articulated in terms of causes, which essentially govern goods of appropriation, nor in terms of grounds, which essentially govern goods of participation. Forgiveness, like investment, attention and devotion, is a *good of offering*. It announces a further metaphysical category and a different philosophical practice, beyond the consideration of causes and grounds: repetition.[18]

Faith may be grasped in terms of repetition. There is something distinctive about investment, attention and devotion: when life has been spent in this way, the life that one receives is the life that one gives. A life may be spent in devotion and service, yet the life that one experiences is precisely the same life: the life that is spent. Even if you spend your life in service of yourself, that life is ultimately spent, and the only life you have is the life thus spent. One does not, at the end of such a life, acquire a 'self'. The notion of repetition in Christian subjectivity has been explained, albeit in an ambiguous and questionable manner, by Søren Kierkegaard:

> Christianly understood, you have absolutely nothing to do with what others do to you; it does not concern you; it is curiosity, an impertinence, a lack of consciousness to mix into things that are no more your business than if you were absent. You have to do only with what you do unto others or with the way you receive what others do unto you; the direction is inwards. For Christianly understood, to love human beings is to love God and to love God is to love human beings. . . . For God is himself really the pure like-for-like, the pure rendition of how you yourself are. . . . God's relationship to a human being is the infinitising at every moment of that which at every moment is in a man . . . everything you say to and do to other human beings God simply repeats; he repeats it with the intensification of infinity.[19]

The one who devotes herself to truth, as in Temple's account of worship, does not, by this means, acquire truth or participate in truth. All that is received is the life of devotion, the life characterised by a love of truth. The mind is therefore under contradictory and incompatible obligations. On the one hand, one must ask: 'What is truly worthy of devotion? What is the richest, most intense, and most rewarding life? What would be the presence of God within this life, mind and time'? Such a question is insoluble and yet necessary; it leads to an infinite questioning of life as it is lived. On the other hand, one cannot stop life in order to pose such a question; one cannot solve the problem of living before one has lived. Time is passing; one is under an inexorable obligation to spend that life. Each moment, then, is a foreclosure of the infinite inquiry into divinity. The unlimited possibilities of ways of living are reduced to a few faltering steps forwards. In this sense, all have sinned and fall short of the glory of God; sin is a short-circuiting of the infinite depths of experience. To live in time is to live in contradiction.

The only solution is faith in the forgiveness of sins. In the context of this question, one can understand this as a release from the obligation to pursue the infinite inquiry into the true wealth of experience. There is no obligation to incarnate God in experience or in this world, except insofar as God is merciful. Yet here we come to the other side of subjectivity: investment, attention, devotion and forgiveness are relational terms. One does not live for oneself alone; the life one lives is mediated by others. One lives only by offering, only in relation to others. For even if one attends to oneself – whether in self-seeking, or in the discipline of Christian duty – the life one receives is not entirely determined by oneself but mediated by the life that one is given. In this sense, sin is no longer conceived as a short-circuiting of the relation to God, for no one has the power to deny or resist time, attention and devotion. On the contrary, sin is a lack of faith, a short-circuiting of the external conditions of experience. The striving for purity is itself sin, a vain attempt to seize mastery over one's own mind. Kierkegaard's formulation requires a little qualification: Christianly understood, what you do to yourself does not concern you; it is curiosity, impertinence, a lack of consciousness to mix yourself up in things that are no more your business than if you were absent. You have only to do with what you do unto others, or what others have done unto them. The direction is outwards. Such worship is not fulfilled through a heightening of subjectivity, but through its self-emptying. Weil is more faithful to the gospel here in her account of the 'decreation of the self': 'If only I could manage to disappear, there would take place a perfect love union between God and the earth that I tread, the sea that I hear'.[20] Consciousness is only fully conscious when it is conscious of what is outside. Faith in forgiveness consists in granting credit to others. On this account, the reward that is given is the reward of life itself – the consciousness of earth, sun and sky, of time, meaning and value. For it is how much credit one has granted that is the basis for how the wealth of one's life will be judged.

CONCLUSION

At last, we are now in a position to articulate the sense in which life is more than food and the body more than clothing. Life is more than the goods of appropriation; life is also more than the goods of participation. Life, on Jesus's account, consists in goods of offering: investment, attention, devotion and forgiveness. Life is the repetition of grace by offering credit. To restrict life to a concern for appropriation or participation alone is to short-circuit life by means of reducing its household to the individual or the community. By contrast, this Christian account of subjectivity is radically exposed to what is beyond. In temporal terms, what lies beyond the self is what comes before, the life that is created and given, as well as what comes after, the life that is judged and rewarded. In spatial terms, what lies beyond the self is the infinite depth within as well as the universe without.

The Christian economy of thinking is a matter of managing investment, attention, devotion and forgiveness with responsibility and accountability. It is by no means a matter of keeping a perfect house. On the contrary, it is always a matter of hospitality, of conducting oneself as at once host and guest, exposed to the chances that come from without or within. *In this respect, keeping the household of thought is not a matter of self-sufficiency, but a matter of exposure to the responses of all the other households in life.* Finally, we move from the archaic sense of the economy, as the management of a self-sufficient household, to the modern one, where the experience of each household is dependent upon the circulation and distribution of resources.[21] The concern is primarily outwards. Of course, modern economics has been far more concerned with the distribution of scarce goods of appropriation than it has with the distribution of scarce goods of offering. Yet might it not be the case that the religious life, as articulated in the economic terminology of Jesus, may only find completion outside itself, in the strictly economic life of the satisfaction of needs? Might there not be a theology that can only be articulated through its economic concerns? Is this not what the Johannine author, in appealing to goods of offering, has proclaimed: 'We know love by this, that he laid down his life for us – and we ought to lay down our lives for one another. How does God's love abide in anyone who has the world's goods and sees a brother or sister in need and yet refuses to help'? (1 John 3.16–17)

Finally, then, we can state four conclusions of this very partial and limited abstraction from the mind of Christ as a 'philosophy of religion':[22]

1. The Christian articulation of its gospel in terms of economy draws attention away from any explicit power to command and persuade; yet once one starts to inhabit life from its perspective, to make sense of experience in terms of its categories, one may find that it has its own inner necessity that becomes utterly compelling and authoritative.
2. This philosophy of religion consists in a mindset for transforming mindsets: in hope, as a principle of judgement, as an eschatological suspension of all received criteria; in faith, as a principle of redemption, as a chiasmic inversion of evaluations; and in love, as a principle of creation, as a work of mutual transformation where each perspective interprets another by which it is interpreted in turn.
3. Life itself can be divided into the dimensions which constitute any experience: goods of appropriation, goods of participation, and goods of offering. Salvation may be achieved by restoring attention to goods of participation and goods of offering. Christian life is economic insofar as it is a distribution of goods of offering: investment, attention, devotion and forgiveness.

4. This mindset entirely lacks any substance or sovereignty of its own; it can only come to make sense when it is handed over, immersed in a field of other mindsets, a wider economy of offering and response. It is a thought which requires mediation, a theology which requires supplementation by economics.

At first, one may simply not know what to make of this philosophy of religion. No exterior criteria of evaluation seem to hold any purchase here. Any test involves finding out what it is like to think in this way. This is where we shall turn our attention next, rearticulating this abstraction from theology in terms of a philosophy.

II

Value and Debt: Philosophical Roots

Chapter Six

Redemption

Why do you see the speck in your neighbor's eye, but do not notice the log in your own eye? Or how can you say to your neighbour, 'Let me take the speck out of your eye', while the log is in your own eye? You hypocrite, first take the log out of your own eye, and then you will see clearly to take the speck out of your neighbor's eye. (Matt. 7.3–5)

There are few more thought-provoking statements of the philosophical task than this. Amongst the rarest and most difficult acts of thinking is taking the log out of one's own eye. For if one cannot even see clearly to take the speck out of another's, how can one see to take the log out of one's own? Indeed, how could one ever know that it is there? Even if one turns to others for assistance, is not the Socratic saviour who promises 'Let me take the log out of your eye' not in danger of becoming an even greater hypocrite, should such a saviour possess no guarantee of their own clarity of vision? Might not those who understand thought through the lens of its propositional content, as something the mind might appropriate, obscure any understanding thought as an act of redemption itself, as something the mind might offer or be offered?

Here is a possible framework for comprehending this predicament. The eye is the lamp of the body: what we pay attention to determines what is noticed, what one thinks, what one desires and how one lives. A healthy eye pays attention to what matters, orienting life in accordance with its light. An unhealthy eye has its vision obstructed, whether by presuppositions, prejudices, habits of thinking, narrowness of focus, undisciplined impulses or self-deceit. The case of the hypocrite is more than a matter of obstruction. It is not that the hypocrite fails to see, evaluate or criticise; the hypocrite cannot see, evaluate and criticise their own powers of vision.

Attention itself has its own economy and ecology.[1] Vision is pervasive in a knowledge economy, where much of the workforce are involved in receiving, processing and adapting information, where entertainment is primarily cerebral, and where social communication consists in constructing images and appearances. Yet the role for the mind here is highly circumscribed: in work, leisure and socialising, cognition is a plastic material, an instrument, a means for the pursuit of extrinsic ends. Vision is not yet thought. Either one sees what one has paid to see, as in consumption, or else one sees only what one is paid to see, as in employment. In either case, it is as though one person inhabits the body of another, adopting their abilities as if they were one's own, while the other, in turn, mimes a display of vision purely for the sake of their employer. Payment frames vision. All becomes hypocrisy in the universal prostitution of knowledge, even when one simply considers the facts. Perhaps Arendt's diagnosis is truer than ever: thoughtlessness is one of the outstanding characteristics of our time.[2]

In philosophical thinking, by contrast, it is the mind which becomes a plastic material, its reasoning and aspirations reshaped by the idea itself. Such thinking is scarce. An idea which is genuinely transformative, which removes the obstacles to clear perception, is, for a philosopher, a pearl of great price. It is at once what matters and what enables the perception of what matters: a reason is at once an obligation and a matter of fact. There is difficulty both in finding such pearls and in making their value perceptible to others. Expending itself in the quest for scarce treasure, philosophical activity can be described as an enterprise. Scarce thinking requires a stimulus or provocation, followed by the expenditure of time, energy and investment. It requires detachment from certain presuppositions, investments and habits of thinking upon which one has previously relied. It requires an extensive process of cultivation, for one can only bring to bear in critical judgement an acquired wealth of knowledge, understanding and experience to engage with the matter at hand. Finally, it requires the formulation of a problem: a lens to enable one to see what is pertinent and what matters. As a whole, philosophical thinking is an investment which wagers its capacity to pay attention on the frameworks it constructs. Each act of constructive thinking has an irreversible effect on the thinker. Apart from this irreversible effect, the return on investment is somewhat meagre: the ideas that flow into a speech or onto a page pass through a hearer's or reader's mind in but a moment, and slip away, leaving barely a trace. Balancing expenditure against income, one might suppose that thinking is pure extravagance. Even so, the impact generated by the few contagious and potent ideas is sufficient to reconstruct the world. There is an unlimited potential to the value of thought.

The cultivated mind hungers for this value. To come across thoughts that might transform oneself or the world: this is a means for feeding the soul. There is a hunger in reading – one lets each formulated thought pass so quickly because it makes such little difference, and rapidly moves on, hoping to discover or accumulate something of scarce value. This hunger is rarely satisfied: if the thoughts one reads are too familiar they do not satisfy, if too strange they are not digested. The thoughts that truly nourish the soul are scarce.

Nevertheless, the philosophical enterprise as a whole offers little guarantee against hypocrisy: it remains hard to distinguish lenses from logs. The problem of hypocrisy is this: in the act of judging others, or in promising to clarify their vision, the hypocrite lays claim to a wealth which they do not in fact possess. One can distinguish between empty promises and those which offer substance by means of their effects or what is actually given. The false prophets, the ravenous wolves in sheep's clothing, consume more than they produce (Matt. 7.15). The task of one who seeks to escape hypocrisy is therefore to offer more than they have received. This simple maxim of leaving the world a richer place, a guide to economic conduct as well as to philosophy, is, of course, extremely hard to apply in practice: For what is the true measure of wealth? Which promises and what vision are grounded in substance rather than in show? How does one know whether one has truly enriched others or only impoverished them? In the absence of a vision of substance one can only make do with signs.

There is one sign of value which holds a nearly universal currency: payment of some cost. Georg Simmel explained the origin of economic value in this way:

> For if any object is valued rather than simply satisfying desire it stands at an objective distance from us that is established by real obstacles and necessary struggles, by gain and loss, by considerations of advantage and by prices. . . . Within the economic sphere, this process develops in such a way that the content of the sacrifice or renunciation that is interposed between man and the object of his demand is, at the same time, the object of someone else's demand.[3]

Logs are heavy to remove; the resistance they offer can only be overcome by effort. A price to be paid – whether in effort expended, goods or services rendered, collateral pledged, people given as hostages, or simple money exchanged – bears witness to the value that has been seen for one to pay such a cost. Especially nowadays, people tend to value difficult achievements irrespective of the purpose they serve. Even when we cannot trust the vision or the words of others, we can at least trust the seriousness of their commitment. The collector of fine pearls sells all he has to gain the pearl of great price. The earnest disciple abandons family and possessions in order to follow their master (Luke 18.28). Even the Johannine author seems to treat sacrifice as a guarantee of love: 'We know love by this, that he laid down his life for us' (1 John 3.16). A price paid is a universally accepted guarantee against hypocrisy. The rationale here is similar to that for trial by torture: no liar would be willing to pay such a price. Ending the torture by false confession risked

further torture, whether in this life or the next. A price that is paid claims to
disclose truth and value. Yet instead of displaying what matters about any
given truth or value, it merely displays an obligation to value the sacrifice:
value is displaced by debt.

Such prices paid form a basis for an economy alongside philosophy. As
Jürgen Habermas once put it, reasons 'are the currency used in a discursive
exchange that redeems criticisable validity claims'.[4] Reasoning is an irreversible investment; it does indeed bear a cost, that of wagering its future capacity to pay attention. It is important to distinguish between a reason which has
currency and a reason which draws its necessity from that which matters.
One draws its value from the sight of others; the other has intrinsic value
irrespective of whether it is acknowledged. The problem, here, is that intrinsic value may be overlooked.

These concerns may be illuminated by how they apply in the case of
material economy; this, too, is a theatre of value. Some receive money as a
sign of labour expended, goods and services exchanged, or pledges accepted;
others receive money, through rent, dividends and interest, as a sign of the
expenditure undergone by others. In each of these forms, money is a record
of the expenditure of a life. In one respect, money's value or desirability is
proven by the sacrifice undergone for it. Nevertheless, there is no direct
correlation between sacrifice undergone and the quantity of money awarded.
One is paid not according to one's own valuations, but according to the
valuations of others. One is paid not for labour expended but for preferences
fulfilled. In this other respect, much effort is simply wasted, for its fruits are
not recognised: enterprises fail, investments are lost, products are replaced
and people lose their jobs. Money is less a sign of sacrifice than a sign of
recognition: it is a record of preferences fulfilled and pleasures undergone.
Perhaps the wastage and sacrifice can only be justified if, as a result, preferences are fulfilled more efficiently and effectively. Even so, the problem,
when it comes to the value of preferences, is that we have hardly more
adequate defences against self-deception than we do against hypocrisy. Even
in the case of enjoyment, one may experience one's own pleasures with a log
in one's eye.[5] According to Pierre Klossowski, for a pleasure that is unintelligible and nonexchangeable, it is once more the cost borne that is the measure
of the pleasure: 'Some basic *resistance* is necessary even if it's only an
illusion: the pursuit of pleasure or enjoyment, ergo the voluptuous emotion,
presupposes an act of resistance, and indeed *the simulacrum is worthless or
ineffectual unless it encounters some form of external resistance*'.[6] Even in
leisure activities, many of the most popular forms of pleasure consist in
overcoming a challenge. If this is what we are willing to pay for, then in both
production and consumption the value that underpins money is the living
currency of the expenditure of life. Indeed, it is very possible that such costs

borne often make ourselves or others poorer rather than richer. One cannot always be sure to leave the world a richer place.

Reasoning is often an expenditure to purchase validity. Such considerations provide an initial clue as to what it might mean to have a 'log in one's eye'. The price that is paid bears no relation to the truth or value that is seen. There is no intrinsic relation between a truth or value and its simulacrum. Yet lacking any guarantee against hypocrisy or self-deception, the one with faulty vision takes on the burden of a labour, expenditure or pledge, as if the price that is paid might persuade in the absence of any common vision of value. To have a heavy log in one's eye is to measure value by the cost of what has been pledged. Since the greater sacrifices are treated as evidence of greater value, any inflationary competition becomes deeply self-destructive. A world where there is no intrinsic perception of value is a world which is passing away.

A pledge or sacrifice offers only a simulacrum of value. This is why we can conceive the philosophical task as redemption of a costly pledge. Such redemption does not consist in further payment of some extrinsic cost or value; on the contrary, the aim is simply to be economical, to liberate from unnecessarily costly pledges and debts. Redemption consists in a transformation of perspective such that any prior costs or pledges no longer seem to matter as a measure of value. Instead, a value is seen which has the power to communicate its worth. The aim of economic life is no longer a matter of fulfilling preferences but one of creating real value. Economics without philosophy entirely lacks direction. Yet even philosophy itself may stand in need of the redemption of its thought. Before turning directly to economic life, the immediate task of this part is to consider how the thinking of credit and faith extracted from the interaction of gospel and economy in the preceding part may offer categories of existence and operations of thinking that steer philosophy towards the task of redemption. The task is to consider how value can be conceived in itself, apart from debt, while the value of values is devalued by its subordination to debt.

Chapter Seven

Value

The task of philosophy is to think the truth, to make thinking conform to being. Yet thought is one thing; actual existence quite another. How can thinking become adequate to being? For a human mind, being, by itself, is not necessarily thought; thinking, by itself, is not necessarily true. Howsoever truth is conceived, it is a third thing alongside thinking and being, a common measure, that by which thinking and being agree, conform or are adequate to each other. Truth is that in respect of which thinking conforms to being, as well as that in respect of which being may be thought. How, then, are we to think this third thing, truth?

According to the gospel, this truth is strictly eschatological. Grounds for truth are neither a matter of recollection nor participation for an inquiring mind. It is important to consider what has been suspended here. For centuries prior to the influence of Francis Bacon, Thomas Hobbes and John Locke, the ground of truth was sought in the idea of perfection: a perfect thinking conforms to being; a perfect being is one which may be thought. By contrast, imperfect thinking was erroneous, while imperfect beings were unintelligible. The idea of perfection led directly to God as perfect thinking and being, while worldly imperfections were often conceived as falling short of God. Diverse philosophies appealed to God, the perfect being, as the ground of truth. As Spinoza put it, 'All ideas, insofar as they have reference to the idea of God, are true'.[1] Yet Spinoza clarified that what was at stake in the idea of God is the idea of substance, 'that which is in itself and is conceived in itself'.[2] Truth, on this account, is grounded in substance, and substance is that whose essence implies its existence. Substance is that which is the same for thinking and being, as Parmenides might have said. But this is only to restate the problem. What is the substance of truth? Is this substance even

thinkable for a human mind? If philosophies agree over thinking truth, they
disagree over how truth is to be thought.

PLATO

It is worth pausing to consider the origins of appeals to perfection. In Plato's
Phaedo, the dialogue set on Socrates's final day, Socrates reports the discovery that set him on his philosophical journey, one found in reading a book of
Anaxagoras: 'It is Mind that directs and is the cause of everything'.[3] In other
words, the ground of existence is thinkable. Reality is the reality of thought.
On this account, 'If then one wished to know the cause of each thing, why it
comes to be or perishes or exists, one had to find what was the best way for it
to be, or to be acted upon, or to act'.[4] Such an idea of 'the best' nourishes
thought by providing it with an entire field of experimentation. Thinking is
oriented by the ideas in which it participates. Thought has ontological priority over existence. For example, Plato cites with approval the episode when
Thales fell into a well because he was looking at the stars, in spite of the fact
that he was made fun of by a Thracian servant girl who said 'he was wild to
know about what was up in the sky but failed to see what was in front of him
under his feet'.[5] For the stars, in their eternal, regular, circular motion, at
least portray something of perfection, unlike feet and wells. Or in a dialogue
of questionable authorship, the *Greater Hippias*, Socrates could explain:

> You all say what you just said, that I am spending my time on things that are
> silly and small and worthless. But when I'm convinced by you and say what
> you say, that it's much the most excellent thing to be able to present a speech
> well and finely, and get things done in court or any other gathering, I hear
> every insult from that man (among others around here) who has always been
> refuting me. He happens to be a close relative of mine, and he lives in the same
> house. So when I go home to my own place and he hears me saying those
> things, he asks if I'm not ashamed that I dare discuss fine activities when I've
> been so plainly refuted about the fine, and it is clear that I don't even know
> what *that* is itself! 'Look', he'll say, 'How will you know whose speech – or
> any other action – is finely presented or not, when you are ignorant of the fine?
> And when you are in a state like that, do you think it is better for you to live
> than to die'?[6]

The voice of Socrates's conscience imposes a demand: it is necessary to
know *what* things such as beauty are before one can make judgements about
them. The substance of thought is understanding what concepts truly mean; it
is a comprehension of the *essence* of things.

This appeal to perfection needs to be understood against the backdrop of
cognition without substance. The task of philosophy is redemption from the
opinions of the crowd or market. Sophistry, according to Plato, simply teach-

es what the crowd approves. Plato compared the convictions that the majority express when they are gathered together to the gestures of a great beast:

> It's as if someone were learning the moods and appetites of a huge, strong beast that he's rearing – how to approach and handle it, when it is most difficult to deal with or most gentle and what makes it so, what sounds it utters in either condition, and what sounds soothe or anger it. Having learned all this through tending the beast over a period of time, he calls this knack wisdom, gathers his information together as if it were a craft, and starts to teach it. In truth, he knows nothing about which of these convictions is fine or shameful, good or bad, just or unjust, but he applies all these names in accordance with how the beast reacts – calling what it enjoys good and what angers it bad. He has no other account to give of these terms. And he calls what he is compelled to do just and fine, for he hasn't seen and cannot show anyone else how much compulsion and goodness really differ.[7]

Plato had clearly been observing the exchanges of Tokyo, Shanghai, Frankfurt, London, New York and Chicago. On his account, the market or beast lacks any conception of the fine, good or just; it just responds according to the compulsion of its nature. It cannot judge or evaluate. In a similar way, the crowd, when gathered together, distils its convictions from the reactions of others, who in turn respond to the reactions of others. The crowd is a phenomenon produced by the laws of group interaction. It does not reason. It acts out of compulsion. It can merely offer praise or blame (or buy or sell):

> When many of them are sitting together in assemblies, courts, theaters, army camps, or in some other public gathering of the crowd, they object very loudly and excessively to some of the things that are said or done and approve others in the same way, shouting and clapping, so that the very rocks and surroundings echo the din of their praise or blame and double it.[8]

Under such compulsion, no individual self-discipline is able to take a stand. The crowd, which exerts compulsion, is therefore entirely subject to compulsion for it has little other knowledge than of itself.

> No indeed, it would be very foolish even to try to oppose them, for there isn't now, hasn't been in the past, nor ever will be in the future anyone with a character so unusual that he has been educated to virtue in spite of the contrary education he received from the mob – I mean, a human character; the divine, as the saying goes, is an exception to the rule. You should realize that if anyone is saved and becomes what he ought to be under our present constitutions, he has been saved – you might rightly say – by a divine dispensation.[9]

Simone Weil understood this point as follows: 'For there is not, there never has been, and there never will be any other moral teaching except that of public opinion'.[10] For her, the essential idea of both Plato and Christianity has been neglected: humanity cannot help but be wholly enslaved to the beast, 'even down to the innermost recesses of the soul', except insofar as it is freed by supernatural grace.[11] It is therefore essential to distinguish between compulsion, insofar as it is produced by the crowd, and freedom, insofar as it is enabled by an understanding of the fine, good and just. The objectivity of value – its givenness, the way it seizes control of thought by imposing itself as an obligation – is the condition for freedom. Plato is invoked against Platonism as proposing redemption from moral ignorance.

Why adopt such an extreme scepticism about human moral judgement? The problem is especially acute when one considers the extent to which all moral development is acquired through faith in the judgements of others. Weil offered various reasons for her preference for moral scepticism. A first reason is developmental. Initially, one has no freedom over what one thinks about: the world is not outside the mind; it weighs upon the mind, inviting an impulsive response.[12] We receive other people's thoughts as if they were our own. It is impossible to have thoughts which are not related to all the other thoughts bequeathed to us through language.[13] In this respect, thinking is largely formed by the crowd; it is rare that thinking can be formed by the good. A second reason is the lack of criteria for selection: the difficulty encountered in sifting such thoughts is that we are not conscious of the evil we do. Weil remarks that, 'human beings are so made that the ones who do the crushing feel nothing; it is the person who is crushed who feels what is happening'.[14] It is the same with praise and blame, and so with criticism – these are not easily anchored in experience of their effects.[15] A third reason is the shaping of thought by interests. Justice and truth might be attractive in principle, but there are always reasons for suspending the quest for these in practice: when their purport is not entirely clear, it is so easy to confuse one's own desires and interests with the aspiration for the good.[16] In attempting to grasp the realm of value, it is all too easy to encourage the most dubious elements in oneself, and dignify them with moral self-righteousness. On this account, then, any philosophy that claims to know the fine, the good and the just, and to judge things on that basis, is absurd.[17] One does not attain to the perfect idea by clinging to the idea of perfection. Or as Jesus put it, 'Why do you call me good? No one is good but God alone' (Mark 10.18).

If direct access to knowledge of value is either impossible or unverifiable without supernatural assistance, then how is value to be known? There is an alternative direction for philosophy: it is necessity that can become an object of knowledge. Weil declared a fundamental reversal of Platonism: 'For the living here below, in this world, sensible matter – that is to say, inert matter or flesh – is like a filter or sieve; it is the universal test of what is real in thought, and this applies to the entire domain of thought without exception; matter is our infallible judge'.[18] Such a reversal of Platonism was taken indirectly from Kant,[19] for Weil borrows his analogy of the dove for the critique of metaphysics:[20]

> The light dove, cleaving the air in her free flight, and feeling its resistance, might imagine that its flight would be still easier in empty space. It was thus that Plato left the world of the senses, as setting too narrow limits to the understanding, and ventured out beyond it on the wings of the ideas, in the empty space of the pure understanding. He did not observe that with all his efforts he made no advance – meeting no resistance that might, as it were, serve as a support upon which he could make a stand, to which he could apply his power, and so set his understanding in motion.[21]

FEUERBACH, MARX AND WEIL

It is precisely such an approach that was developed by Ludwig Feuerbach in his manifesto *Principles of the Philosophy of the Future*. He sought to question the primacy of the question of essence in all the forms of idealism running from Plato to Hegel. His task was to lead philosophy 'from the realm of "departed souls" back into the realm of embodied and living souls; of pulling philosophy down from the divine, self-sufficient bliss in the realm of ideas into human misery'.[22] Thought should be concerned primarily with what is not thought: the relation between thinking and being is not achieved by an effort of thought, but is already present from the simple fact that the mind exists. Just as breathing involves a necessary relation to what is outside itself in the world, so also the empirical sciences make their essential business the external world – irrespective of perfection. Modern thought is the practical negation of theology insofar as it no longer concerns itself with the philosophical God.[23] Feuerbach announced the conversion of thought from a concern with essence, which is a purely abstract thought, towards existence, which has meaning and rationality for itself even without being put into words. 'Where words cease, life first begins, and the secret of being is first disclosed'. For existence itself is not a concept but a reality: 'I owe my existence never to the linguistic or logical bread – bread in itself – but always only to *this* bread, to the "unutterable"'![24] Real seriousness requires a reality beyond the idea, 'an object, not only for thinking, but for not-thinking'.[25] For Feuerbach, this not-thinking that demonstrates material existence is sensation – the air which I breathe and the bread that I eat make my existence possible insofar as they affect me. Thus it is in feelings that the deepest and highest truths are concealed: 'only passion is the hallmark of existence. Only that which exists which is an object – be it real or possible – of passion'.[26] This is an entirely relational understanding of existence. 'The reality of man depends only on the reality of his object. If you have nothing, you are nothing'.[27] The task of philosophy, then, consists 'not in leading away from the sensuous, that is, real, objects, but rather in leading toward them, not in transforming objects into ideas and conceptions, but rather in making visible, that is in objectifying, objects that are invisible to ordinary eyes'.[28] Feuerbach even appeals to an explicitly Christian inspiration for this turn towards the sensuous: 'only the truth that became flesh and blood is the truth'.[29]

Karl Marx believed that he was completing the revolution announced by Feuerbach: while the affective relation to existence is still purely contemplative, humanity actually produces its existence through feeding itself. Baking and eating are more significant than the taste of bread. Once the eternal truth has been suspended, the relation of thinking to existence is purely temporal and practical. Socially conditioned labour is the source of human production, just as naturally conditioned labour is the source of human reproduction. Where idealism had sought to bring redemption from mere opinion, naturalism sought to bring redemption from any debts to transcendent ideas. Yet once value is measured by passion, one is in danger of returning to the thoughtless world of praise and blame. This is why Weil, appearing to follow Marx, regarded manual labour in the natural world as the condition of access to the truth. There was, however, one practical difference between Weil and Marx: her thoughts were more often put to paper after a day spent labouring in the vineyards of Provence than after a day spent reading in the British Library. In her efforts to be an authentic worker, she bore witness to a conception of truth as authenticity, a conformity of being to thinking achieved by the will. Where socialism sought merely to change the world, existentialists sought to change themselves. Yet what Weil learned while attending to vines is the necessity of detachment or suspension of the will. Her restatement of the philosophical task has decisive importance for the role of economic life within the operation of philosophy itself:

> The concept of value is at the center of philosophy. All reflection which bears on the notion of value and on the hierarchy of values is philosophical; all efforts of thought bearing on anything other than value are, if one examines them closely, foreign to philosophy. For that reason the value of philosophy itself is beyond discussion. For, as a matter of fact, the notion of value is always present to everybody's mind. Everybody orients his thoughts about action towards some good and cannot do otherwise. Moreover, value is exclusively an object of reflection. It cannot be an object of experience. . . . Knowing how to judge between values is for everybody the supreme necessity. . . . At each instant our life is oriented according to some system of values. At the moment when it directs our actions, our system of values is not accepted with conditions or provisionally or reflectively; it is purely and simply accepted. Knowledge is conditional, values are unconditional; therefore values are unknowable.
>
> But one cannot give up on knowing them, for giving up would mean giving up on believing in them, which is impossible, because human life always has a direction. Thus at the center of human life is a contradiction. . . .

> Everything that can be taken as an end cannot be defined. Means, such as power or money, are easily defined, and that is why people orient themselves exclusively towards the acquisition of means. But they then fall into another contradiction, for there is a contradiction of taking means for ends. [30]

To have a 'log in your eye', on first reading this account, is to take means for ends. Thinking conforms to being only when the mind senses what matters. Values exist in a system or hierarchy – some matters are more important than others – and the mind is inevitably oriented by a system of values, yet one can only reflect on a value and judge it in relation to others by an effort of detachment. This entire account is beset by apparent contradictions: values are unknowable yet absolutely certain; failing certainty about ends, one attributes value purely to means; the effort of detachment required to free oneself from values that lack intrinsic value is itself an attachment to means. Weil celebrated each of these contradictions for they are signs that something has been understood at the wrong level. In other words, to have a 'log in your eye' is to err in one's metaphysics of value; it is to be confused in practice about the hierarchy of values. Philosophy, then, is a striving towards the good, an effort of detachment to free itself from the limitations of its own understanding:

> The detachment needed for philosophical reflection consists in being detached, not only towards the values one has adopted beforehand, whether yesterday or a year ago, but towards *all* values without exception, including the ones that are guiding one's actions right now. An athlete who, at the very moment when he is breathless while concentrating on winning, ranks rest equally with winning, pleasure with eating well, work well done, friendship, or any other possible object of desire, and then compares these diverse objects impartially, well, then, *he* would be the picture of detachment. That would be a miracle.
>
> One sees quite well by that illustration that philosophy does not consist in accumulating knowledge, as science does, but in changing the whole soul. Value is something that has a relation not only to knowledge but also to sensibility and action; there isn't any philosophical reflection without an essential transformation in sensibility and in the practices of life, a transformation that has a bearing on how one sees the most ordinary of circumstances and also the most tragic ones of life. Since value is nothing but an orientation of the soul, posing a value to oneself and being oriented towards it are one and the same thing. [31]

The substance of philosophy, where thinking and being become indistinguishable, consists purely in an orientation towards value. As in Paul, the thinker lives life as an athlete, yet this athlete runs by a transformative miracle of detachment which can only be conceived as 'grace.' [32]

LAGNEAU

Weil followed Jules Lagneau in treating value as the substance of philosophy. Notes on his lectures were published in 1925 by his former students
under the title *De l'existence de Dieu* [*On the Existence of God*], and here
one may find a central source of inspiration for Weil's thought on necessity,
value and grace.[33] In this work, Lagneau offered a third alternative to the
conception of reality as existence or essence: he thought of substance as
value.[34] In many ways, his solution offered a reconciliation of the philosophies represented by Plato and Feuerbach within a framework provided by
Kant, but a reconciliation which set them to work in a new direction. As
Harry Frankfurt later explained a similar insight: modern philosophy has
largely concerned itself with *what to believe* and *how to behave*; there is also
an inquiry into *what to care about*.[35]

On the one hand, Lagneau began with the Platonic love of beauty: beauty
manifests an interior reality that is more real than its material truth. A Shake-
speare play is not explained by an arrangement of words; a Bernini sculpture
is not explained by an arrangement of stone. Then to think is to judge; it is to
make judgements about the value of this interior reality. Thinking begins
with the love of beauty. Lagneau rejected the materialist reduction of love to
an irresistible, blind and natural force on account of the judgement the mind
makes in approving of love. To love perfection, on this account, is to raise
oneself above nature, for nature only imperfectly participates in beauty: to
love, in spite of imperfection, demonstrates the free act of the mind. Beauty
in the object and love in the subject exceed all natural determination. While
each of our thoughts affirms the reality of the perfect, and the mind can only
move towards perfection, 'the truly real act is the act of love'.[36] Perfection
may be posited as a condition of moral progress; but this does not demonstrate that perfection actually exists.

On the other hand, Lagneau turns to atheism: atheists deny God because
they have a higher idea of God than their contemporaries, and so are moved
to deny the reality of what they see as imperfect. Negation is a condition of
progress, just as is affirmation and believing. God is not given as a sensible
reality, nor is God given as an intelligible essence. God is neither contingent
nor necessary. From this point of view, it is not appropriate to speak of the
existence of God, for to exist is not simply to be conceived, but to be an
object of perception. Existence is only properly said of things, not of God. To
argue for God's existence is to attribute the same reality to God as to an
object of sense.[37] But likewise, to argue for God's essence is not sufficient by
itself, for being involves a relation to existence. Truth is a relation. If one
endeavours to argue for a necessary being, then one annihilates thought: for
thinking endeavours to understand the reasons to affirm something, and so
must feel itself satisfied; but an absolute necessity would have to be ac-

cepted, irrespective of thought. He suggested that thought can have no relation to absolute necessity; absolute necessity is a self-contradiction.[38]

The originality of Lagneau's proposal lies in seeing thought not simply as a passive contemplation, affirming the truth of what it encounters, nor simply as a logical operation, tracing out necessary truths: thinking is a human action, and the idea of action is not exhausted by sensation or necessity. Thinking is a moral act; when it affirms existence and essence, there is also the value of the moral act by which one affirms. A thought which is determined by nature or by reason alone lacks a certain reality which belongs to liberty: if an act of devotion is necessary, it is no longer an act of devotion. Instead, the orientation of action is offered by value: 'Value is being, the real being, for liberty'.[39] What we search for in reality is neither existence nor essence but value. 'At the ground of all judgement affirming the truth of something, there is an approval of the mind which, at its heart, considers itself as free, and affirms itself not only as existing, as being, but as having to be'.[40] Once thinking is no longer considered a response to causal or logical necessity but as an action, then value, felt as obligation, is the true substance of thought.

This element of obligation at the heart of the moral act of thinking enables a striking reversal: it is not simply that the moral act of thinking chooses a value to affirm; it is rather that value affirms itself in the mind. One cannot debate the existence of value; one can only respond to or deny its claim.[41] One could say that moral actions depend upon formations of subjectivity: they cannot simply be taken up or discarded at will. Yet the subject is formed through its perceptions and affirmations of value. This reality, the reality of value, is an absolute value, neither given by the senses nor by reason. Lagneau does not shirk from calling it 'supernatural' for the simple reason that it exceeds theoretical and practical reason; existence and essence depend on this superior reality that is value or obligation. This superior reality of value over essence and existence pertains to God. 'We cannot say that God exists, nor that he is'.[42] It is not that the mind attains God, but 'God attains himself in the act itself by which we pose any thought whatsoever as true'.[43] Thinking is no longer a question of postulating God, but in a strange reworking of Descartes's ontological proof: 'It is to participate in the act itself of God; to put it better, it is to offer the place to God himself in us . . . It is God who descends in us, who poses himself in us in our self-positing, that is to say that we attain in this act of reflection the absolute region of creative power, we enter into the creative act'.[44] On first reading, this seems to be extraordinarily dangerous: few greater evils are committed than those based on moral self-righteousness. But Lagneau's point is that thinking operates within the moral sphere of devotion and obligation: value itself has a reality superior to the mind. He explicitly refuses any infinite progress towards value; the idea of an absolute end is self-contradictory. What is real in the ideal of perfection is the attachment we have for it, the value we confer on it.[45] God is essentially incomprehensible. The true relation to the absolute is not the physical relation of effect to cause, nor the logical relation of consequent to antecedent, but that of true appearance to reality.[46] Insofar as the mind desires value, it perpetually endeavours to distinguish the reality of value from its appearance. It asks, 'What is really valuable here'? It is only by the feeling of love that one is certain of the reality of God. Love is at once liberty and necessity; someone who truly loves *has to* love.

What is of immediate interest here is less what Lagneau said about God but what he said about thinking. For the question of the reality of God is that of the absolute value of thinking. For 'to know if God is, is to know if thought is as it should be, if thought has an absolute value'.[47] To reflect is to ask if thought is as it *should* be. In this respect, thinking is a continual expenditure or sacrifice. Instead of sacrifice being offered as evidence of value, sacrifice is offered in response to value. Lagneau exhorted his students: 'Realise yourselves; be as minds; detach yourselves at each moment from the pleasures that stop you, fix you in place; do not cease the effort because you feel what that effort costs you; know that you must sacrifice the present to the future'.[48] For it is only sensibility that tells us that we are nothing but the present, a purely individual reality. By contrast, what constitutes us in reality is not a succession of actions and feelings, but the relation one has with all other beings. Thinking is the reflection that sacrifices itself, out of devotion, to the reality of value that it seeks to separate from appearance. The development of life is nothing but the perpetual sacrifice of present reality. Scepticism is a form of egoism, a refusal to love.

Nevertheless, this love for reality is made possible by the reality of value. Lagneau speaks of prevenient grace: it is as though 'there is at the heart of nature a deposit of grace which makes possible the moral life'.[49] This grace manifests itself as a feeling with two faces, one turned towards reality itself, the other towards other beings; the feeling that makes the moral act possible is joy and love.[50] The reality that one feels within is the basis for the reality one encounters without. For one for whom the world appears to have no sense, then it has no sense; for one for whom it has no value, then it has no value.[51] In this respect, the deposit of grace is subject to creative investment: the reality of value that one finds in the world is the reality that one has put there. Yet the return one receives of a valuable world is itself really valuable; it manifests the reality of value.

What Lagneau's thought suggests, therefore, is a practice of philosophy constituted by an economy of thinking. The substance of thought, what thought must think, is value: it is what matters, what is real, insofar as reality is no longer considered in terms of individuality, according to sensation, nor considered in terms of universal and necessary laws, according to reason. What matters, what is real, is what loves, what invests in other realities in order to find the value of that deposit of grace located in nature. This practice of thinking involves a perpetual labour and expenditure (for Lagneau evil is essentially idleness),[52] a quest to discern the value of each reality, a perpetual sacrifice of all present appearances in the hope of discovering the relations of value behind appearances. This practice of thinking also involves a return on investment, a sense of joy in life and love of life, which is the sentiment of the value in reality itself. Lagneau's philosophy of value suggests an economics of thinking.

Drawing on Weil and Lagneau, it is possible to suspect that something of value is lost in Marx's transformation of Feuerbach, something relating specifically to Feuerbach's Christian theological heritage: the socialists have only sought to change the world; the point is to love it. The relation between thinking and being may be a matter of investment, attention and devotion. Of course, passion is not an infallible guide to value. Philosophy would have to begin again with a critique of passional reason. Indeed, the entire tradition of Western philosophy can be re-read as a spiritual exercise or critique of passional reason, starting with Platonic eros as passion for the truth. The philosophy of God which begins with the idea of perfection may be complemented by the philosophy of God which is grounded in desire. Indeed, for Augustine and Aquinas, human desire may have a better understanding of God than the human mind. Nevertheless, our task here is not to reappropriate the history of philosophy from a distinctive point of view – at least, no more than has just been performed – but to draw from some striking instances in the history of philosophy to illustrate some dimensions of the philosophical task. It is at last time to schematise the philosophical project undertaken here, and to show exactly what kind of athleticism is at stake. It will be seen that the substance which brings thinking together with being is far too rich to be grasped under any simple concept, whether conceived in terms of perfection, sensibility or action. It is not in this way that the divine enters directly into human thought. It involves, at the very least, many operations of thinking and many dimensions of being.

THINKING THE SUBSTANCE OF VALUE

The task of philosophy is to think the truth – that is, to offer a thinking of value and a value to thinking. *Thinking the truth is orientating thought towards value.* Much human cognition bears little relation to value, neither recognising nor offering it. In seeking to orient itself towards value, the mind can fall into various self-constructed traps. These constrain it to undertake efforts which in themselves lack value. Such traps consist in giving credit to signs of value rather than attending to the substance of value; it is matter of storing up treasure on earth rather than in heaven. Here we are concerned with three traps. There is the trap of worldliness: by placing faith in the value judgements of others as signs of value, others who in turn respond to judgements of still others, one postpones any inquiry into the true substance of wealth. Thinking is short-circuited by relying on extrinsic evidence rather than sensing intrinsic value. In direct opposition to this, there is the trap of unworldliness: positing a perfect, unmediated relation between thinking and being, whether Parmenides's One, or Plato's Forms (defined by being what they are), or Aristotle's Unmoved Mover which merely thinks itself, or Spinoza's substance which is in itself and is conceived in itself; perhaps only with Hegel's Absolute Spirit does such philosophy start to open itself to mediation.[53] The problem, diagnosed by Schelling in his critique of Hegel, is that existence itself is short-circuited by a self-thinking thought.[54] In other words, life itself is suspended in this purported meeting of thinking and being; such truths may be suitable for the contemplative activity of gods, but as ideals for mortal thinking they substitute themselves for the sensing of intrinsic value. Then, as we have seen, there is the further trap of sacrifice: in the absence of any ability to think and communicate value, one exchanges some extrinsic sign of evident value as proof of the inarticulable value that has been sensed. Once extrinsic signs substitute for intrinsic values, then value is no longer something received but something expended.

The philosophical reading of the gospel's announcement through the medium of economic concerns in the previous part was constructed to address precisely this set of predicaments. The three operations of thought named by theological virtues are reorientations in respect of value. For it is not that what matters can be directly stated or shown; instead, thought may only be reoriented by and towards value. As the chiasmic restoration of intrinsic values over extrinsic signs, faith liberates from sacrifice. As the eschatological suspension of all ultimate criteria of judgements, hope liberates from unworldliness. As the crystallisation of new relations between beings, love communicates actual value and liberates from worldliness. These theological virtues, understood as operations of thought, fulfil the philosophical tasks bequeathed to us by Plato, Feuerbach, Marx and Weil. From Plato, we have learned that the task is to escape the worldliness of the judgements of the crowd. From Feuerbach, we have learned that the task is to escape unworldly thoughts through a passional relation to existence. From Marx and Weil, we have learned that the task is to escape sacrifice, whether in the substitution of commodities for the substance of value or in the substitution of means for ends, by means of a thinking which is mediated to itself only by engagement with the external world. Such philosophy becomes a task, a way of transforming thinking and living, rather than a doctrine claiming the authority of a revealed truth. The point here is not to claim that the gospel offers a perfect or true philosophy – that would be a prerogative of divine wisdom alone – nor a philosophy more adequate than others, nor a reconciliation of apparently contradictory claims. The point is to proceed with the work of redemption by whatever means possible.

Nevertheless, before proceeding with the task, it is worth pausing once more to consider how this orientation in thought given by theological virtues brings to light a certain material of existence.[55] Indeed, the most valuable work is accomplished in the pauses when one stops thinking and waits, for thinking only comes back to itself through its relation to existence. It is now possible to roughly sketch five dimensions of existence through which thought is mediated to itself. Since these are the nonthought within thought itself, precision here is impossible; one can only deploy signs. Each time one endeavours to speak the truth, one should endeavour not to overlook any of these dimensions of being. The sketch is merely laid out to orientate thought within the differing levels or dimensions of existence for the sake of resolving contradictions and confusions. What is stated below is merely taking stock of the preceding discussion of how life is more than food and the body more than clothing, and it is offered as a schematisation of existence for a practical philosophy which is more multidimensional than any simple division into means and ends.

1. Existence itself is temporal. The human mind is a steward; never a master in its own house. Thoughts are guests which come and go. The passage of time is experienced as forgetting, but also as the welcoming of new opportunities and arrivals. Needs and preferences, recently fulfilled, recommence imposing their imperious demands. Such an observation is sufficient to realise that the logic of mastery, whereby the mind seeks to posit its own ends, depends upon self-deception: the mind has little power to hold its ends constant amidst the changes that come from within and without. In other words, thinking is largely mediated to itself by alien entities beyond its control. Nevertheless, the temporality of existence has value both in freeing the mind from what it has thought and in offering new opportunities for existence in relation to other beings.

2. Existence lends itself to appropriation. The human mind dwells in an external world which is a condition for its existence. Needs and preferences are fulfilled by the labours of production and consumption. Temporal life, for humans, necessarily involves investment and appropriation. The value of this exposure of the mind to what is outside thought is that it perpetually renews the need for contact with reality. The correlate of this need is the desire to appropriate.

3. Existence is an experience of participation. The human mind does not simply hold its ideas as private property; with greater or lesser facility, it enters into an understanding of ideas which exist only in order to be

shared. Ideas are not self-subsistent beings or objects of appropriation; on the contrary, the conditions for the existence of ideas is that they may be participated in and expressed. To have an idea is to participate in common understanding with others for some duration. Temporal life, for humans, necessarily involves attention. The value of this exposure of the mind to what is inside thought is that it facilitates the communication of value. The correlate of this expression of value is the desire for friendship with others.

4. Existence is a matter of offering. The human mind is oriented towards value, yet every step along its path is an offering of value. For thinking is a temporal activity which does not last. The mind does not simply store up thoughts of value in order to make an offering, but every step towards value receives value only in offering it. Temporal life, for humans, necessarily involves devotion. The value of this devotion is that it gives credit to others, enabling other existences to flourish. The correlate of this devotion is the love which desires to give.

5. Existence is characterised by grace. The substance of value is not an object of appropriation, participation or offering without first being given. The human mind, in this respect, is entirely passive towards value just as it is entirely passive towards time. Time and value are the unthinkable dimensions of human existence which exceed the orientation, capacities and desires of the human mind even as they function as conditions of existence for the orientation, capacities and desires of the human mind.

Here, then, we have a tentative orientation for thought. To think the truth about any object of thought is to inquire into the temporality of that object, the value appropriable from that object, the value participatable in that object, the value offered through that object, and the value given in that object. It is enough to enumerate these dimensions of existence to raise the possibility of a critique of all existing philosophy and theology. For any account of reality which does not recognise all five dimensions and their value is necessarily partial. To consider only that which can be appropriated as an object of the mind, whether a proposed definition, a piece of evidence, or a piece of private property, is to overlook the temporality and value of existence. Given facts, however verified, are not in themselves true, for reality is given to us not as fact but as value. Yet the danger of pursuing such a critique is that of becoming caught up in a short-circuit of thinking which merely exposes false values without offering new ones. Instead of clarifying these dimensions in themselves, it is far more urgent to offer them to an understanding of economic life.

Here our concerns are delimited to credit: How is the grace of value transformed into the burden of debt? Instead of conceiving practical delusions as the simple substitution of means for ends,[56] one can conceive them as the substitution of one dimension of existence at the expense of another. Three delusions will be explored by critical revisions of three significant discussions in modern philosophy:

- The consideration of time as freedom in abstraction from the time of necessity, drawing from Kant's philosophy of religion;
- The consideration of goods of appropriation apart from goods of participation, drawing from Marx's discussion of estrangement;
- The consideration of promises apart from trust, drawing from Nietzsche's discussion of debt.

Chapter Eight

Necessity and Freedom

What happens when time as freedom is considered in abstraction from time as necessity? It was Immanuel Kant who demonstrated the inadequacies of both materialism and idealism, both empiricism and rationalism. For his work was set in the context of the clash between the rise of modern science, with its determinist view of human nature understood as following given laws, and the purposive realm of human freedom and history, where actions are undertaken to obtain desirable ends. It would seem that human beings participate in both realms at once, leading to a conflict of the faculties which remains with us today: Should decisions be grounded in economic science, which gives priority to the working of means, or moral philosophy, which gives priority to the selection of ends?[1] For all of Kant's influence, the lessons of his critique have hardly been learned by those who implicitly continue to construct a metaphysics out of means or out of ends today.

According to the Kantian critique, science cannot give us an account of how the world actually is; it only offers an account of how the world appears to us from a given perspective. For perspectival phenomena, such as left-handedness and righthandedness, or having an actual location in space and time, are irreducible in experience; they are not explicable by general laws such as those used by science.[2] If one supposes that a law or model gives a full account of the world as it is, one cannot explain how the law or model applies to this situation here and now. 'Objects of the senses therefore exist only in experience; whereas to give them a self-subsistent existence apart from experience or before it is merely to represent to ourselves that experience actually exists apart from experience or before it'.[3] Science does not give us being; it remains pure thinking. To build a worldview from science is to make an empty, ungrounded, metaphysical reduplication. Kant therefore saw his critique as severing the root of materialism and atheism.[4]

Likewise, metaphysical reason cannot give us an account of how the world actually is. For concepts and ideas are used to link representations; one cannot step outside of representation by means of a concept, moving from essence to existence. To think of God in terms of perfection, for example, as the original being, highest being, or ground of being, is to regulate our reason to search for the origin, the higher form, or the reason for each matter we consider. Again, there is a redundant reduplication in supposing that the perfect origin, highest being, or ground of being exists. For if we were to attain this thought, we would no longer seek an origin, higher form or reason for it, and so we would undermine the principle by which we posited it.

While Kant set limits to a purely theoretical reason, so that it concerns the interpretation of experience alone and does not transgress over into the realm of moral freedom, he also likewise purified practical reason, so that it concerns the determination of the will alone and does not transgress into those areas that can be decided through experience by pleasures or goods. The outcome was a sharp separation between nature and freedom, where each is to be conceived independently of the other. Yet this sharp dualism between nature and freedom, fact and value, means and ends, economic law and moral choice, is merely a feature of the critical employment of our reason; it does not grasp the substance of reality as it is in itself. In practice, thinking longs to rediscover the lost unity, the substance of truth. For moral action does not simply require that the will be pure; it also hopes for the outcome of happiness within the world. Where experience shows a mismatch between moral conduct and happiness – being moral is hardly a guarantee of being happy – morality longs for a reconciliation: one acts morally in the hope of making others or oneself happy. Moral conduct involves action in the world that generates experience. This reconciliation can only be achieved by acting in faith.[5] The effect of Kant's critiques is to restore the significance of a critical religion, one that determines conduct not simply by reason but by faith, hope and love. The overall effect of his critique is 'to deny knowledge in order to make room for faith'.[6] Such a philosophical religion or religious philosophy is not primarily concerned with the analysis of experience or even the self-control of the will, but with the generation of experience. It is within such a field that we may locate an economic philosophy of value.

The task, then, is to see how an economic philosophy of value, after Lagneau and Weil, can reconcile necessity and freedom without confusing the two. The temporal and relational aspects of existence are at once necessary yet free. Necessity can be conceived in terms of freedom; freedom in terms of necessity. Problems arise when one treats either in isolation. Notions of necessity as mechanical causation and notions of moral value as what is worthy of praise or blame may not be adequate to the task – the apparent clarity of such notions has a tendency to blind with light. More modestly than efficient causation or logical entailment, necessity can be considered in terms of *conditions of existence.*[7] Such conditions are contingent and external: there are basic needs that have to be fulfilled for the survival, health and growth of the physical organism.[8] While there may be variations between individuals as to what they might need to maintain and enhance the balance of their organism – some might need more sleep than others, for example – the kind of balance required by a human being as a result of sleeping is largely universal. There is a kind of necessity, then, which is a relation between an enduring existence and its conditions. At the same time, the benefits offered by the fulfilment of such basic conditions are typically individual: my sleeping is unlikely to refresh your mind, unless it contributes to your sleeping. In this respect, these benefits are goods of appropriation: sleeping will only refresh me if I make it my own. It is not that you can benefit directly from stealing my sleep; but I can lose out if you do so. Moreover, the goods that fulfil such basic needs are typically temporary and consumed in appropriation; it is necessary to repeat their consumption, just as one repeatedly breathes in the air. A first sense of necessity is the need for conditions of existence to be provided.

Alongside such basic individual needs, however, one may speak about social needs for inclusion and participation. In this case, what is needed for participation in a particular society will be differentiated by the technologies and norms in operation in that society.[9] In some social groupings, participation requires a tattoo; in others, an automobile; in some, competence in the use of electronic media; in others, the practice of an art of persuasion; in some, emotional self-expression; in others, the cultivation of a habit of submission. Whichever is the case, inclusion and participation open up a realm of recognition, where a person is valued insofar as they participate in socially accepted ideals. However, here the relation of need is reversed: in order for social institutions to exist, it is necessary that people participate in them virtuously and carefully, with concern for the common good. Social necessity is reciprocal, whether as a mutual relation of dependence between individuals, or whether in the mutual dependence of the society as a whole and its component individuals. The enduring good of an institution, beyond the arrival and departure of its members, has to be expressed in terms that exceed individual need – and thus as ideals. Such ideals are typically goods of participation, values that are only valuable insofar as they are accepted in common. In a given society, considered as a social realm defined by its ideals, the people may come and go, but the ideals remain as obligations. Such obligations may differ between societies, but their obligatory force remains. A second sense of necessity, then, is social obligation.

Freedom, by contrast with necessity, seems to pertain primarily to living in time. Whatever one's felt needs and obligations, freedom consists in an allocation of time. Freedom is intentional: it adopts an object for investment, attention and service, and in this choice, it is gratuitous. Even so, one can discern here a third sense of necessity: it is the compulsion exercised by time itself. For although the time given to us is purely gratuitous – we need not be given time to live, no more than we need be given care by others – it is necessary that the time given to us is spent. On the spending of time, we have no choice, whether we spend it wisely or foolishly, in work or in rest, on others or on ourselves. The experience of time reconciles necessity and freedom: on the one hand, in time we pass, subjecting all to necessity; on the other hand, an orientation must be chosen, granting freedom. Time reconciles ontology and ethics, for my life is essentially the time that is given to me; on the other hand, my task is paying attention, giving my time, and the life that I live is only the life that I make through my attention. Time reconciles renunciation and fulfilment, insofar as its passage requires total expenditure, yet we possess no other wealth than our experience in time.

In this respect, freedom requires orientation, and orientation, if it is to be more than an arbitrary impulse or decision, requires cultivation of a life deemed to be good.[10] In addition to the distinction between basic and social needs, a further differentiation can made between social needs for inclusion and the needs of cultivation: in both cases it is a question of what is necessary for maintaining a certain way of being, for fulfilling a vision of the good life. But while the ideals that set out what a good life is might be socially mediated, their fulfilment requires individual appropriation. Cultivation requires individual expense: the love, care and devotion through which life is expended in fulfilment of a vision of the good life are goods of offering. What is needful, in order to cultivate one's life, is a sense of value. There are goods which are worth expenditure, which demand the offering of investment, attention and service. It is through such cultivation that the good life is sought.

Now, in any society based on cooperation, it may be difficult to differentiate strictly between these three kinds of necessity: basic needs, social needs, and cultivated values. For example, insofar as there is any division of labour, and individuals do not simply work to fulfil their own needs, social inclusion may be a condition for biological survival as well as for pursuit of the good life.[11] Moreover, in many cultured societies, some form of cultivation, a recognised attempt to fulfil a given social vision of the good life, may be a condition for social inclusion.[12] In this respect, one cannot simply assume that basic needs have to be fulfilled first, before social obligations and cultivated values. Much depends on the rules of distribution within a community. The satisfaction of cultural values may be a condition of inclusion and participation, and so also a condition of the satisfaction of basic needs.

Such considerations offer an understanding of necessity: necessities are conditions of existence; they include physiological, social and cultural goods. Freedom, in such a context, would be the cultivation, adaptation and refunctioning of the conditions of existence.[13] Freedom is exercised through work.[14] It aims, first of all, to cultivate the fulfilment of basic, social and cultural needs.[15] In this respect, necessity is a condition of existence for freedom; without needs, there would be no freedom, no material upon which to work. Yet at the same time, the fulfilment of needs depends upon the production and distribution of the basic, social and cultural goods through which they are to be fulfilled. The success of this fulfilment, under changing conditions of existence, depends upon freedom. Necessity and freedom, compulsion and value, can only be thought in terms of each other.

The question remains as to whether freedom itself can be cultivated. But there is no other freedom than cultivated freedom. Freedom is cultivated through attention to necessity, imagination of possibility, and invention as work or actualisation. The faculties of attention, imagination and work are the most adaptable of faculties, the most easily cultivated, adapted and re-functioned. Yet here we must qualify such materialism: the critical principle guiding attention, imagination and work is the promise of the value to be found through their cultivation. In this respect, the economic life of humanity is not driven by need, want or choice alone, but by the sense of value that it first divines and then demonstrates. Economic life is a matter of credit, investment and reward.

A temporal life, lived as credit, investment and reward, is an uncertain and precarious life. No amount of scientific understanding can bring knowledge of the future under changing external conditions. No amount of moral criticism can ensure the outcome of choices in a complex external world. While science and morality may be necessary conditions for the success of credit, investment and reward, they are not sufficient. A life lived forwards can only be guided by faith, hope and love. Theology, as a discourse that conditions the goods of offering – time, care, attention and devotion – complements morality and politics, as discourses that condition the goods of participation, and science, as a discourse that conditions the goods of appropriation. In brief, human beings, who live life forwards, have a need for theology, just as they have a need for science, morality and politics. For value is only approached through faith, hope and love. Where these are lacking, in an uncertain and precarious world, a theology may be constructed out of science or politics. Cultural values become subordinated to social obligations or basic needs. Goods of offering are directed to goods of participation or goods of appropriation. In such circumstances, confusion abounds.

Under such confusion, a little clarity may be established by discovering how faith, hope and love are in fact distributed and regulated. For, since life must be lived forwards, there is little doubt that they will be there. Everyone, for good or ill, lives by an implicit theology. A critique of implicit theology, seeking a religion within the limits of reason alone, may seek to distinguish a theological reason from both a theoretical reason, grounded in sensation, and a practical reason, grounded in ideas. For a pure theological reason will endeavour to direct faith, hope and love towards that which matters, to the substance of value.

Chapter Nine

Estrangement

What happens when goods of appropriation are considered apart from goods of participation? Like Plato with his great beast and Kant with his light dove, Karl Marx also employed the notion of the 'animal' for what was less than fully rational. What distinguishes Marx's philosophy from that of his predecessors, including Feuerbach, is that he situates reason in the context of labour; that is, free work in regard to natural necessities. Labour is irrational if it is not proportioned to need. If factory labour is not the direct satisfaction of a need, but merely a means to satisfy needs external to it, then it no longer expresses the intrinsic nature of humanity. As a result, the worker

> only feels himself freely active in his animal functions – eating, drinking, procreating, or at most in his dwelling and in dressing-up, etc.; and in human functions [i.e., working life] he no longer feels himself to be anything but animal. What is animal becomes human and what is human becomes animal.
>
> Certainly eating, drinking, procreating, etc., are also genuinely human functions. But taken abstractly, separated from the sphere of all other human activity and turned into sole and ultimate ends, they are animal functions. [1]

Acts of consumption, here, are treated as animal insofar as they are *abstract* – not the acts of a moth, wombat, turkey or slug, but of an animal. Or rather, to take acts of consumption as ultimate ends is to become a solitary animal, turning these into animal functions. The consumer, however wealthy he or she may be, may live as an animal; that is, in abstraction. In a remarkable inversion of Feuerbach's materialism, Marx treated sensuous reality as abstract. Estrangement is not simply understood as estrangement from any intrinsic individual nature with its bodily and social needs; it is estrangement from 'the sphere of all other human activity'. For humanity is a social animal: in conditions that are not those of estrangement, eating may offer a framework for companionship or family, drinking for socialising, procreation for intimacy and parenthood.

The human value, here, is less a matter of appropriation than a matter of participation. The workplace may offer value to the worker insofar as it offers a framework for a life. Perhaps, then, the value of a workplace cannot be evaluated purely by the rate of profit that it offers to investors or by the goods and services that it produces for others; the value of a workplace may also include the life it offers to its workers. The irony, here, is that if the quality of working life became the sole criterion for the evaluation of a workplace, then work itself would be reduced to consumption or entertainment, and so would be taken abstractly, separated from the sphere of all other human activity, from service of others. The context for human activity is a network of needs.

This purely social understanding of estrangement might seem to be a by-product of a more fundamental alienation understood traditionally in Marxism through the production of capital as accumulated labour. As Marx had outlined previously in his manuscripts of 1844, workers produce capital as an accumulated stock or as a means of production; they work for capitalists. Now the more they produce, the greater the supply of accumulated stock or the more efficient the means of production, and the greater the supply brought to the market. As a result of the balance between supply and demand in the employment market, the more the worker produces, the greater the supply produced, the less the worker will receive in the form of a wage. In this respect, since their products are appropriated by the capitalists, the workers produce their own poverty: 'More and more of his products are being taken away from the worker, that to an increasing extent his own labour confronts him as another man's property'.[2] This Marxist conception of alienation starts with the alienation of labour: products for sale are alienated labour, an objectification of the life and energies of the worker, yet this objectified life in the product, what actually gives it value, is appropriated by the employer. In capitalism, the external social world is not produced by the worker out of his own need; it is alien to the worker in that the worker first receives work from it, is offered employment, and then receives a wage as a means of subsistence. But what is such a worker alienated from? It is easy to think that Marx imagines a direct relationship to nature, in which the worker fulfils his intrinsic nature by providing for his own means of subsistence through his work.[3] Yet insofar as nature, here, is conceived as the nature of an individual, then labour is taken in abstraction, estranged from the sphere of all other human activity. It may be claimed that such naïve humanism was abandoned by the later, scientific Marx. But this analysis has hardly changed in the theory of exploitation of surplus value: the worker can only be exploited if he owns his labour time, and therefore sells it for less than it can produce.[4] To regard labour-time as private property, as a good of appropriation, already expresses a fundamental estrangement: time is taken in abstraction from the sphere of human activity.[5]

It is notable that while the early Marx attempted, rather unconvincingly, to derive the concept of private property itself from the estrangement of labour[6] – as though he had already decided rather dogmatically that the human essence consists in labour[7] – the first manuscript of 1844 breaks off after re-posing the question: 'How does *man* come to *alienate*, to estrange his *labour*? How is estrangement rooted in the nature of human development'?[8] This is, of course, the vital question. The later manuscripts of 1844 offer an alternative answer when they seek the essence of humanity not in labour but in society: 'The *human* aspect of nature exists only for *social* man; for only then does nature exist for him as a *bond* with *man* – as his existence for the other and the other's existence for him – and as the life-element of human reality'.[9] Value is somehow constituted in society, in the bonds established between workers, beyond that of their immediate products and the fulfilment of their immediate needs. Here, of course, we must be cautious: where Plato had described the mob as 'the great beast', Marx, following Aristotle, understands the bonds between people as constituting the human essence. Yet it is not the social relation as such that constitutes the human essence, but only the nonestranged or reappropriated relation. But in Marx's positive description, the social person, constituted by activity in direct association with others, may be enriched and transformed even in the senses, for social influence is the condition for aesthetic education: 'Only through the objectively unfolding richness of man's essential being is the richness of subjective *human* sensibility (a musical ear, an eye for beauty of form – in short, senses capable of human gratification, senses affirming themselves as essential power of *man*) either cultivated or brought into being'.[10] Only in society can one cultivate a sensibility for value, for what matters; Marx is treating estrangement, here, as estrangement from the goods of participation. It is against this norm that estrangement is measured, such that, for example, the starving person is only concerned with the abstract existence of food, food in general, any food at all, not the human form of food as a bond between persons established by cooking for another.

In this slightly later account, it is private property itself that is the mechanism of the estrangement of the senses, of the individual from society: 'Private property has made us so stupid and one-sided that an object is only *ours* when we have it – when it exists for us as capital, or when it is directly possessed, eaten, drunk, worn, inhabited, etc. – in short, when it is *used* by us'.[11] Estrangement, here, consists in a loss of sensibility for the goods of participation, for human value, and its replacement by a sensibility only for goods of appropriation, for use value. This occurs when one replaces the bonds of dependence upon other people as the source of one's food and

necessities with a bond of dependence purely on the abstract workings of the
productive order, the impersonal framework of pure necessity.

> As soon, therefore, as it occurs to capital (whether from necessity or caprice)
> no longer to be for the worker, he himself is no longer for himself: he has *no*
> work, hence *no* wages, and since he has no existence *as a human being* but
> only *as a worker*, he can go and bury himself, starve to death, etc. The worker
> exists as a worker only when he exists *for himself* as capital; and he exists as
> capital only when some *capital* exists *for him*. [12]

So estrangement does occur on the basis of capital. Capital, of course, is a
social relation, a means for mediating the bond between persons. Yet it is a
blind, mechanical, and impersonal social relation; it has no sense for value,
for what matters. Labour is estranged when its product is no longer that of a
bond between persons, but simply a means for the satisfaction of animal
needs. Marx therefore regarded capital as the ultimate limit and downfall of
this private property relationship in which estrangement is fully realised:

> There is the production of the object of human activity as *capital* – in which all
> the natural and social characteristic of the object is *extinguished*; in which
> private property has lost its natural and social quality (and therefore every
> political and social illusion, and is not associated with *apparently* human rela-
> tions); in which the *selfsame* capital remains the *same* in the most diverse
> natural and social manifestations, totally indifferent to its *real* content. [13]

According to Marx, this estrangement, this indifference to the real content
of human life, to value, or to what matters, has become the creed of the
political economists. Insofar as the worker is expected to save, then the
worker is expected to become a minor capitalist managing their own life. [14]
For political economy only attends to capital as the 'wealth of nations'. Marx
accused it of a simple moralism: the more you save, the greater your capital.
This is a religion of asceticism or self-sacrifice. The renunciation of life and
of all human needs is its principal teaching: 'The less you *are*, the less you
express your own life, the more you *have*, i.e. the greater is your alienated
life, the greater is your store of estranged being'. [15]

Marx's critique of alienation is grounded on Feuerbach's critique of
religion:

> For on this premise it is clear that the more the worker spends himself, the
> more powerful becomes the alien world of objects which he creates over and
> against himself, the poorer he himself – his inner world – becomes, the less
> belongs to him as his own. It is the same in religion. The more man puts into
> God, the less he retains in himself. The worker puts his life into the object; but
> now his life no longer belongs to him but to the object. Hence the greater this

activity, the more the worker lacks objects. Whatever the product of his labour is, he is not. Therefore the greater this product, the less is he himself.[16]

As an account of capitalism, this is highly pertinent. As an account of religion, it is somewhat partial, for here religion is taken abstractly. For in Feuerbach's account of Christianity, it is not primarily human labour that is put into God, but the essence of human subjectivity that is attributed to God. If the human subject is the capacity to judge the true, the good and the loveable, and these ultimate criteria are projected externally and used to judge human conduct, then humanity will appear false, sinful and undesirable. Thus Feuerbach wrote that, 'To enrich God, man must become poor; that God may be all, man must be nothing. But he desires to be nothing in himself, because what he takes from himself is not lost to him, since it is preserved in God'.[17] This Feuerbachian formula works abstractly, if the human essence is considered theoretically as a collection of subjective properties, but the situation is transformed significantly if the human essence is considered concretely in terms of labour or socially in terms of the bond between persons. For then one would need to analyse different dimensions of religion. Now religion is no longer a question of merely judging the true, the good and the loveable, but of bringing them into being. Under such active conditions, religious life may be considered under a model of capital – as credit, investment and reward – rather than under the model of alienation, the projection or objectification of an essence. Indeed, considering the value of capital as *trust* rather than as productive capacity or alienated labour completely changes how one evaluates economic life. For all its powers of estrangement, capital may facilitate the creation of certain bonds of trust even while it dissolves others.

'The worker puts his life into the object'. What is the essential object of labour? Here our categories of existence may help. If the essential object is a commodity or capital, then the worker's life is in the commodity or capital; it will be appropriated by another. If, by contrast, the essential object is the bond with another person, then the worker's life still endures in the lived bond with that other person. And yet the life that is spent, the life of labour, is not the same life as the life that is subsequently lived, the life of the bond. It is of the nature of time to pass. 'The worker puts his life into the object; but now his life no longer belongs to him but to the object'. Life is not a good of appropriation; the worker cannot appropriate her life, and neither can the object. Even under conditions of full emancipation, labour remains sacrifice, renunciation, so that the true, the good and the loveable might be brought into being. What is lacking in Marx, but intimated in the later Feuerbach, is an understanding of the economy of religion. For if the religious person as a worker devotes herself to making visible things that are invisible to ordinary eyes, to actualising value, then the situation may be entirely reversed: the more a person puts into value, the more valuable her life becomes. If life is essentially relational, if its reality depends upon the reality of its object, then life is essentially service, devotion to the object. Thus a religious conception of life can understand human fulfilment in terms of freedom, fellowship and service.[18] The more a person puts into God, the more she becomes herself. It is not that religion is unambiguous. The critical question lies in knowing whether her conception of God itself has value – that is, whether it will give her value in return. Estrangement, which is in fact all too prevalent in religion, is essentially estrangement from freedom, fellowship and value.

In the same way, capital too has an ambivalence. It estranges relationships for the sake of producing trust. If capital were the full extinction of all natural and social relationships, the elimination of all qualifying characteristics, then capitalism would have destroyed itself long ago. Perhaps one day soon there will be money and finance recorded in machines but no people; yet this day has not quite arrived. For better or worse, capital remains a social relationship, one that mediates all relations on the basis of its own nonrelation. Capital offers an alienated structure, just as the world offers material necessity, and freedom can only be constructed in relation to such necessities. In spite of its tendency towards depersonalisation, towards the annihilation of all natural and social relations, capital remains a framework for the growth and emergence of natural and social relations – in this respect, the laws of physiology and the laws of economics are alike. They may not recognise value, but they are conditions for the existence of value. Capital remains ambivalent, just as all social bonds are ambivalent.

For this reason, it is not sufficient to pose the problems of estrangement and emancipation purely at the social level. To do so leads to an outright condemnation of that which both disrupts and facilitates social bonds. But all social bonds, like the bond of capital, are deeply ambivalent – only when participatory goods are lacking, when oppressed by social need, are we likely to mistake social bonds for absolute goods. One would need something beyond society, something like the idea of justice, in order to evaluate the ambiguity of any social bond. One cannot seek salvation in the immediacy of relationship any more than in the mediation of relations through the impersonal operations of the mechanics of capital. All relations are ambivalent.

For labour is not the sole good of offering, the sole perspective from which life can be judged. For the capitalist investor, as also for the worker, time is filled with trust. The complexity of relations of class or power, and their influence in determining the relative distribution of labour, credit and reward, need not deter us from distinguishing relations of trust from relations of power, separating investment from politics. For, in the long run, labour, desire, investment, care, attention and devotion, while deeply imbricated with relations of power, have a substance and value which is independent of it.

Chapter Ten

Fidelity

What happens when promises are considered apart from trust? David Hume wrote of a dilemma encountered by two farmers:

> Your corn is ripe today; mine will be tomorrow. 'Tis profitable for us both that I shou'd labour with you today, and that you shou'd aid me tomorrow. I have no kindness for you, and know that you have as little for me. I will not, therefore, take any pains on your account; and should I labour with you on my account, I know I shou'd be disappointed, and that I shou'd in vain depend upon your gratitude. Here then I leave you to labour alone; You treat me in the same manner. The seasons change; and both of us lose our harvests for want of mutual confidence and security.[1]

One can only imagine the sorry history that had led to such estrangement between two neighbours. Caught in the prisoner's dilemma described by game theory, each can do little to save their own harvest.[2] There is nothing elementary in such a vignette of social life. Yet purely by its absence, the story discloses one of the necessary conditions for cooperation: trust. For instead of proposing that people cooperate purely on the basis of reciprocal exchange, as in market transactions, this scenario introduces a time delay between one harvest and the next. The temporal interval can only be bridged by trust. All economic relations take place over time, and therefore involve an element of trust.

Friedrich Nietzsche drew attention to consciousness of the past and future as that which distinguishes the human from the animal. At the opening of his second essay *On the Genealogy of Morality*, he proposed: 'To breed an animal *which is able to make promises* – is that not precisely the paradoxical task which nature has set herself with regard to humankind? Is it not the real problem *of* humankind'?[3] Humanity is the remembering and promising ani-

99

mal, related to its own past and future: 'It is an active *desire* not to let go, a
desire to keep on desiring what has been, on some occasion, it is the *will's
memory*'.[4] How is such a memory achieved, given the opposing tendency to
forget – not simply a passive forgetting, such as that of an animal who lives
in the present, whether camel, dragonfly, carp or crane, but an active forgetting as the precondition for any concentration, any reasoning or attention?
Nietzsche's answer is notorious: 'A thing must be burnt in so that it stays in
the memory: only something which continues *to hurt* stays in the memory'.[5]
He even attributed the origins of asceticism and religion to the solemn and
cruel attempts to fashion a memory for humanity.

The context for this emergence of promises, memory and pain is treated
by Nietzsche as an economic one: the contractual relationship between creditor and debtor.

> Precisely here, *promises are made*; precisely here, the person making the
> promise has to have a memory *made* for him; precisely here, we can guess, is a
> repository of hard, cruel painful things. The debtor, in order to inspire confi-
> dence that the promise of repayment will be honoured, in order to give a
> guarantee of the solemnity and sanctity of his promise, and in order to etch the
> duty and obligation of repayment into his conscience, pawns something to the
> creditor by means of the contract in case he does not pay, something which he
> still 'possesses' and controls, for example, his body, or his wife, or his free-
> dom, or his life.[6]

What we have, here, is a description of unequal exchange, a promise of
life in return for a loan. If only Hume's farmer had demanded such a guarantee, perhaps his difficulties would have been solved; but perhaps Hume's
selfish farmer, who only imagines the impossibility of an equal exchange,
would have found such unequal terms barbaric. No doubt such expedients
have often been necessary, but one cannot help but suppose that more often it
has been the creditor, not the debtor, who has demanded such terms, whether
as a prior condition for a loan or whether to extort payment of tribute by
postponing the threat of death. Such formal contracts between creditor and
debtor occur more commonly under conditions of unequal resources or unequal power and in the absence of trust. The basis for trust, on this account,
would be the exercise of naked power.

Of course, the threat of force offers little real basis for the victor to trust
the vanquished. It is here that Nietzsche invokes the phenomenon of guilt,
the bad conscience through which the powerless person directs aggression
against herself: only the person with a 'bad conscience' is reliable.

> I look on bad conscience as a serious illness to which man was forced to
> succumb by the pressure of the most fundamental of all changes which he
> experienced, – that change whereby he finally found himself imprisoned with-

in the confines of society and peace. It must have been no different for this semi-animal, happily adapted to the wilderness, war, the wandering life and adventure than it was for the sea animals when they were forced to either become land animals or perish – at one go, all instincts were devalued and 'suspended' . . . those regulating impulses that unconsciously led them to safety – the poor things were reduced to relying on thinking, inference, calculation, and the connecting of cause with effect, that is, to relying on their 'consciousness', that most impoverished and error-prone organ! . . . All instincts which are not discharged outwardly *turn inwards* – this is what I term the *internalization* of man: with it there now evolves in man what will later be called his 'soul'. The whole inner world, originally stretched thinly as though between two layers of skin, was expanded and extended itself and gained breadth, depth and height in proportion to the degree that the external discharge of man's instincts were *obstructed*. . . . Animosity, cruelty, the pleasure of pursuing, raiding, changing and destroying – all this was pitted against the person who had such instincts: *that* is the origin of 'bad conscience'.[7]

It is most improbable that there was any such evolutionary transformation. Humanity, as a social animal, evolved from other social animals. Trust and suspicion, fight and flight, care and self-limitation have been with humanity from the outset. What is of interest in Nietzsche's account, here, is the way it exposes the fact that environmental, technological and social changes devalue existing habits and impulses; change requires the weak powers of calculation, consciousness, decision and freedom. Reason only develops in response to crisis; thinking is scarce. So it is those in crisis, the vanquished, who first become capable of calculation and cunning. The problem with attempting to rule by brute force is that such force can often be manipulated for extrinsic ends. Blind force is incapable of ruling insofar as it has no ends, no relation to the past or expectation for the future. Similarly, a consciousness which only knows its past and future as a will, a promise or decision, has no knowledge of changing circumstances and external necessities. Indeed, promises can even be seized and manipulated for entirely extrinsic ends.

The fundamental problem of humanity as a social animal, then, adapting to the circumstances offered by changeable others, is less a matter of making promises than that of discerning how changeable people can nevertheless be trusted. Trust, the basis for all cooperation, is the fundamental human and economic problem. For it is hardly the case that 'the oldest and most primitive personal relationship there is' is that between buyer and seller, or creditor and debtor, as Nietzsche claims.[8] Marx is more realistic in treating the relationship between man and woman as the more primitive, as the condition for human reproduction.[9] Yet even men and women have parents. Relations to parents, partners, peers and progeny, insofar as they continue through time, are relations of trust. Perhaps there is no distinctively human problem, here, for humans, like many other species, have been bred for both trust and suspicion. The human problem is less a matter of forming bonds of trust that endure through time than that of discerning where such trust is appropriate in times of crisis.

The advantage of Nietzsche's formulation of the primitive personal relationship as that between creditor and debtor is that it stages the encounter in conditions of radical uncertainty, balanced between trust and suspicion. This situation differs from that between buyer and seller in several significant respects: as we have noted, the relation between creditor and debtor is one that will have to endure through time; but in addition, it is formulated as a social relation between persons rather than as a direct and mutual comparison of things. Furthermore, the context for the emergence of debt is not simply the comparison of preferences but an expression of need. While the strength of an individual might be measured by the superfluity of their resources in proportion to their preferences, the weakness of an individual is measured by the urgency of their need as contrasted with the risks they would be willing to undergo in order to meet it – only a person in extreme circumstances hazards their own body, wife, freedom or life. Nietzsche is realistic in relating economic life, and even differences of power, to degrees of compulsion. In such encounters between strangers, there is a mutual sizing up of each other: 'here person met person for the first time, and *measured himself* person against person'.[10] If a trade is to be negotiated, then it will be one which assesses relative need and relative sufficiency.

> Fixing prices, setting values, working out equivalents, exchanging – this preoccupied man's first thoughts to such a degree that in a certain sense it *constitutes* thought: the most primitive kind of cunning was bred here, as was also, presumably, the first appearance of human pride, man's sense of superiority over other animals. Perhaps our word 'man' (*manas*) expresses something of *this* first sensation of self-confidence: man designated himself as the being who measures values, who values and measures, as the 'calculating animal as such'.[11]

What Nietzsche's account exposes is the employment of such calculation in the service of cruelty, in taking advantage of another's need. For in the context of trust, there is no need to calculate. Moreover, when compensation consists in an entitlement to cruelty, there is no direct equivalence between the wrong committed and the pleasure received – these matters are entirely incommensurable.[12] The calculation of equivalents as a form of justice is for the purpose of setting limits to revenge.[13] In this respect, the one who legislates, who imposes a law of justice upon others, is first of all one who imposes this law of justice upon themselves. Legislators, who are also bound by their promises, are like the debtors, who are bound by theirs. They calculate:

> But what a lot of preconditions there are for this! In order to have that degree of control over the future, man must first have learnt to distinguish between what happens by accident and what by design, to think causally, to view the future as the present and anticipate it, to grasp with certainty what is end and what is means, in all, to be able to calculate, compute – and before he can do this, man himself will really have to become *reliable, regular, automatic*, even in his own self-image, so that he, as someone making a promise is, is answerable for his own *future*! [14]

In other words, the one who makes promises is committed to behaving according to necessity, as if she were imitating inanimate matter. While a promise may involve calculation prior to it being issued, a promise is in a certain respect a promise not to think. One who promises their own body, wife, freedom or life, who evaluates their urgent need as more significant, is also promising not to reevaluate their decision: such promising involves an active forgetting, a refusal to attend to the value of body, wife, freedom or life. Such fidelity is inhuman.

The contraction of a debt, under conditions of unequal resources, unequal need and unequal power, is the moment at which the vital relationship of trust is replaced by a simulacrum, the debt contract, under conditions of distrust. Distrust, then, is the condition for the exercise of power. Now Nietzsche has this relationship between distrust and power inverted, for his entire account is based on his theory of the will to power.

> A sort of *pleasure* is given to the creditor as repayment and compensation, – the pleasure of having the right to exercise power over the powerless without a thought, the pleasure '*de faire le mal pour le plaisir de le faire*' ['to do evil for the pleasure of doing it'], the enjoyment of violating: an enjoyment which is prized all the higher, the lower and baser the position of the creditor in the social scale, and which can easily seem a delicious titbit to him, even a foretaste of a higher rank. Through punishment of the debtor, the creditor takes part in the *rights of the masters*: at last he, too, shares in the elevated feeling of despising and maltreating someone as an 'inferior'. [15]

What is at stake in this morality of the school playground is purely a matter of prestige. As Nietzsche indicates, the pleasure of cruelty is desired primarily by those who themselves have had masters which have been cruel. Only a damaged person takes pleasure in such an exercise of power. What is distinctive about Nietzsche's theory of the will to power, however, is that he extends it from the purely human relations where it belongs to the entire field of nature:

> Life itself is *essentially* appropriation, injury, overpowering of the strange and weaker, suppression, severity, imposition of one's own forms, incorporation and, at the least and mildest, exploitation. .... 'Exploitation' does not pertain to

a corrupt or imperfect or primitive society: it pertains to the *essence* of the
living thing as a fundamental organic function, it is a consequence of the
intrinsic will to power which is precisely the will of life. [16]

So on the one hand, for Nietzsche, the one who promises has to behave as
if their will were a piece of fate, a natural necessity. On the other hand,
however, nature is no longer considered in terms of necessity, but in terms of
the active freedom to exploit pleasure from cruelty. There is no doubt some
degree of confusion between freedom and necessity is here – most predators
do not treat their prey as domestic animals – but it is one born of a significant
insight, for freedom can only be articulated in terms of necessity. There
remains, however, a clear metaphysical difference: necessity is a compulsion
that is purely present, while freedom consists in proportioning anticipation to
recollection. In considering the promise as a memory for the will, Nietzsche
articulates freedom in terms of necessity and nature in terms of freedom.

Weil can assist us in sorting out the confusion. In her account of the social
struggle for power, concerned with privilege, obedience and oppression,
Weil wrote of the necessity that belongs to the exercise of force as such:

> The preservation of power is a vital necessity for the powerful, since it is their
> power which provides their sustenance; but they have to preserve it both
> against their rivals and against their inferiors, and these latter cannot do other-
> wise than try to rid themselves of dangerous masters; for, through a vicious
> circle, the master produces fear in the slave by the very fact that he is afraid of
> him, and vice versa; and the same is true between rival powers. [17]

The masters too have needs, have conditions of existence, and these are
the source of their strength as well as their downfall. Yet this is a distinctively social relation: in the relation between humanity and nature, there is no
fear, no threat nor promise. For the relation between humanity and nature is
an entirely present one; it is not extended by recollection or anticipation on
the part of nature. Of course, humans feel the pressure of natural necessity,
and meet with resistance and obstacles in their endeavours to fulfil their
needs. Yet this struggle is entirely asymmetrical: the natural world does not
defend itself against human intervention. It neither anticipates nor fears. [18]
Like a perfect Stoic, nature manifests an acceptance of necessity, and so does
not collude with any power based on the threat of force. As a result, the
struggle is set within real limits, for once an effort is successful and a need
fulfilled, the struggle is over. This is not the case with the social struggle for
power, for to exterminate one's slaves would be to exterminate the source of
one's power, and to exterminate one's rivals would be to exterminate one's
prestige. Social power is essentially unstable:

For, owing to the fact that there is never power, but only a race for power, and that there is no term, no limit, no proportion set to this race, neither is there any limit or proportion set to the efforts that it exacts; those who give themselves up to it, compelled to do always better than their rivals, who in their turn strive to do better than they, must sacrifice not only the existence of the slaves, but their own also and that of their nearest and dearest.[19]

The struggle for prestige, unlike the struggle against nature, is an unlimited quest. Even if the masters dream of moderation, they can only practise it at the risk of being overcome by others. Under the conditions of such an unlimited struggle, the strongest survive only until they overreach the conditions of their power.

Now, according to Weil's account of the natural order, all beings are limited by their conditions of existence.[20] Far from power being a matter of will, it is a matter of resources, and those who exhaust their resources will lose their power. Since everything exists only in relation, everything exists within given proportions and limits. In this respect, to regard the natural order as a matter of preference or will is simply to extrapolate the conditions of the social struggle for power into the natural order. It is to treat the natural order as though it made calculations, recollecting the past and anticipating the future. It is to treat it as though it senses fear, threat and promise. Yet even the social order is a part of natural necessity and operates within its own limits and conditions: a power that overreaches itself will destroy itself. So the social struggle for prestige is itself constituted by illusion, since it seeks recognition by others rather than knowledge of its own limits and conditions of existence.

In placing such an emphasis on the will to power, Nietzsche appeals to prestige. In this he is not alone, as Weil indicates in her critique of all existing moral values:

We all choose for treasure those values that have their substance in social prestige. This is true even for the desires which seem only to have reference to individuals. So is the desire of the lover. 'Love without vanity is only an invalid', said La Rochefoucauld. The pleasures of eating and drinking are much more social than they seem at first. Riches, power, advancement, decorations, honours of every kind, reputation, recognition, are values of an exclusively social order. Under the names of beauty and truth almost all artists and scholars seek social prestige. The etiquette of charity, of love for one's neighbour, is generally a cover for the same article.

Social prestige, as the name itself indicates, is pure illusion, a thing which has no existence.[21]

Here we return to our original philosophical question: What is the substance of value? From what does the value of values derive? Where Nietzsche offers the will to power, it is all too easy to see a yearning for prestige.

The quest for prestige is a social necessity, for insofar as we are dependent for survival on cooperation with others, that cooperation is largely only forthcoming in response to the offer of reified prestige, or money. Even debts may function as reified prestige. For under conditions of distrust, the primary aim in the quest for power is no longer to offer trust, but to appropriate the trust of others. Nietzsche exposes the power dynamics of such an appropriation: to appropriate the promises of others is to appropriate a claim on their future time. Far from being an offering to the future, a promise, contract or debt becomes a claim upon the future.

CONCLUSION

The purpose of these re-readings of Kant, Marx and Nietzsche is to open out the potential for thought. Freedom may be understood as working with necessities; appropriation may be understood as a way of engaging in participation; promises may be understood in terms of offering trust. These are ways of being attentive to the varied dimensions of being. When it comes to the consideration of economic life, credit, expressing trust, brings with it the substance of value that is absent when credit is considered purely in terms of debt. A debt requires the disciplining of the future to conform to the promise: it is as though, in some strange way, the future holds an obligation to the present. On the contrary, when credit is considered apart from debt as the trust given to the trustworthy, then credit is an offering towards the future. The difference between these perspectives changes the entirety of what we see when we examine economic and religious life.

The key issue, as Nietzsche shows us, is who will be considered as trustworthy. Here, the freedom to offer credit should be guided by some sense of necessity. In practice, credit and debt are deeply imbricated with each other in economic life. The task is to explore how credit can nevertheless remain an offering and not simply an exercise of power.

Chapter Eleven

Light and Repose

In conclusion to this part, let us consider the costs to thinking of substance and value achieved by reliance upon debt. This might seem a strange connection to make, for one might suppose that either debt has little to do with thought, or else at most it merely concentrates the mind. Yet the latter is precisely the point: the content of thought is shaped by attention, evaluation and trust. If value is that by which thinking is made to conform to being, trust is that by which one strives to make being conform to thinking. When trust is enabled through debt, then what is, what is valued, what is counted and what is produced derive directly from the experience of debt. An anonymous thirteenth-century manuscript consulted by Jacques Le Goff in the Bibliothèque Nationale in Paris explains the reasoning for the prohibition of usury as follows:

> Usurers sin against nature by wanting to make money to give birth to money, as a horse gives birth to a horse, or a mule to a mule [*sic*]. Usurers are in addition thieves, for they sell time that does not belong to them, and selling someone else's property, despite its owner, is theft. In addition, since they sell nothing other than the expectation of money, that is to say, time, they sell days and nights. But the day is the time of clarity, and the night is the time for repose. Consequently they sell light and repose. It is, therefore, not just for them to receive eternal light and eternal rest. [1]

In this account, usurers are accused of selling someone else's time. What is presupposed is that time does not belong to the debtor any more than to the usurer: time belongs to God. In practice, this ownership alludes to religious obligation: the day should be devoted to contemplative prayer, prefiguring eternal light, the night to rest, prefiguring eternal repose. Day and night, light and repose, are offered in proportion. To sell that time is to steal from God;

but it is also to steal light and repose. So to enter into debt is to sell one's own illumination and inner peace; it is to deprive oneself of the divine.

Throughout history, the life of a debtor, lacking light and repose, has been a precarious, driven and industrious one. For so long as the debtor has pledged a little of their own substance as security – perhaps a home, a child, a wife, one's freedom or one's life, or simply an expectation of future earnings – then light and repose must wait until the pledge is redeemed. David Graeber comments on what debt has meant to the majority of people for most of human history: 'the terrifying prospect of one's sons and daughters being carried off to the homes of repulsive strangers to clean their pots and provide the occasional sexual services, to be subject to every conceivable form of violence and abuse, possibly for years, conceivably for ever'.[2] Debtors are motivated to be industrious; they may also be motivated to sell anything which they own. Graeber also observes that much of the labour that built the modern world, once seen from an international perspective, was not free labour contracted to work in a factory, but slaves, serfs, coolies, indentured labourers and debt peons.[3] Debt offers a powerful motivation for work and exchange.

What the conduct of time lacks, when it is calculated in terms of money, is any sense of limit or proportion. In a world of scarce resources and a life of finite needs, economy is concerned with the allocation of industry and effort in proportion. If it were simply a matter of human ownership of time, then the greater the time, the greater the industry and productivity, the more that can be allocated to meeting basic, social and cultural needs. Likewise, the greater the overall productivity, the larger the population that can be supported, and the greater the overall productive potential. If, by contrast, humans are involuntarily appointed to their time, then there might be reasons to set limits to overall quantitative increase. If there is industry to excess, what is it that is lacking?

Our medieval source suggests where to seek an answer: what might be lacking is light and repose, illumination and peace. There is an intimate relationship between time and understanding. Few have articulated this relationship better than Weil. Let us start with what she said about misunderstanding: 'People used to sacrifice to the gods, and the wheat grew. Today, one works at a machine and one gets bread from the baker's. The relation between the act and its result is no clearer than before. That is why the will plays so small a part in life today. We spend our time in *wishing*'.[4] For all the benefits offered by the division of labour, people are placed in an entirely dependent relation upon others for their conditions of existence, and this leaves them in ignorance of the network of economic relations that makes their existence possible. Society presents a screen that interrupts the relation between humanity and nature. This is certainly convenient – just as one does not need to understand the inner workings of one's physiology in order to breathe, eat and play, so one may not need to understand the outer workings of society. So long as society can be trusted to provide for one's needs, why not direct attention to more urgent matters? The problem that Weil sees is that those who are maintained in dependent ignorance are infantilised, capable only of wishing: their time is regulated for them. They cannot proportion their will to reality. Likewise, if the particular distribution of necessities is founded on injustice, with some barely able to fulfil their basic, social and cultural needs, then the position of helpless dependence offers no opportunity to seek justice. Instead of the value of justice, other compensations motivate effort. Lacking knowledge of justice, of social duty, and of conditions of existence, the dependent person can only be induced to work by the offer of praise or blame, of social approval. Smith and Hume called it 'sympathy'. Weil called it 'prestige'. It is expressed in material form as money. In any case, society demonstrates its approval of industrious behaviour by offering a reward, a claim upon its resources; it demonstrates its disapproval by withholding the means to obtain the necessities of life. Unlike a great beast, people are easily tamed and made compliant by such careful handling. Society produces its own morality: cooperation with social norms is deemed good, while anything that fails to serve social demands appear evil. Lacking any understanding by which such norms can be proportioned or made relative, society produces transcendent judgements of good and evil. 'The Great Beast is the only object of idolatry, the only *ersatz* of God, the only imitation of something which is infinitely far from me and which is I myself. . . . Only one thing can be taken as an end, for in relation to the human person it possesses a kind of transcendence: this is the collective'.[5] Indeed, Weil argues that anything one seeks for oneself, such as money, power, prestige or privilege, in fact derives from the social element. There is no egotism possible apart from introjection of socially produced values. All evil results from the social simulation of value.

> That which we want is the absolute good. That which is within our reach is the good which is correlated with evil. We betake ourselves to it by mistake, like the prince who starts to make love to the maid instead of the mistress. The error is due to the clothes. It is the social which throws the colour of the absolute over the relative. The remedy is in the idea of relationship. Relationship breaks its way out of the social. It is the monopoly of the individual. Society is the cave. The way out is solitude.[6]

Society manifests itself as a cave for the factory worker and the debt-bonded labourer: all that is seen are shadows of value, the things that generate social approval, as opposed to the things that answer to needs and necessities. For industrious activity under threat of losing the substance or necessities of life concentrates the mind largely on the present. Weil's reflections here echo her experience of the extreme concentration required for factory piecework:

> What counts in human life are not the events that dominate in the passing years – or even the months – or even the days. It is the way in which one minute is linked to the following one. And what this costs for each one in body, in soul – and above all in the exercise of the faculty of attention – to bring about and maintain this linkage minute by minute.[7]

For Weil, a 'man is only real, in his innermost self, when he forms the connecting link between the past and the future. Whoever deprives him of either of these (or of both) does him the greatest possible injury'.[8]

The emphasis placed upon the individual, here, rather than on the person whose relations to herself are mediated entirely by social approval or disapproval, has a twofold significance: in the first place, only the individual mind can directly encounter nature as obstacle or resistance, just as Kant's dove senses the air that holds it up. In this respect, only the individual mind can gain knowledge of the idea of relationship and proportion: 'this is good in so far as . . .', 'in relation to . . .', or 'under these circumstances and limitations . . .'. The operation of intelligence is required to conceive relationships, limits and equilibria. A crowd can conceive and represent isolated and abstract values, but it cannot add things together. It can deal with generalities, but it cannot conceive complex relations between particulars. For Weil, the operation of the intelligence is strictly individual. In the second place, only an individual is a singular moment in time, being this, here and now, capable of recollecting the past, anticipating the future, and linking them together. However changeable it might be, society is not in time in quite the same way. Society does not have the same ontological and temporal status as the living person. What is at stake, for our discussion, is not the relationship between society and the individual, but what might be left out when time is measured by money: a certain clarity consisting in knowledge of proportion, and a certain repose in time or waiting. For waiting, like work, is a condition of a kind of knowledge.

Weil often drew an analogy with Lagneau's discussion of a cube: a cube is not visible in all its three dimensions from any single vantage point – a photograph would render its aspect in only two dimensions – yet as one walks around a cube, and multiplies perspectives, its three-dimensional structure has to be posited to make sense of the whole. Perhaps a house or a building is a clearer example, as one would have to pass around it and through it to gain a sense of the whole. Similarly, dispassionately waiting can multiply perspectives in time, as differing impulses rise and fall: 'Time brings modifications in us, and if throughout these modifications we keep our gaze directed onto a certain thing, finally what is illusory is dissipated and what is real appears; always provided that our attention consist of a contemplative look and not one of attachment'.[9] By paying attention, and waiting, things may change and a new perspective may be revealed. 'Duration discriminates between the diabolic and the divine. That is the meaning of the parable of the wheat and the tares'.[10] It is only by attention, waiting and change that a further dimension becomes visible: the further dimension is not what I may do, but what time will bring. It distinguishes conjecture from that which is actually thought.[11]

It is the clarity of this contemplation that is the cost of subordinating time to money. Such clarity is required above all in the realm of value. For what is the purpose of all the toil and bustle in the world if it is merely directed to the competition for prestige, and not directed to the fulfilment of basic, social and cultural values? Industry without clarity is blind. For in repose, the mind can become centred, grounded, accepting of its conditions of existence. The relation it builds to the past is one of rootedness. In clarity, the mind directs attention to its object: it waits to see what its object will prove to be. In both cases, time is required to be free, undetermined, simply waiting. This is superfluous, supererogatory time. It is time as grace.

By contrast, the perpetual twilight of the debtor invokes a rather different relation to both past and future. The inheritance from the past, far from simply providing the roots or conditions of existence, is regarded as a set or resources to stake and a set of tools and strategies to employ. Concern for the future, far from offering an openness to reality, is restricted to the possibility of meeting the terms of payment or gaining a socially sanctioned reward. In short, such a perpetual twilight consists in a short-circuiting of attention. Debtors make very poor philosophers, having little attention for what matters.

What matters exists prior to the mind: it exceeds the capacities of the mind as the past exceeds the present. The mind awakens to find itself thrown into a world of cares: it does not choose its concerns any more than it chooses its relatives. What matters takes hold of the mind. In the same way, what matters exceeds the mind as the future exceeds the present. What is possible depends largely upon external conditions. At best, the mind can endeavour to serve the future by realising the possible. Yet this is a matter of service, rather than the will's mastery, for each act is only a minor contribution to a multitude of conditions that make any given future possible. The past matters, the future matters, and the present – this has value insofar as it forms a connecting link between past and future. In order to be decisive, to be a point of reference that matters, to contribute towards the good whether or not this is ever recognised, it is incumbent upon the human mind to care for what matters in the past and the future, to perceive what matters from its own given point of view. It is not the case that we could ever come to a decisive judgement about what really matters; consensus is not what matters here. It is rather the case that by multiplying perspectives, what really matters comes to stand out in relief, as though in a fourth dimension: what matters becomes more clearly visible. Thinking is the art of making what matters sensible. Thinking recovers the past and enables the future; as it does so, it contributes more light.

Now the human mind is born in darkness. It invests credit, trust and desire in what it takes to be good, but it starts without an understanding of the conditions of existence of those goods. In this respect, the mind is drawn from what matters to what is necessary. It becomes concerned for the conditions of existence of what matters. Goods of appropriation are good for the sake of those who appropriate them. Goods of participation are good for the sake of those who participate in them. It is only the goods of offering, the time, investment, care, attention and devotion that are offered, that constitute the mode of being of the one who offers them. It is only these goods that constitute bonds between persons and through time. The human mind matters as it participates in a network of things that matter. It fulfils its nature of being local and temporal by concerning itself with what is local and temporal.

Now the human mind has limited attention. Here, then, is a vital component of thinking economically: it is to attend to the way in which the network of interdependent conditions that constitutes reality responds to our actions and interventions. It is to sense reality as the dove senses resistance from the air by means of being attentive to any diminishment of the conditions of existence. Thinking economically, then, is concerned with value, with necessity, with proportion, with relation, and with responses of augmentation and diminishment. It is fundamentally oriented to what actually happens in the world. This is what it means to stand there in the light, blinking, with a few specks in one's eyes, attending to reality, the substance for thought. To think uneconomically, by contrast, is to think excessively or wastefully. It is to be concerned with values anticipated in exchange as opposed to the value of what matters. It is to be concerned with preferences instead of necessities. It is to be concerned with maximisation rather than with proportion. It is to be concerned with abstracted objects of investment or consumption instead of the relations that constitute conditions of existence or manifestations of care. It is to be concerned with how reality might be changed in 'creative destruction' rather than with what might be augmented or diminished in unintended consequences. This is what it means to stand in the darkness, unblinking, staring blindly, with one or several logs in one's eye. It is to short-circuit one's thinking, to enter a hall of mirrors where one only encounters oneself. It is to become blinded both to what matters and to what happens in the world.

III

Credit and Creation:
Economic Roots

Economic life is normally concerned with scarce goods – that is, goods of appropriation where what is mine cannot also be yours. While such goods may be multiplied through production, exchange itself is a zero-sum game. Market exchange may extend distribution, enabling production to answer to need, but it does not, purely of itself, increase production. In practice, production is increased by institutions which complement the market: human cooperation through productive enterprise and the division and organisation of labour. Wealth is multiplied when tasks and knowledge are shared. Of course, there are limits to how complex an institution can become, how large a group of common interests can be pooled, and how far knowledge can be appropriated and understood. Nevertheless, participation in a common life largely increases production. Such goods of participation depend upon relationships which endure for longer than a simple exchange. Insofar as economic life is composed of enduring obligations and commitments, rather than a sum of instantaneous transactions, then it is founded on trust. Now trust is a good of offering. Where goods of appropriation are essentially zero-sum, and goods of participation multiply towards a limit, goods of offering such as trust admit of exponential increase, even if the time, attention and care with which they are expressed do not. The more trust one offers, the more one is trusted, and the more one is trusted in turn, the more the credit or trust one offers to others can be taken seriously, in a virtuous cycle of growth.

These differences in dynamic qualities between kinds of goods point towards a hierarchy and complementarity of values. For a healthy and dynamic economy where people are able to determine their own courses of action, the offering of credit makes the decisive difference. The goods of offering, increasing in virtuous cycles, are for that reason fundamental for goods of participation, increasing themselves as they are shared, in turn generating goods of appropriation. It may not always seem so. For one in desperate need or debt, the order is reversed: goods of appropriation are needed first, followed by goods of participation and goods of offering. It may be rather unwise to take such conditions of desperate need as determining the order for economic management. In either case, one is dealing with cycles, not with ends in themselves. The order of goods offers a complementary order of reasons, where each dimension is necessary for the whole. Economic goods, political and moral goods, and theological goods are necessary dimensions of a healthy life.

Each good has its own kind of desire, its own kind of freedom, and consequently, its own kind of rationality for orienting that freedom. The freedom to appropriate may be distinguished from the freedom to participate, and this in turn from the freedom to offer. There are many who, in the tradition of John Locke, regard the human being as essentially a proprietor, elevating freedom to appropriate over the constraints imposed by participation. There are many who, in the tradition of Aristotle, regard the human being as essentially a social animal, elevating freedom to participate over the constraints imposed by desires for appropriation. There are many who, in the major religious traditions, regard the human being as essentially a worshipping animal, elevating duty to God over the constraints of worldly life. What easily gets overlooked in each perspective is the mutual interdependence of such dimensions, for humanity is a temporal and relational animal. Many seek salvation by endeavouring to restore awareness of either economic, communal or spiritual goods. Yet such measures alone are insufficient, for each dimension can go astray: economies can consume their conditions of existence; communities can be based on short-circuits of exclusion or on mutual estrangement; worship can be based on the value signified by sacrifice, rather than responding to what matters. The task is a reintegration of theological, political and economic life, guiding credit by faith and orienting faith by credit.

In this respect, to think, to offer thought to what matters, is to be guided not by abstract ideas but by actual relationships. The theological dimension enjoys no mastery here. It is not enough to make promises or offerings in order to become holy, for promises and offerings simply generate their own constraints. Instead, it is necessary to feed a virtuous circle – to make an offering which in turn empowers others through trust. A redemptive theology, freeing people from debt, finds its fulfilment in a detour through economic life. Dependent upon the actual responses of others, such a theology involves a loss of control. If this is the implicit agenda of our unfolding discussion, the explicit agenda involves uncovering and reorienting the theological dimension of economic life.

A fresh perspective on economic life may be constructed by considering the dynamic role of credit. The starting point for considering credit in economic life is the intimate sphere of the home, prior to exchange. Christian theology, with its concern for offering, does initially elevate this intimate sphere over the political sphere of action and participation as well as the economic sphere of exchange and appropriation. Indeed, centuries of Christian teaching have endeavoured to keep the family sphere of intimate community sacrosanct against incursions from political authorities or against the undermining effects of usury. Nevertheless, the fate of an offering is to be handed over, to be subjected to other powers, and this very expenditure inspires trust.[1] When credit is offered as a sign of trust, a whole set of intimate meanings and associations may be lost for the sake of extending wealth. Offerings are reconceived in terms of participation; common goods are reconceived in terms of appropriation – this becomes evident in the range of meanings attributed to the word *credit*. In economic life, credit given, understood as endowing with attention, value and trust, may be transmuted into the virtue of creditworthiness, understood as integrity and reliability;

this, in turn, may be transmuted into credit given, understood as expectation of deferred payment. Offerings and virtues may be transmuted into transactions, while transactions may link strangers beyond the bounds of intimate community. Furthermore, where one might accept deferred payment from someone one trusts, one is more likely to accept a bank note when faced with a stranger – a promise of deferred payment from a known and trusted institution. Banks offer credit to facilitate exchange. Unlike intimate relations within the home, however, credit is only offered by a bank in exchange for some collateral or debt. The paradox of credit is this: credit may only lead to wider creation when it is offered beyond the intimate sphere of the home; in doing so, the value of credit is gradually displaced, so that it is underwritten, not by virtue, but by debt. This handing over of credit and its new foundation upon debt is a necessary part of economic life. Credit loses its theological sense when it is conceived purely in terms of debt. Yet to complete the circuit and fully enhance trust, there would have to be an inverse movement, a redemption from debt and an extension of the intimate sphere. Redemption is normally conceived as a settlement of debt, a resolution and closure of the relationship of credit. An alternative understanding of redemption, to be explored in *Metaphysics of Trust*, would see it as an extension of the intimate sphere, where debts no longer matter.

In this part, the outward movement of credit from the home to public institutions will be explored. In this process, goods of offering come to be conceived purely in terms of goods of exchange. Such forgetting of the theological dimensions of economic life extends their reach while leaving them somewhat disorientated. This process is deeply ambivalent: it multiplies human powers of creation by at once augmenting and restricting human freedom. It is also a process of discovery: while concerned primarily with a conceptual progression, we shall have occasion to illustrate this progress by appealing to a range of thinkers, including the first theorist of value and capital, the thirteenth-century Franciscan Peter of John Olivi, and the first theorist of credit as the key to wealth, the seventeenth-century alchemist William Potter, before turning to the embodiment of their ideas in the institutions created in the English Financial Revolution. Institutions forged upon these models still determine the character of economic life in the global economy today. This inquiry will prepare the ground for the second volume, *Economic Theology*, by directing us where to look to find the theological dimension of contemporary economic life. For the economy is not primarily a market, distributing goods of appropriation, nor is it primarily a set of contests for power between institutions, striving for goods of participation. The economy is fueled by trust in the form of credit. Perhaps the notions of the 'free market' as exchange and 'capitalism' as accumulating the means of production have always been partial distortions of the dynamic forces of economic life. If so, then reforms aimed at restoring the natural operation of 'free market capitalism' have always been in pursuit of a chimera.

Chapter Twelve

Credit as Offering

Household Economics

What does it mean to invest? In what ways might credit open up opportunities for creation? While one might be expected to turn directly to finance to address this question, such an approach delimits any answer either to profits expressed in monetary values or processes of production of goods and services for consumption. Here we are concerned with goods of offering, the higher values at stake in investment, both in their expression and their suppression. Let us start instead with a pair of examples, one from household life, the other from Christian practical theology, each of which situate investment within the context of care.

> *A parable*: A plum tree grew in a garden. Some of its fruit attracted maggots, fell early and rotted. Others reached maturity, fell to the ground and rotted. And rarely, very rarely, a large animal would eat one of the fruit and transport the stone for some distance.
>
> And a man took one of the fruit and offered it to his young daughter. Always reluctant to eat, she exchanged the plum with her stepsister for the best seat at the table. The older girl rubbed the plum's soft and smooth skin. The man turned to her and shrugged. Then the older girl went out into the garden, picked another fruit, and offered it to her younger stepsister, who ate it up.
>
> Later, the older girl ate her plum in the car on the way to school and threw the stone out of the window. A wild plum began to grow by the roadside.

The young daughter needs to eat: what she needs is not the plum itself, but the substance of the plum, its carbohydrate, fibre, vitamins and minerals. Substance responds to need. What the girl perceives is the colour, odour and texture of the fruit, its distinctive differences from other plums, fruit and foods she has seen, and she expresses a preference for position over substance. Difference responds to preference. What the father thinks is that the girl needs the fruit; his authority consists in both his wisdom, his conforming of preference to substance, thinking to being, and his care, his offering of the fruit. The younger girl sees no reason to trust in her father's authority: lacking an understanding of substance, she believes that he is simply being fussy and interfering again, imposing his own preferences. She does not see the value in eating the fruit. Yet along with the fruit, the man has also offered a simple substance and wisdom: it is good to eat fruit. But the older stepsister trusts the man and reads his shrug as a gesture of impotence where she believes she might have power. She imitates the man. As a result, because the younger girl trusts her stepsister, already has her favourite seat, and can send a defiant message to her father to stop interfering, she will eat the fruit. The older sister, through trust, has gained what the young girl has not: both have gained the substance of a plum, both have fulfilled their different preferences for plums, but only the older girl has gained the higher values: wisdom, in proportioning preference to need; a bond of authority and trust, in having her offering accepted; confidence, through taking initiative; and friendship, in sharing a common mind with the man. All this is achieved in response to a simple shrug. This shrug is an offering of credit; it symbolises a whole set of practices of investment. The higher values that it offers are wisdom, authority, confidence and friendship; these values are achieved through a creative response. This is the kind of credit offered by the good Samaritan who presented far more than two denarii to the innkeeper by saying, 'Take care of him; and when I come back, I will repay you whatever more you spend' (Luke 10.35). Such a blank cheque is an offering of trust.

Such is the complexity of household economics: it embeds needs and preferences within a deeper set of values. For so long as there is a division of generations or a division of labour, whether within the household or beyond it, then economic relations require credit, creation, care, wisdom, authority and trust. While a theological economics can concern itself with such aspects of economic life, the practical outworking of such concepts in economic life can be used to refine a conceptual understanding of them. In the following illustration, credit is not merely what is offered, but also a response to an offering.

The Anglican pastoral writer and theologian W. H. Vanstone offered a purported 'phenomenology' of love.[1] He suggested that with love it is not the same as with food: while those who are hungry will be satisfied with anything, a child deprived of love is the most demanding and discriminating – there is a universal longing for love. Such a child is prone to distrust and cautious to give credit, resenting anything else that masquerades as love. While one cannot say exactly what authentic love is, Vanstone attributed to all the practical capacity to recognise inauthenticity in regards to love, and derived a conception of love from such distrustful, testing and defiant behaviour. Vanstone identified three criteria of inauthenticity, the first of which is limitation, for, in line with the Christian theological tradition, only love is infinite:

> When love is expected, no kindness, however lavish, satisfies: for it is known that, however much is given, something is being withheld. A locked room or a locked box will affront someone to whom, in the name of love, all the rest of the house has been made open: a secret of which one will not speak will offend someone to whom, in the guise of love, one will disclose everything else.[2]

Of course, it is only distrust that is offended by secrecy; loving trust accepts that secrecy has its reasons. Divine love might be infinite, but humans are finite and have competing cares. Yet the mark of limitation perhaps pertains more accurately to inauthentic forgiveness, as Vanstone notes: however much love is tested or rejected, it does not cease to show its care.[3]

Vanstone's second mark of inauthenticity is that of control: love is entirely distinguishable from power:

> Love is activity for the sake of an *other*: and where the object of love is wholly under the control of the one who loves, that object is no longer an other. It is a part or extension of the professed lover – an extension of himself. . . . In the care of children a parent is peculiarly aware that each step of love is a step of risk; and that each step generates the need for another and equally precarious step. In each word of encouragement lies the danger of creating over-confidence: in each restraint the danger of destroying confidence.[4]

Love, then, is precarious and easily frustrated in its goal. Love is liberal in the sense that it allows to the other their own authentic development and mode of being: it does not claim to own or control the beloved.[5] In this respect, love must wait to see if its precarious endeavours may come to fruition; it must continually adapt in response to what it finds. Vanstone compares love to the creative work of an artist, one whose true ability lies in incorporating the brushstroke that has gone astray into a greater whole. This theological position expresses a modern Anglican kenotic Christology that takes the doctrine of creation seriously: creation involves willing the otherness of the created being, endowing it with a power over against oneself.[6]

Yet it is Vanstone's third mark of inauthenticity that opens up a connection to a third metaphysical register, a register of value: love cannot be unaffected by that which it loves. Kindness that is self-sufficient, that withholds from the other power over the feeling self, is inauthentic. In the care of children, only when patience fails and gives way to anger can children be reassured that they have the power to affect the carer, and so that they matter.

Where there is no such surrender or gift of power the falsity of love is exposed. The human power of discrimination is constantly exercised to discern this mark of falsity. The commonplace question, 'Do I matter'? is the question of whether I have the power to affect the person who professes to love me or to whose love I feel myself entitled: and a huge range of human behaviour may be interpreted as a variety of attempts to answer the question. Our doubt about the authenticity of love is most commonly raised by, and focussed upon, the apparent detachment of one whose love is sought or expected: and our testing of love is most commonly a testing of the reality of this detachment.[7]

Love gives to the one it loves the power of meaning: they have value for the lover. Love, in this sense, is an investment which is vulnerable; it may not be returned. It is not that love is vulnerable in the sense that it can be eliminated or destroyed if the investment fails, for the power to affect the lover only continues to the extent that love is undiminished. Yet love is distinguishable from control in that it involves a power to be affected. Love is infinite in its power to suffer.[8] Vanstone's God is revealed only in the crucifixion: 'Love that gives gives ever more, / Gives with zeal, with eager hands, / Spares not, keeps not, all outpours, / Ventures all, its all expends. / Drained is love in making full, / Bound in setting others free; / Poor in making many rich; / Weak in giving power to be'.[9]

These, then, are Vanstone's marks of authentic love: it is infinite or un-limited; it is creative and precarious; and it is vulnerable and affected. It may seem a strange procedure to derive these from the unruly and testing behaviour of children who crave love; nevertheless, Christianity has always followed this kind of negative path in deriving the meaning of love from the crucifixion. The Trinitarian nature of this infinite, kenotic and mattering love is made explicit by Vanstone in his subsequent discussions.[10] Rather than pausing on such deliberations, my suggestion is rather to follow a route indicated by Vanstone: it is when love fails, when creation expresses its autonomy, when credit invested does not receive its expected return, that one might meet with the test of reality. Just as a deprived child may test for authentic love, just as Kant's dove is held up by air resistance, so it may be that economic life, rather than metaphysics, may offer a framework for the refinement of theology. Instead of understanding love through God, a Christian theology 'from below' may understand God through love, and love through its outworking in offering credit and creating value in the context of trust and hope.

So, on the one hand, daily economic life invokes issues of credit, care, wisdom, authority and trust, the most significant of theological concepts. It can be considered theologically in relation to these, rather than simply in relation to needs and substances, preferences and differences. On the other hand, the Platonic strategy of seeking the most perfect conception of credit, care, wisdom, authority and trust can be deferred – or approached indirectly – by exploring how these might operate in practical life. The value of love is only known by the way in which it deals with the obstacles to love. A theology only reveals itself in its response to sin. Here, Vanstone's conception of love offers an account of credit. It is not the case that credit is unlimited in its offering, for just as goods of appropriation are limited, so also will love impose limits on what is offered. Credit is not love, but the offering made by love, a limited sign of care which is vulnerable to misinterpretation. Yet credit, in the home, is creative and precarious, vulnerable and affected, hoping for the response of trust. Vanstone's account of love illuminates credit insofar as it is a handing over of responsibility, leaving room for self-determination. As such, Vanstone stands in a long tradition of liberal theology which is ultimately Franciscan in origin: what is truly loved is the freedom of one's friend, their active power to attend to and affect their own conditions of existence.[11] In this respect, theology finds a 'terminative cause', what it is about, in economic life.

Chapter Thirteen

Credit and Participation

Interest

In the medieval era, theological treatises included teachings on economic life as an inherent part of theology. Thomas Aquinas summed up a long tradition of Christian reflection on the acquisition of wealth by observing that, 'One man cannot abound in external riches, without another man lacking them'.[1] It was a matter of distributive justice. Wealth, in a largely cyclical agrarian economy, is a zero-sum game: the person who possesses an estate has appropriated all the efforts of those who have built it, service it and labour for its produce. Without the assistance of fossil fuels and elemental energies, all wealth was produced through the work of labourers, animals and plants – and so, dispensing with the myth of a directly divine origin of wealth as blessing, an anonymous Pelagian observed in the fifth century that all accumulation of wealth comes from theft or exploitation, or inheritance of the benefits of theft or exploitation.[2] Even if the Pelagians expressed this point more acutely than others, the origin of all wealth in landed estates was the context for the early Christian suspicion of wealth, expressed sharply in the preaching of Ambrose of Milan and Basil of Caesarea. In the Roman Empire, wealth had been attained largely through conquest, theft, slavery, tribute, patronage, taxation, lending, or by appropriating the benefits of these as a middleman. It was only around these primary wealth-generating activities that secondary markets could grow. At the origins of Christianity, there had been little role for the 'honest merchant' of the medieval towns: the economy was largely based on extraction through conquest, taxation and tribute. In such an economy, the gospel command to 'sell one's possessions and give to the poor' was clearly intended to make restitution and redistribute wealth, as in case of Zacchaeus.

The resultant use of wealth as an instrument of piety, whether in almsgiving or endowing the church, inherited aspects of Roman pagan piety expressed in endowing temples, monuments and games. For Augustine, the primary concern was to remove the lust for glory from the exercise of wealth: get rid of pride, and riches would do no harm.[3] Indeed, the church required regular giving for its maintenance and support for the poor, not one-off acts of dramatic renunciation. If the origins of wealth were thought to be opaque, this mattered little once wealth was offered to God as a regular act of penance, and to the church for management on behalf of the poor.[4] In effect, bishops and deacons acted as stewards of the church's income, whether from endowed land, trade or ongoing almsgiving. For such wealth was a blessing, the result of divine charity in its original bestowal and human charity in its donation to the church for the sake of God and for the poor. In its usage, it opened a path to a heavenly reward as well as providing for human need. Moreover, since all could give according to their means, rich and poor alike were united in sharing in the work of redemption. Of course, this ideal model of the circuit of wealth was not always strictly adhered to, for opportunities to manage wealth attracted desires to enjoy wealth. In later centuries, bishops, clerics and monks often enjoyed luxuries at the expense of the poor. Most subsequent theological controversies were rooted in the context of the use of wealth. Some reformers protested about the use of wealth to buy forgiveness, others the exploitation of the common people through rents, tithes and taxes. Their opponents sought to maintain an order of power to ensure governance by virtue and a stable use and distribution of wealth.

In Aquinas's day, on the one hand, the mendicant orders sought to renew the gospel life of radical renunciation while, on the other, centuries of management of offerings informed the practice of the mainstream church. Aquinas drew on the bishop's role as overseer to replace Roman notions of the private property of the *paterfamilias*. Property could be regarded as stewardship rather than dominion in that a person 'ought to possess external things, not as his own, but as common, so that, to wit, he is ready to communicate them to others in their need'.[5] Stewardship is not merely a matter of redistribution: it is clearly important that estates are managed effectively and productively so that all needs can be met – ownership arrangements help facilitate this. Yet stewardship also encounters further qualifications: the order of charity requires that each person must look after himself or herself first of all, and those for whom one has responsibility next, but out of one's surplus one may give to relieve the needs of others.[6] The practical problem would then lie in determining one's basic, social and cultural needs, and then seeing what is left over for the unlimited needs and demands of others, however grave or urgent. In medieval life, a balance was conceivable: for to the extent that populations are static there is some limit to their demands and needs. Yet once populations and goods become highly mobile, the weight of external need becomes unlimited. In modern life, with free movement of goods, services, people and capital, the traditional Christian teachings on wealth are thrown into crisis – both by the accessibility of unlimited need and by the possibility of new creation of wealth. In other words, the Aristotelian vision of a participatory order based around mutual interest is no longer preserved by intrinsic balances and limits.

Christian economic practice may itself have contributed to the rise of a dynamic economy. Following the collapse of the Roman Empire, much mobile wealth and coinage was offered to the church and melted down into plate, leaving the economy in a rather static state in Western Europe.[7] Yet just as feudal warfare stimulated the economy with its demand for castles and city walls, so did the far more extensive programme of building stone cathedrals and village churches.[8] For these religious projects inspired credit and liberated precious metals from their stored forms for minting as coins, just as did warfare and mining. Costly and unproductive as such enterprises were, the money and credit coined to pay for them continued to circulate and, in many cases, led to the founding of medieval towns and cities. Even the most unproductive expenditure, if it elicits the investment of trust, may make a positive contribution. By the thirteenth century, a dynamic economy involving extensive use of coin had emerged. While charity may offer a model for grace in an agrarian economy, credit and investment may offer a model in a dynamic one.

It is clear that economic life is not entirely static: crops grow, animals breed and surpluses multiply under careful management. Agriculture has never been a zero-sum game; manufacturing even less so.[9] It is agriculture which, since the time of Aristotle, has offered the primary contrast for coinage: coinage is sterile, it does not reproduce.[10] Given a fixed amount of coinage in circulation, one person cannot accumulate coinage without other people lacking it. Likewise, given a finite number of labourers, one person cannot accumulate wealth without it being extracted from the labour time of others. It is for such reasons that scholastic arguments against usury treat the practice as like making coinage breed coinage, an action against nature. The usurer, by definition, takes more than he gives. Typically, then, the underlying rationale for the prohibition against usury was a matter of balance and justice: as Bernardino of Siena, the Franciscan economic thinker and preacher, rationalised: 'Usury concentrates the money of the community in the hands of the few, just as if all the blood in a man's body ran to the heart and left the other organs depleted'.[11] Aquinas himself had already offered a refined version of such an argument: money measures the worth of other things; it is the unit of account. On this monetary scale of values, there should be a formal equivalence of money lent and money returned, for both measure the same activity, whether before or after. To take more for less money is to 'diversify the measure':[12] in offering a 'spread' between offer and bid prices it is as though one were using lighter weights when goods are taken away and heavier ones when they are returned. It results in unequal accumulation. Aquinas also offered a comparison with wine: just as the only use of wine is to consume it, and one does not charge for the use of wine as well as its ownership, the only use of money is to exchange it, and after exchange, one does not have it any more. One does not rent wine because one drinks it; likewise, one should not rent money because one spends it. So to charge interest for the use of money is charge for it twice: once for the principal, which is to be exchanged for the same sum when returned, and once for the usage.[13] Even if one objects that, unlike wine, coinage can be used to make a profit, Aquinas replies that it is human industry, not money, that is the principal cause of profit. It is hardly surprising that in a metaphysics grounded on 'Pure Act' that human activity is seen analogously as the source of value, anticipating Locke's conception of property and Ricardo's labour theory of value.

There's an obvious problem in this argument: there is far more demand to borrow money than there is to rent wine. People in need are inclined to borrow money in the expectation of acquiring money in the future, or simply to postpone the inevitable and buy some time, or in the desperate hope that the consequences of default may be less severe than the consequences of lacking money. It is the introduction of time that fundamentally changes any account of what is 'natural', adding a dimension additional to substance and use. There is the question of what money is intended for. Even with a given amount of coinage in circulation, economic reality is more complex than arguments about sterility suggest. For the use of coinage is to spend it, as Aquinas says. It is one thing for a usurer to accumulate coins, to continually relend what is received in interest, and so increasingly draw the means of exchange away from the wider economy so that people have nothing left to trade with. It is quite another matter for a capitalist to spend or invest those coins, and then for merchant to trade with merchant, accelerating the rate at which the coins pass from hand to hand, before returning briefly to the capitalist to be invested once more, and so increasingly adding to demand and trade. In the first case, money is sterile; in the second, it underwrites creative investment. Even with coinage, let alone with more complex monetary instruments, the key question is not who owns it, and not simply how fast it circulates, but where it circulates: whether its distribution is increasingly broad and inclusive or whether it circulates in ever narrower circuits, excluding many from the opportunity of spending it and making their demands effective. The coin that passes from hand to hand assists human cooperation, trust and the meeting of needs; the coin that lies idle in a treasure chest fails to assist the meeting of needs – unless it functions as a reserve to guarantee a credit note that circulates in its place. One should perhaps be cautious about judging credit and interest too promptly: when credit and interest facilitate a broadening distribution of effective demand, then they accomplish a kind of distributive justice with far more lasting effects than merely selling one's possessions and giving the money to the poor. For if all are included in economic life and circulation, this offers an element of distributive justice. By contrast, if the poor are only included via mere 'charity', then once the poor have spent their money, it can quickly return to the rich, leaving the poor to wait for the next charitable gift. Even in those economies where the poor can keep the money received circulating only between themselves, preventing it from returning to usurious accumulators, such circulation does not necessarily expand to include wider groups of the poor.

Peter of John Olivi, about two decades after Aquinas, set out one of the first strictly economic treatises, *A Treatise on Contracts*, in order to draw a clear distinction between usurious exploitation of the poor and the mutually beneficial investment practices of merchants. Usury is evil because it devours the temporal substance of one's neighbour, feigning compassion while intending profit.[14] Olivi affirmed unequivocally the established scholastic objections to usury, including those stated by Aquinas. In the loan of a fungible good, to be returned in an equal quantity, the substance and use belongs to the receiver, not the lender, so to charge for usage is to sell the same thing twice. To ask for more is an injury to equity, selling someone their own industriousness.[15] Moreover, usury incites an infinite passion for gain, corrupting friendship, resulting in idleness, a love of this life and a despair of the other.[16] In addition, Olivi described usury as the selling of grace, a category mistake: 'To give a loan, as it is a strict donation, is an act of grace . . . in usury the grace of the loan is sold'.[17] A grace is a gift or favour, but if something else is demanded based on what is owing according to justice, then it is no longer grace but an exchange. Drawing on Luke 6.35 ('But love your enemies, do good, and lend, expecting nothing in return'), Olivi distinguished between the evangelical counsel of perfection of a supererogatory offering with a view to a heavenly reward, and a loan, with a view to an earthly one.[18] The problem is treating goods of offering as if they were goods of appropriation.

When it comes to merchant practices, however, many estimates have regard to the future time of the thing in question, such as the productive power of a horse or a field which is leased, where payment is appropriate for future time.[19] Just as a person who pays up front for a box ordered from a craftsman owns the box when it is made, an increased price can be charged for those who defer payment after receipt of the good, so long as it remains within the just price.[20] For Olivi, there were a wide range of factors which affect price setting: the composition, durability and satisfaction offered by the goods; their relative scarcity or abundance; the labour involved in making goods available; and, when it comes to recompense, the dignities of the office involved, whether in the greater experience, industriousness and thoughtfulness required, or whether in the greater expenses of office. As such, there is no possible direct measure of value, and considerable latitude in price due to different estimations.[21] Overall, the ultimate measure of contracts must be the common good of all.[22] These considerations of latitude in price and contribution to the common good enabled Olivi to develop a theory of capital: money is capital when it is set aside for commerce, and, as such, 'compensation for the probable profit was contained in a certain way casually and, as it were, like a seed in the aforementioned capital inasmuch as it is capital'.[23] This character of capital, the seed of profitability, can be sold in addition to the money loaned, without selling the same substance twice. The meaning of money is not its substance; it includes what the money is for. Possibilities, enabled by attention and credit, may exist as much as discrete substances.[24] This is close to an ontological description of capital as credit.[25] Seminal reasons are 'the potentialities of matter to forms that are to be educed from it by an extrinsic agent.'[26] There is something more to reality than the substance of things; it is a precursor for what we have called 'value', something which is added by temporal and relational existence to a thing. All this may sound rather mysterious and metaphysical, but it emerges from concrete practices. If someone places an order from a craftsman or merchant without paying in full up front, the craftsman or merchant will engage in labour and acquire materials prior to payment: they give the customer credit. Similarly, if they do not have the money in advance to acquire what they need, the order itself can count as proof of the possibility of future payment. Such transactions take place by means of an advance; moreover, if someone advances money itself to facilitate such transactions, where trust is otherwise lacking, then such an advance catalyses a possibility which would not otherwise occur. Here, money is the 'seminal reason' for the existence of things. Credit is the source of wealth.

In any given set of circumstances involving customer orders, providers of goods and services, and their own suppliers, what makes a difference is credit. This can be embodied in money, but what is essential is possibility: not what exists, but what people are thinking. Olivi likewise acknowledged the vital role of attention and intention in cognition: a thing does not simply impress its form upon the intellect, but the intellect actively seeks it out.[27] This introduction of an active role in perception enables a decisive change in metaphysics which presages modern thought: for if the object is present in the mind as a 'terminative cause', what the thought is about, rather than as an active cause which impresses an imprint as if the mind were passive matter, then the reality which corresponds to freedom is possibility.[28] In economic life, things are not simply what they are; things are what they mean in relation to other things: a plum is not merely a plum, and a shrug is not merely a shrug; each is a sign with a definable meaning. Where Aquinas attributed value to industry, Olivi also attributed value to attention and intention. His nascent theory of capital offered a justification for interest: for there is no limit to the new meaning and value that can be created.

There are profound theological issues at stake here: Is grace best modeled on the charitable, redistributive gift, or is it best modeled on credit and investment? Does it make merely an accidental and extrinsic difference to its recipients by providing objects of consumption, or does it effectively transform their mode of being and relations with others? Does it fulfil needs for consumption or also needs for participation and offering? For all the associations of credit with debt, sin and guilt, it is not clear that credit should be ruled out in advance on religious grounds. Credit may even include a charitable dimension: it may incorporate elements of giving to those in need out of superfluity. Insofar as credit is not compelled, it may incorporate an element of grace. Credit is at once the superfluous dimension of the economy and also the most necessary.

Moreover, there are also profound ontological issues at stake here: What is the ontological status of credit which, lacking substance in itself, is a complex relation of trust between persons? Is it merely ephemeral and derivative, or is it determining in the last instance? Might not a Christian ontology be willing to follow Paul: 'God chose what is low and despised in the world, the things that are not, to reduce to nothing the things that are . . .' (1 Cor. 1.28)? Perhaps things which lack a substance of their own may occasionally constitute the highest realities. In order to explore such theological and ontological issues, we will turn to explore the role of credit in economic life.

The key practical issue, however, is how one may distinguish between a usurious debt which consumes a person's wealth and capital investment which may add to it. Scholastic considerations against usury may still be illuminating here. The first developed statement of the argument against usury on the basis 'selling time' was formulated by William of Auxerre, who pointed out that 'each creature is compelled to give himself; the sun is compelled to give itself to illuminate; similarly the earth is compelled to give whatever it can, and similarly the water. Nothing, however, so naturally gives itself as time'.[29] Credit may be offered as a gift out of superfluity to relieve the need of one's neighbour. Yet the very same act, under the guise of kindness, may also seek to profit out of another's need. As Peter of Tarentaise put it, 'It is wrong that that which was instituted as a favour should be turned into an injury'.[30] A lender stakes a claim on possible future wealth irrespective of whether that wealth is forthcoming,[31] and irrespective of whether there are more urgent claims on the borrower's time than accumulating a surplus to return to the lender. Usury profits from another's suffering and fear of loss. For even if a borrower is willing to borrow at high rates of interest, he or she does so with a 'forced will', an act performed for fear of greater evils,[32] compelled by need and the lender's refusal to lend for nothing. Lending, in all its ambivalence, has to be measured by charity. A charitable creditor will be primarily concerned with the lasting fulfilment of the debtor's need. In this respect, the decisive difference determining what was permitted by Olivi was whether the investor's capital was at risk in the venture.[33]

Interest may signify a mutual benefit enabled by participation. It is the actual usage of coin, not its substance, which determines whether it is merely an instrument of exchange facilitating consumption or it enhances the means of production. What matters about any particular sum of money is what it will prove to have been through time. It is where it circulates, not who owns it at any particular time. Of course, one cannot necessarily judge the outcome of time in advance.[34] Yet one can take into account the economic forces that bear on any situation at a particular time.

Chapter Fourteen

Appropriating Credit

Tokens of Value

Credit, as invested trust, is encountered in the intimate spheres of the attentive mind or the home. The value it divines is communicated through tokens: a shrug, a gesture, an offering, a promise, or perhaps even a sum of money. While an insignificant shrug might vanish in the course of time, an enduring token, such as a written promise or a sum of money, may travel far beyond its initial place and time of issuance, being reissued or reinterpreted with an entirely different significance. Such tokens are inherently ambivalent: without them, one could hardly communicate value at all; using them, one can hardly be certain of what message of trust and value is passed onwards. Just as it is in the nature of credit to give some measure of autonomy to the recipient, it is also in the nature of credit to be exposed to an economy of tokens which may transmit to the recipient a rather different set of evaluations. Without a foot in each camp, credit would be reduced to either a personal trust which lacks power or a public value which lacks trust. Yet the consequences of this dual nature have further consequences: on the one hand, the act of offering credit may be reinterpreted as part of an incomplete exchange, creating a specific obligation or debt; on the other hand, such tokens of value, once exchanged, may function as the condition for a general view of value. Indeed, credit is a bridge between the intimate sphere of personal relations and the public sphere of generalised relations. It is a bridge which leads from theology to economics.

Let us take, first of all, the case when credit is seen as an incomplete exchange, a debt. The contemporary anthropologist David Graeber suggests that in most human economies one would not buy or sell one's most important possessions for the same reasons that one would not buy and sell people:

they are unique objects expressing a web of relationships with human be-ings.[1] To sell a household object, to make an exchange or to substitute for it, is to let go of all the memories and obligations associated with it – who made it, who gave it, on what occasion and for what reason. An object is never an object; it is a nexus of human relationships, memories and possibilities, re-plete with meaning. Yet exchange destroys the meaning by cancelling such relationships: it 'allows us to cancel our debts. It gives us a way to call it even: hence, to end the relationship'.[2] Graeber points out how rare exchange relations have been in the course of human history and the variety of its cultures, citing the authority of Caroline Humphrey, who concludes the defi-nite anthropological work on barter by declaring: 'No example of a barter economy, pure and simple, has ever been described, let alone the emergence from it of money; all available ethnography suggests that there never has been such a thing'.[3] In traditional societies, most economic relations were either 'communist' – from each according to ability to each according to need – or 'hierarchical' – relations of patronage where a complex web of tributes and favours is distributed between powerful individuals and their hangers-on. Direct exchange, when it occurs, largely takes place with people outside the community, people one might not wish to feel any obligation towards. 'Swapping one thing directly for another while trying to get the best deal one can out of the transaction is, ordinarily, how one deals with people one doesn't care about and doesn't expect to see again'.[4] Only when commu-nal or hierarchical relations are reconceived in terms of debt, as though they could be measured by money and given a specific cost and timeframe, does exchange become the dominant paradigm. Each object no longer signifies the bond to the one who has given it; it signifies the obligation that is owing. Debts, as obligations, emerged in history long before money.

To illustrate this transformation towards a society conceived in terms of exchange, where communal and hierarchical bonds are kept out of mind, Graeber cites Rabelais's satirical character Panurge, whose philosophy of life consists in being perennially in debt. Debt is good, for Panurge, for without the bonds of debt that keep creditors concerned for the welfare of debtors in the hope that they might be repaid, Panurge believes that human life would be no better than a dog fight.

> Amongst human beings none will save another; it will be no good a man shouting Help! Fire! I'm drowning! Murder! Nobody will come and help him. Why? Because he has lent nothing: and no one owes him anything. No one has anything to lose by his fire, his shipwreck, his fall, or his death. He has lent nothing. And he would lend nothing hereafter.
>
> In short, Faith, Hope and Charity would be banished from this world.[5]

What is missing, in this image of life, is any conception of faith, hope and charity that is not conceived in terms of debt or exchange. Graeber attributes the same consequences to a vision of society as a market consisting primarily in relationships of exchange. For this vision tends to impose the bleak alternative of either ongoing debts (incomplete exchanges), or the complete absence of any human bond:

> If we insist on defining all human interactions as matters of people giving one thing for another, then any ongoing human relations can only take the form of debts. Without them, no one would owe anything to anybody. A world without debt would revert to primordial chaos, a war of all against all; no one would feel the slightest responsibility for one another; the simple fact of being human would have no significance; we would all become isolated planets who couldn't even be counted on to maintain our proper orbits. [6]

To view the primary human bonds as those of exchange, then, is to regard them as destined for dissolution once the exchange is complete. Exchange, on this account, consists in the destruction of the human meaning and value of things, leaving them simply with a use-value, dependent on their nature, and an exchange-value, dependent on what could be substituted for them. In a human, meaningful economy, by contrast, to make something into a commodity is to tear it out of its context. [7] Graeber attributes the spread of a market economy to the actions of burglars, conquerors, mercenaries, debt collectors and slavers: 'Who was the first man to look at a house full of objects and to immediately assess them only in terms of what he could trade them for in the market likely to have been? Surely, he can only have been a thief'. [8] Equivalence, whether of value or quality, only seems rational when people or objects have been severed from their contexts to the extent that they can be treated as substitutable for something else. Comparison, equivalence and substitution produce an exchange-value that substitutes itself, not only for use-values, but also for human-values – intrinsic human bonds. The issues raised for philosophy by such reflections could hardly be more grave: When does an appeal to fungible substances and concepts, as well as to differences and quantities, substitute in human thought for irreplaceable bonds, memories, obligations and possibilities? Is Western reason from its outset entirely structured for exchange? [9]

Of course, people are not the only thieves: we are all equal before death. The passage of time brings moth and rust, erases memories and deprives those who remain of their companions. All objects within a human economy are subject to a continual loss of meaning and value. Time rips people and objects away from their contexts and makes slaves of us all. Objects become mere tokens of the value they once held. Nevertheless, this effect is not without its ambivalence: for all that the passage of time might steal, it also gives: it gives time, so that we, in turn, can receive this time by spending it. To live is to redonate the time we have been given. Yet we cannot give time to everything that is worthwhile at once, so to save time, it is helpful to invest in those people or things that matter to us with a sense of importance, whether implicitly remembered or explicitly marked. We give credit; we invest; we give something of ourselves, our meaning and our time, in the objects we pass on, at once creating and losing meaning. Credit, here, is no longer to be understood solely as an act of offering, an investment of time, attention and devotion. Credit, as an offered token or memento, is the creation of a sign of value.

As Bernard Stiegler has pointed out, the basis for credit is studious leisure time (*otium*), involving libidinal investment and the direction of attention, and drawing on all forms of memory as well as anticipating the future.[10] Yet once we materialise this time of consciousness beyond consciousness in a cultural symbol, such as in gestures, words, writing or a price to assist with memory, then the result is deeply ambivalent: on the one hand, tokens serve as reminders; on the other, the words or marks focus our attention, leading to a loss of experience, memory and knowledge – much of what we care about goes unmarked. For at the same time, marks of credit do not necessarily reawaken the perception of value that gave rise to them. When signs substitute for meaning, it becomes possible to exchange the signs instead of investing in their meanings. So it is not merely theft, trade or time that tears things from their context, resulting in the loss of meaning and value: our very attempts to preserve meaning and value by marking them can lead to their loss. As Martin Luther expressed it in his 95 Theses: 'It is blasphemy to say that the insignia of the cross with the papal arms are of equal value to the cross on which Christ died'.[11] Yet could that cross have communicated its value without the papal arms or the printed word?

Marks of credit can easily lead to a reversal: the sense of importance seems to derive from symbols of value – thus price becomes a mark of quality, words become a proof of truth – rather than value deriving from our investment, where quality gives rise to price and truth gives rise to words. Stiegler generalises Socrates's famous argument for the superiority of speech over writing from the *Phaedrus*: culture is characterised by a process of grammatisation, an externalisation of psychic experience, where structures, processes and records intervene to short-circuit psychic individuals and their direct investments.[12] Our aids to memory may be at once remedies and poisons. The problem arises when the attention is captured by signs of value and is no longer offered to its human substance. For Stiegler, the successful reliance on signs, structures, processes and records leads to a disinvestment in human relations in contemporary society. Just as Panurge views a society without debt as catastrophic, so does Stiegler view a society without interpersonal investment: the capture of attention by work and entertainment leads to a failure of people to spend time together and invest in each other at a psychic level. He describes the consequences in psychoanalytic terms, but the message is similar to Graeber's version of estrangement. Between the generations, the failure of adults to attend to and care for youth leads to a failure of children to build their character through a primary identification with adults. Instead of seeking the higher goods of culture, there is a progressive disenchantment and desublimation of the libido into its component drives. In place of human investment, financial speculation and drive-based obsessions are substituted.[13]

For all Stiegler's pessimism, it is also important to appreciate the positive significance of grammatisation, of techniques for recording, remembering and repeating value. For these are the conditions of possibility for freedom, reason and religion alike: no self-determination is possible without some extrinsic means for recording, remembering, repeating and assessing value. Such signs simply need to be invested with value; they are given credit, and they are given as credit. Even reason itself may be situated in relation to the work of self-determination through modes of cultural memory. For philosophy originated in the West as a work of self-determination through living life in accordance with reason.[14] For example, the ancient Greeks saw the regular movements of the heavens as exhibiting the regularity of nature, disclosing the reason underlying the cosmos, where everything moves in harmony and proportion. The aim of reason, then, was to live life in accordance with nature. But reason itself was only made thinkable, made explicit, by being projected onto the order of the heavens.[15] Life is only subject to rational self-determination when it can be measured against an external sign. By contrast, an entirely different conception of the *logos* was at work in the Reformers, who removed the sacred from the natural order and confined it to scripture, preaching and individual conscience. For the Reformers, the divine *logos* was encountered in the text of scripture itself, and the aim of religion was to live life in accordance with the will of God. The printing press enabled the recording, repetition and distribution of scripture: the sacred, for them, was no longer present in nature, but only in word and thought. Cosmos and printing press produce very different effects as means of recording, remembering and repeating. Modern reason has combined both means of recording: the power of printing, enabling a science that can be recorded, distributed, repeated and tested, with the regularity of nature, as the object of enquiry and modification. As such, modern reason has sought to rationalise and modify productive practices, economic relations, and even individual conduct in pursuit of the collective goal of the production of wealth. Yet such self-determination requires certain preconditions: the rituals and technologies that allow us to record, repeat and remember, the spiritual practices through which life is perpetually reconstructed, the collective goals of human endeavour – each of these were formerly developed in religious life.

Self-determination requires that a meaning must first be condensed into a symbol, sign or medium. The external material, here, has a dual function: if it is first an expression of a preserved meaning, it must then become a criterion that gives shape and form to subsequent conduct. One thinks in and with and through this material of expression. Bodily markings, speech, religious rituals, chants and astronomical movements may all function as forms of 'writing'. Nevertheless, while writing may organise life, and grammar may organise writing, the advent of the written word enables the sedimentation of a 'writing within writing', a mode of ordering how writing should be – the consistent determination of written signs as concepts. Metaphysics, the order of being, is a 'writing within writing', enabling philosophical reason as the ordering of life in line with the idea. Philosophical ideas become fundamental organising categories of experience insofar as they duplicate the recording of experience and function as the ultimate criteria by which what is real can be judged.[16] Even if modern thought has become oblivious to its grounding in metaphysics as objective philosophical presupposition, this does not mean that its extrinsic grounding is any less firm: subjective presuppositions, embedded in assumptions about what it means to think and know, become inscribed within cultural institutions such as the university and the literary form of the scientific paper. Our 'writing within writing' is embedded in genres and practices as well as in concepts.

One should therefore recognise the deep ambiguity of tokens of value: they record values in signs, so that life can be regulated by means of them; yet they also erase the specific, local and human meaning of such values insofar as a sign circulates beyond its original context. For example, to describe the courageous action of a friend as 'good' is both to mark its significance and to mask its specificity or goodness. It enables comparison with other good actions, and yet comparison reduces them to their lowest common denominator. This was Nietzsche's most fundamental objection to metaphysics: it devalues values.[17] There is, however, little prospect of successfully hoarding and preserving value just as there is no prospect of hoarding and preserving time. Like time, it is the nature of value to give itself: values are bestowed. The exchange of tokens is part of the bestowal of value. Where metaphysics relates to the social activity of preserving common goods in which all minds may participate, economics relates to what happens outside the mind. For in the act of thinking, we can only make offerings of value; in the act of living, we receive the value that is bestowed upon us. There is no doubt a relationship between what one gives and one what receives, even if this is not an entirely necessary relationship. The economy of value concerns what happens to values through their interactions with the rest of existence. Such an economy takes place outside the sphere of direct mental control. It is what happens when we offer credit. Yet it also has a value that exceeds simple exchange. Every exchange, insofar as it is actively preferred, marks an act offering credit. Even though a market economy may appear alienated from human meanings, such meanings are still present and may still be read. There remains a complex dialectic between credit and exchange which requires careful analysis. For this, we need to turn to a historical example where exchange was facilitated by credit as deferred payment.

Chapter Fifteen

A Culture of Credit

Let us return to promises as expressions of credit. Walter Powell of Gloucestershire, in a pamphlet of 1645 campaigning against the swearing of oaths entitled *A Summons for Swearers, and a Law for the Lips*, wrote:

> If wee walk unblameable in our lives; if we so highly value truth, that we sell it at no rate; if we keep touch, and observe promises, though to our hinderance; our word, even in our weightiest businesse, will be credited, and need no superior confirmation: for it is not the oath which give credit to the man, but the man to the oath. . . . speak the truth without an oath, and . . . thy word shall be taken by itself; otherwise thou art like an ill credited borrower, that ridest up and down the country with sureties. [1]

Powell was clearly concerned that an oath, a declaration of one's sincerity before God, was a poor substitute for character, putting duty before inclination. It is not at all the principle behind the oath that offended Powell – that there is a God who is offended by lies but approves of faith and truth – so much as explicitly drawing attention to this principle that was accepted by all at the time. If there is such a God, then one is judged on one's word, not simply on one's formal oaths; the invocation of God therefore reveals a practical atheism in the rest of one's doings and discloses an untrustworthy character. Powell's campaign was aimed at the religious improvement of poorer sort of people, 'oaths being the common sureties of the basest of people, even the scum of highways, Alehouses and Taverns', those associated with vagrancy, debt, idleness, indulgence and dissipation. Yet what is presupposed in such a campaign is that piety is associated with probity, and honouring promises is not simply a matter of personal morality, but the very basis for the common wealth of the people as a whole – if there are some whose word cannot be trusted, then one ought to be miserly with trust, and everyone is poorer. What seems so foreign to the economic culture of England in the twenty-first century seemed entirely natural in the seventeenth: that religious faith should underpin the economic order.

Craig Muldrew offers an explanation in his account of the credit economy in early modern England from 1530–1720. The context, here, was one of rising prosperity: the Tudor policy of encouraging wool manufacture, replacing arable lands with sheep, setting households to work in spinning and weaving, selling the manufactured cloth abroad, while forbidding the export of raw wool, seemed to be paying off.[2] Such a concentration led to increasing returns, a division of labour, greater synergies within towns, new knowledge and the emergence of a free internal market concentrated on market towns. Since farming sheep was less labour intensive than farming crops, many were displaced from working the land directly, but at least some of these found employment in growing craft production. With a rise in population, and households increasingly engaging in market activities, there was an acute shortage of coinage throughout the period.[3] For out of the coins in circulation, many were centuries old, most were clipped, and the good ones were consequently hoarded by merchants for important transactions. Moreover, coins had to be accumulated for rents, tithes and taxes, for use in emergencies, for lending to those with pressing obligations or whose reputations were in decline, for landowners to pay large bills, and for merchants to engage in overseas exchange, with the result that they did not circulate frequently. Credit expanded rapidly to take the place of money in daily transactions in the form of deferred payment for goods and services.[4] Debts were often not of borrowed coins at all; they were incomplete transactions. Payment dates were also subject to continual renegotiation, balancing the needs of creditors against debtors. Wherever possible, reciprocal debts contracted between various interested parties over a number of months could then be 'reckoned' or canceled against each other, with only the remaining balance paid in coins. In this way, credit accelerated the velocity of money: Muldrew estimates that in the East Anglian port town of King's Lynn in the 1680s every pound, as an abstract unit of account, would have changed hands once every ten days, while the majority of coins would have been retained by the rich merchants.[5]

Many writers of the early modern period attested to the fact that private credit, rather than coinage, was the main basis for the transfer of goods and services: one 'bought upon credit, and sold upon trust'.[6] The result, as both diaries and legal records show, is that all, whether rich or poor, had a multitude of debts owing to them as well as themselves owing debts to others. A typical example is the great London cloth merchant Gregory Isham, who owed £5,000 when he died in 1558, was owed £6,000, but only had £145 cash in hand. Much later, at the beginning of the eighteenth century, Daniel Defoe in *The Complete Tradesman* argued for the impossibility of carrying on trade successfully without giving credit: 'He that gives no trust, and takes no trust, either by wholesale or by retail, and keeps his cash all himself . . . so no body is in debt to him, and all his estate is in his shop; but I suppose the Tradesman that trades wholly thus, is not yet born, or if there ever were any such, they are all dead'.[7] The phrasing is revealing: an estate is not 'in his shop', an inventory or a collection of coins, a private stock in his own possession, but with other people in their obligations towards him. Even land was not ultimately a protection against debt, for it could be sold off to keep debtors out of prison. The only significant form of wealth was 'credit' understood as a reputation – one for honest dealing, for care in repaying debts, and for 'sociability' or being obliging to others in their needs. Muldrew explains: 'Wealth in this period is thus better thought of as a series of personal relationships with neighbours and God in which virtue, providence and fortune were all socially understood to be factors contributing to the condition and *estimation* of wealth by others'.[8] *Wealth was not a possession but an attitude.* Defoe made this difference between wealth as cash and wealth as credit explicit:

> Of what fatal consequence then is the raising of rumours and suspicions upon the credit and characters of young tradesmen? and how little do those who are forward to raise such suspicions, and spread such rumours, consult conscience, or principle, or honour, in what they do? how little do they consider that they are committing a trading murther, and that, with respect to the justice of it, they may with much more equity break open the tradesman's house, and rob his cash-chest, or his shop? and what they can carry away thence will not do him half the injury that robbing his character of what is due to it from an upright and diligent conduct, would do: the loss of his money or goods is easily made up, and may be sometimes repaired with advantage; but the loss of credit is never repair'd; the one is breaking upon his house, but the other is burning it down; the one carries away some goods, but the other shuts goods out from coming in; one is hurting the tradesman, but the other is undoing.[9]

The difference from what was to follow is extraordinary. To be wealthy was less a matter of having access to money than it was a matter of having access to credit. One's wealth was not one's property but one's social standing; conversely, one's social standing was one's source of property. As such, it was insecure: in every sale on credit, in every act of standing surety for an associate or relative, one was exposed to the fortunes of others. An ability to pay one's own debts was only partially dependent on oneself; it was also dependent on the actions of others. In each transaction, then, it was important to estimate the credit of the counterparty. If one did not sell upon credit, one would have no customers; if one did, one was exposed to the customers' fortunes and degree of honesty. In this respect, wealth was interdependent. It mattered far less what one had in one's shop, or that one enjoyed the benefits of luxury, than that one enjoyed the benefits of reputation, and could call on others whenever need arose.

The dynamics of this economy of obligation were very different to the dynamics of free market competition based upon self-interest. For there was no complete estrangement of economic from social life: wealth consisted in social relations, or specifically, in one's credit as estimated by others, and in one's debtors' ability and willingness to pay. If rumours went around that one was unwilling to pay debts, dishonest in transactions, spending beyond one's means or too idle to provide for oneself, then the ability to trade could quickly evaporate – few would advance goods. As a corollary, if one was slow in paying one's debts, then rumours about one's character might start to circulate. This economy of obligation was extremely insecure. Credit as reputation was far more valuable than cash in hand: the diarists of this period, such as Samuel Pepys, were not kept awake at night by the fear that some of their debtors might never pay, for they expected to have to write off a portion of what was owing to them due to the misfortune or poverty of their debtors. What kept them awake was their own debts, for a reputation for paying honestly was the basis for their credit. Account books were very poorly kept, but debts, sworn in front of witnesses, were seared into memory. There was little need for the extraction of a pledge to guarantee payment, for every purchase on credit involved staking one's entire reputation. People cared more for their social standing than they did for their profits, for their creditworthiness was the basis for their survival. As Defoe explained:

> CREDIT . . . 'tis the choicest ware [a tradesman] deals in, and he cannot be too chary of it when he has it, or buy it too dear when he wants it; 'tis a stock to his warehouse, 'tis current money in his cash-chest, it Accepts all his bills; for 'tis on the fund of his credit that he has any bills to accept . . . in a word 'tis the life and soul of his trade, and it requires his utmost vigilance to preserve it. [10]

These are heartfelt words: Defoe had gone bankrupt and was writing to earn to repay his debts.

Yet this is only part of the story: it regards credit from an individual point of view. A person's trustworthiness was the concern of whole towns and villages because of the extensiveness of credit and the potential domino effect of default. The more reliable people were in paying debts, or delivering goods and services as promised, the more secure the chains of credit, and the greater the chance of material security for the whole community. [11] An interest in the moral conduct of others was a concern for all: this is why there were campaigns to improve morals. The word *interest* itself was not used in the sense of self-interest, but in the sense of mutual advantage. Honest trade was sociability and cooperation. It was conducted through extensive conversation and negotiation.

The growth of credit, even if an expression of a growth of cooperation, also led to a growth in risk and instability. Misfortunes such as a poor harvest, fire or death, whether they struck one's family, one's debtors or simply one's customers, could have a significant effect. Instability was certainly a spur to competition, but competition was not simply for wealth or customers, but especially for credit. For among the misfortunes that could strike must be counted dishonest, lazy or profligate neighbours. In reaction to this, moral competition was far more apparent than economic competition: one had to cultivate a reputation for paying dues, honesty, diligence and thrift. In addition to this, the main economic effect was competitive piety – religious belief, virtue and honesty were regarded as the basis of moral virtue. For the basis for trust in promises in early modern England stemmed from the shared culture of Christian belief: one could trust one's neighbours as fellow believers. [12] One would trust above all others those who were most devout – and for the purposes of trade, unlike those of politics, the variety of Christian devotion itself was less significant than its authenticity. [13]

One should perhaps register some ambivalence in regards to this economic drive towards religiosity. On the one hand, only a reputation for piety counted, and outer signs were more significant than inner belief. On the other hand, one was also judged on actual conduct, so that honesty, diligence and thrift were really cultivated. Indeed, many were devout believers, and regarded their fortunes, so dependent on circumstance and others, as in the hands of God. It was less a matter of salvation-anxiety that inclined people to work and save, as in Weber's questionable thesis, than it was a matter of reputation-anxiety. Saving was for the sake of maintaining one's credit by giving one the power to pay debts on time; there was little other motive to accumulate wealth, which might give one a reputation for miserliness, than to provide for one's children in the event of one's early death. Overall, piety was highly regarded, and was pursued for the sake of material security and wealth. Yet material wealth itself was only an object of pursuit for the sake of credit or social wealth. Honesty, diligence and thrift were pursued for the sake of God.

One cannot take either the lack of estrangement or the genuine piety of this era as reasons for supposing that this was a golden age. Those who cared for the finest virtue in all their dealings at home could behave very differently when released from social estimation while abroad, whether as merchant adventurers, colonists, slave-traders, privateers or pirates. Even at home there were two other important dynamics arising from the economy of obligation. One was social polarisation between those with credit and those without. Those who were too poor to pay their debts were suspected of moral deficiency. While the forgiveness of the debts of the poorest was widespread and a part of Christian charity – Muldrew estimates that perhaps twenty times as much was offered to the poor in this way than in charitable donations and poor law payments – deference to 'one's betters' was expected as the price of debt forgiveness.[14] Since credit derived from virtue, the poor, as we have heard from Walter Powell, were suspected of bringing their fate upon themselves through profligate spending in alehouses and in idleness. In this context, the poor laws were not simply motivated by compassion but by practicality – they benefited wider society by offering the poor a minimum predictable income, giving rise to less need for credit, and less credit risk.[15]

The other dynamic of this economy of obligation was the massive rise in litigation for unpaid debts and broken contracts. This reached its peak in the 1580s, when there were perhaps as many as over four hundred thousand lawsuits per year in England, as many as there were households.[16] Lawsuits continued in significant volume throughout the early modern period, and did not decline until the eighteenth century. They affected all parts of society: even the poor were active in initiating litigation. In the vast majority of cases, such litigation was a threat to force payment, leading to a settlement out of court. Only 4 percent of such cases proceeded as far as judgement.[17] The decision of whether to proceed to judgement and have it enforced was left in the hands of the plaintiff, and there was little point in going to the expense and effort of forcing a judgement against someone who was entirely unable to pay. Law was expected to be tempered with mercy; the litigious were regarded as cruel and unsociable, and so lost credit on their own account.[18] Imprisonment for debt was numerically rather small, for all the bad reputation that debtors' prisons later acquired: it was either used to force someone unwilling to sell their property to do so, or as a last resort to keep chronically untrustworthy individuals out of the credit process of society.[19] Its severity was used primarily as a deterrent. Nevertheless, an economy resting on moral probity alone was inadequate without the threat of law to enforce contracts.

The culture of credit offered an economic life that now seems remote: while sociability, leniency, charity, forgiveness and virtue were all encouraged, there was a competition for reputation in religious zeal, prurient interest in the conduct of neighbours, and frequent recourse to the law. Economic life was unstable, and ruin, when it came, affected both the economic welfare and the moral standing of the individual, as well as the ability of many others to pay their own debts, and hence their moral standing as well. Those who thrived in such a culture regarded themselves and each other as good, while the unfortunate or those who lacked opportunity were suspected of moral failings. While debts owed were remembered, there was little attempt to keep accurate books, little attempt to calculate in Nietzsche's sense, very little estimation of overall rates of profit, and little sense of self-interest apart from the interest of the whole community. Above all, economic concerns were primarily religious or moral. There was no need or scope for an economic science in the modern sense because economic life was regulated by religious and moral prescription, not calculable profit.

Change, when it came, was brought about by an increase in the money supply through the use of bank credit as money, by the availability of insurance, by the institutionalisation of economic life through the emergence of large state or private enterprises and institutions that engaged in planning, and by the intensification of self-discipline in personal conduct so that people became predictable; it was supported by the repatriation of profits from slave-trading and sugar plantations, and by the advance of technologies of production and later by the use of fossil fuels. Nevertheless, the religious and moral dimensions of economic life from this period have not simply dissipated away; their echoes are very much present in the twenty-first century, even if they are institutionalised in rather different forms. Contemporary banks are as bound together in credits and debts as seventeenth-century merchants. The dilemmas of maintaining reputation and systemic risk from credit are as significant now as always. This is why we may continue to speak of a theological dimension in economics. Nevertheless, this economy of credit has largely been rendered invisible; even public morals have been transformed since the Financial Revolution. It is such a transformation that facilitated the origins of modern economic science. The key issue, here, is how an economy of credit could be rendered invisible within an economy of exchange.

Chapter Sixteen

Measure for Measure

An abiding fascination with the skill of the wordsmiths of the Tudor and Stuart eras may be due, in part, to the heavy burden words had to bear in the daily interactions of the time – not merely in entertainment, as in the theatre or intrigues at court, but in the quotidian business of negotiating credit and exchange. Business negotiations would last for hours, and consisted of elaborate speeches appealing to need, conscience, morality, religion and mutual interest.[1] By contrast, how efficient, elegant, articulate and, above all, concise must have seemed those negotiations conducted by the offer of money. For where requests for credit could only offer vague assurances of future value, money could offer the substance itself. Money talks. But what does it say?

A radical new idea was proposed by William Potter in 1650: when money speaks, it endows its possessor with credit. For money serves as:

> an *Evidence* or *Testimony*, to signifie how far forth men (by their joynt Agreement to take it, being otherwise of no worth, for Commodities of real value) are Indebted for, and engaged, to recommence the fruits of their labours or possessions, in some other Commodities or Necessaries instead of those, that for such money they parted with.[2]

Money was treated here as simply a token of credit or purchasing power. Potter, like Powell, was mainly concerned with the problem of the poor, and sought a solution in honesty, diligence and thrift. Unlike Powell, however, he saw the problem in systemic terms as the failure of trade to elicit productive capacity – a shortage of trust caused a shortage of trade and production. Given opportunities for trade, people would sell goods as fast as they could prepare them, and the mutual advantages of trade could lead to the growing wealth of all. Wealth was primarily desirable as a protection against poverty:

while a poor person had to use up their estate or the estates of others upon their subsistence, impoverishing them and others further, a wealthy person could deploy their surplus in the creation of wealth. This is a dynamic vision of the economy, where poverty is a self-perpetuating threat, while wealth multiplies like a fire.[3] The wealthier the economy as a whole, the lesser the overall numbers of the poor, and the more productive the economy would be. The principal obstacle to wealth creation, then, was the hoarding of coin by the rich – an act which impoverished them by slowing down trade. Prices being equal, Potter speculated that an increase in available money by a factor of ten would encourage such trade as to increase monetary circulation like-wise by a further factor of ten. Potter had discovered this multiplier effect of trade as a key to wealth, a veritable gold mine. Like a real gold mine, the prospect of future wealth could be used as a security for the advance of credit within a mutual society, and such credit could be used in the absence of money to multiply trade. If what money whispers is a promise of future wealth, then the shortage of coin could easily be made up by the provision of credit, in the sense of a paper instrument or means of exchange. Indeed, private credit had effectively substituted in part for the shortage of coins, but it was limited in that such credit instruments could not easily be transferred: the law only permitted the initial creditor to sue the debtor.[4] It was not the creative power of credit as such which Potter discovered so much as a means to organise and coordinate credit.

Many potential schemes to multiply wealth through credit were devised over the following decades such as land banks, backing paper credit against the value of land. Yet much as the aim was to make up for the shortfall of coinage with paper, the essential role of coinage resurfaced as a measure of value. John Briscoe, a prominent advocate of a land bank, was to argue in a pamphlet of 1695, *A Discourse of Money*, that gold and silver possess intrin-sic value. Briscoe even attributed a lack of productivity to the parlous state of England's coins, ancient, worn, clipped and highly underweight as they were – people would work for a fine, beautiful and correctly minted new coin simply for its intrinsic value, but would not be willing to labour for the worn and underweight.[5] Of course, the ideas of this pamphlet were relatively insig-nificant in comparison to John Locke's effective arguments for a thorough recoinage,[6] but they are, at least, illustrative of attitudes at the time: a cor-rectly weighted coin is the antidote to all suspicion and hypocrisy. When discussing the advantages of collective depositing to form a bank, Briscoe observed: 'For in such a case men are ingag'd by stronger Bonds than can be had from Conscience, Religion, Honour, or any other specious Tye; because in these we may be sure there may be Hypocrisie, but in Interest we know there is none'.[7] Likewise, when trust is sorely needed, how much more reliable it is to place one's trust in a coin than in a character.

Yet how radical to take this truthful speech of money in merchant's negotiations and turn it into a theory of language to displace all prior metaphysics. This is precisely what had been done four decades earlier by Thomas Hobbes: 'Words are wise men's counters, they do but reckon by them; but they are the money of fools, that value them by the authority of an Aristotle . . . or a Thomas'.[8] More formally, Hobbes expressed his account of the merchants' reasoning that was to replace the cleric's metaphysics like this:

> In what matter soever there is place for *addition* and *subtraction*, there also is place for reason; and where these have no place, there reasoning has nothing at all to do. . . . REASON, in this sense, is nothing but reckoning . . . of the consequences of the general names agreed upon for the *marking* and *signifying* of our thoughts.[9]

Just as in merchants' negotiations, knowledge, for Hobbes, consisted in taking an agreed object of the senses, clearly defined, and finding a numerical value for it. There is no place here for moral philosophy or metaphysics.

It was Thomas Hobbes's one-time protégé, Sir William Petty, who applied this reasoning to invent the science of 'political arithmetic', and who was therefore regarded by Marx as the founder of classical political economy. Petty was one of the founding members of the Royal Society in London but was unique amongst them in applying empirical investigation to economic matters. Although gaining a chair in medicine at Oxford at the age of twenty-seven, he was disillusioned with clerical influence in the university and its suppression of the new science, so he took a post as the physician to Cromwell's army in Ireland, and then volunteered to undertake a thorough survey of the entire land and economy of Ireland so that those who had funded the expedition, the so-called Irish Adventurers, could be paid in equitable portions of land – some 2.5 million acres.[10] Petty worked out his economic ideas through a painstaking survey of the conquered land and its livelihood. Petty was an ambitious political man, rather than a merchant, but he sought to apply the merchant's morality of truth-telling, diligence, and thrift to a whole nation through scientific calculation. The colonisation of comparatively undeveloped Ireland – Petty estimated that 85 percent of the population engaged in virtually no commodity exchange at all[11] – provided the perfect opportunity for the application of political arithmetic. For Petty was convinced that Irish poverty was no more a result of their character or land than Dutch wealth was a result of theirs – it was simply a matter of organisation and opportunity to work.

Petty sought the basis of value in natural rent and necessary labour: the production of a subsistence living. This is to be preferred to any monetary comparison or measure, for money itself can vary in value, whether in place, time or in the quality of its coinage. He suggested that one man could pro-

duce enough corn to provide subsistence for nine others apart from himself –
this was the necessary labour, and the natural rent was the surplus product in
addition to basic subsistence. The key political question was how to handle
this surplus. Petty recommended redistribution through taxes, taking the surplus from the landed and idle and rewarding craftspeople and the industrious.
Since thrift was the only way to enrich a nation, this would naturally be a
consumption tax. The wealth of the public is diminished if tax goes the other
way, and is imposed on 'the Stocks of laborious and ingenious Men' for the
sake of supporting 'such as do nothing at all, but eat and drink, sing, play and
dance; . . . such as study the Metaphysicks, or other needless Speculation; or
else employ themselves in any other way, which produce no material thing,
or things of real use and value in the Commonwealth'.[12] Specifically, Petty
sought to reduce expenditure on defence, public offices, universities, clergy,
lawyers and physicians, but also considered that the numbers of merchants
and retailers in England could be significantly reduced. By contrast, the
unproductive poor could be provided for out of the surplus, although it would
be better if the able-bodied among them could be put to work improving
highways, clearing rivers, building bridges and planting trees. This is thrift
and industriousness considered on a national scale.

Of course, there are enormous oversimplifications involved in any attempt to put figures on such values.[13] In particular, all labour is compared
with simple, subsistence labour, as though skilled labour did not make any
difference; similarly, subsistence products are assimilated to corn. The problem of making comparisons of heterogeneous values has not been solved.
Petty was aware of such simplifications, but quoted simple estimates of
figures in order to demonstrate his underlying principles.[14] Clearly, a
wealthy nation was not necessarily one that had the highest per capita production of corn. After all, food is perishable, and Petty had a hierarchical
notion of kinds of wealth based on degree of perishability, from food,
through commodities, to property, land and unperishable gold and silver.[15]
For all his interest in the division of labour and technological improvements,
he still lacked a conception of capital as the means of production that is itself
produced. Yet what is striking is that Petty, who invented the concept of the
'velocity of money', did not estimate the wealth of the nation in terms of its
possession of durable coinage any more than by its possession of perishable
corn. The quantity of money was not a measure of wealth. For just like a
merchant, a nation lacking in coin is not necessarily poor, 'For as the most
thriving men keep little or no coin by them, but turn and wind it into various
Commodities to their great Profit, so may a Nation also'.[16] He even calculated a quantity of coin needed for circulation; if a nation had too much, it could
easily melt some down for plate, or send it out for trade where it is desired, or
lend it out at interest. More pressing, in his day, was the converse problem of
too little money, and on this issue he followed Potter in being both optimistic

and prophetic: 'We must erect a Bank, which well computed, doth almost double the Effect of our coined Money: And we have in *England* Materials for a Bank which shall furnish Stock enough to drive the Trade of the whole Commercial World'.[17]

For all Petty's seminal ideas concerning intrinsic value in relation to subsistence, labour and land, and their subsequent influence, via Cantillon and Quesnay, on Smith, Malthus, Ricardo and Marx, it was perhaps the monetary revolution in England that succeeded in making his science possible by providing a measure for measure.[18] Petty had already given one of the strongest arguments for a thorough recoinage back in 1682:

> Qu. 1. *Whether the old unequal Money ought to be new coined, and brought into a new Equality?*
> *Answ.* It ought. Because Money made of Gold and Silver is the best Rule of Commerce, and must therefore be equal, or else it is no Rule; and consequently no Money, and but bare Metal which was Money before it was worn and abused into Inequality.

For alongside credit and litigation, commerce requires a measure for payments, a unit of account. Without a consistent measure for money, there could be no consistent calculations of profit and loss – and this is perhaps why English merchants had so rarely made such calculations up until this time. The great recoinage agreed in 1696 was a crisis measure in response to the rapid depreciation of English coinage, for foreign coins, whose value was judged by weight, were preferred. More lasting effects were perhaps achieved by the issue of paper by the newly founded Bank of England. This epochal event was also a crisis measure, for the recoinage had reduced the silver currency in circulation from six to four million pounds sterling, rapidly intensifying the shortage of reliable currency. The crisis was contained only by recourse to paper.[19] It proved to be a fortuitous arrangement, for a paper note, since it is merely the promise of money, has none of the disadvantages of wear, debasement and clipping – it offers a stable unit of account.[20] Moreover, paper notes can be printed in sufficient quantities to meet the requirements of trade and commerce. The decisive cultural transformation which took place in the eighteenth century as a result of the monetary revolution is that an increasing proportion of trade took place as an instantaneous exchange by means of the transfer of paper securities rather than by spoken credit agreements. Trust in paper with an institutional backing was more secure than trust in the individual who stood before one pleading. As a result, people proved their integrity by paying with money; and more transactions over greater distances could be conducted. Money, it would seem, offered the substance rather than the mere promise of value; and yet the money that was offered was still credit: it was the promise of a bank.

It was in this way that both the success and the insecurity of the credit economy of the seventeenth century set the demand for money. The initial impulse of the demand for money was competitive piety: the ability to pay in money was useful to prove one's credit, one's honesty, diligence and thrift. To pay with cash was to outdo one's neighbours in respectability. This was the 'intrinsic' value that merchants saw in gold and silver: not simply that it was desirable in exchange, but that it could be used as an immediate offer of lasting worth. Moreover, money was desired as a public good: the greater the proportion of transactions effected immediately by money, the less the outstanding debts, and the more secure all would be from contagion by default.[21] Such may have been the motivation for mercantilism, the policy of endeavouring to increase the stock of money in the country by subsidising exports of goods in exchange for money, and restricting imports.[22] There was also a strong political case for the establishment of a bank. Yet as if by an invisible hand, public benefits were transformed into private vices, for one could best contribute to this aspect of the common good – economic security – by means of the private pursuit of money. The greater the private accumulation of wealth, the more secure one was as an individual, and the greater the contribution one could make to the security of society by paying for one's needs with money. Money, as opposed to deferred payment, turned the principle of thrift upside down: it was through avarice and luxury that the wealthy could best contribute to the common good. The satirist Bernard Mandeville's 1705 *The Grumbling Hive* (later republished with a commentary as *The Fable of the Bees, or Private Vices, Public Benefits*) describes this situation with the causality inverted because, in his opposition to moral education of the poor, he started with production as the fundamental reality: for him it was greed which, through trade and exchange, led to hard work to produce commodities for the common good. He delimited the common good to goods of appropriation. By contrast, those whose primary concern was for the moral state of the commonwealth and the security of its credit could sanction the pursuit of individual wealth for the sake of contributing to economic security and prosperity.[23] It was hardly surprising that such a standpoint could be suspected of hypocrisy.

Most significantly, following the financial revolution and the printing of secure paper money, money could at last start to fulfil effectively its traditional role as the measure of values. For paper money merely signifies an abstract quantity. The value that it signifies is purely metaphysical. Of course, the value of that paper depends on trust in the bank's ability to pay. When Sir Isaac Newton established the gold standard for the Bank of England's note issue in 1717, the effect was not that people presented their bills for payment in gold, but quite the opposite: trust in the backing of paper by the 'intrinsic value' of gold was quite sufficient to lend value to paper. Of course, neither the paper nor the gold itself held any intrinsic value – the whole charade was a confidence trick. In economic life, things hold value only if sufficient people believe that they do; those who believe, however, can rarely acknowledge this without dissolving the basis for credit. Yet the basis of banking is quite simple, as J. K. Galbraith has explained:

> The original depositor could get his money, for it was still there. So, alternatively, could the man to whom the deposit was lent. Both could not. The marvel of banks in relation to money – the wonder of creating deposits or issuing notes that so served – was suspended on one silken thread. That was the requirement that depositors or noteholders come in decently small numbers for the hard currency that the bank was under obligation to pay.[24]

Credit, when institutionalised by the establishment of a bank, does not cease to be credit. The measure for measure remains a degree of trust or credulity. Subsequent economic expansion, with its multitude of financial crises, never ceases to remind us of this fact.

Perhaps the new morality of self-interest reached its ultimate consequences in the South Sea Bubble of 1720. The South Sea Company had been founded in 1711 for providing a loan to the state: the company undertook to provide the money due to the army and navy in return for security on various duties and a monopoly on trading in the Pacific Ocean. But in 1720 it offered to take over all the debts of the State, estimated at over £30 million, in return for an interest rate of 5 percent for seven years, 4 percent thereafter. Such a scheme was extremely attractive to those who could afford to invest: the success of the initial subscriptions caused its share prices to rise from £126 in 1719 to £2,000 by June 1720. In response to this, a host of fraudulent companies were set up with share prices that also rose rapidly. On the basis of this rapid increase of merely nominal wealth, there was greater spending and overall growth. As a result of the rising prosperity and inequality, speculation fever took hold of the entire nation, with perhaps £300 million subscribed in total to different projects.[25] Many of those who shared in the fever knew perfectly well that it was all a fraud, but hoped to make a profit by withdrawing before the others did. Even Sir Isaac Newton was dragged in, against his better judgement, and lost a considerable amount. The bubble was finally pricked by the South Sea Company itself, when, alarmed by the success of these other projects, it obtained a writ from the Lord Justices to dissolve the bubble companies. As everything collapsed, and thousands of families were bankrupted, the panic spread to its own shares. A handful of individuals were enriched at the expense of many. The ultimate result, however, was a shaking to the foundations of an economy based on personal credit, thrift and sociability, for most had contributed to the destruction of the public welfare by their own self-seeking. While each might have repented of being caught up in the folly, the basis for personal trust could never be as solid as before. Payment, in the future, would be increasingly expected in the form of money.

It was the national debt and the Bank of England that survived. And in spite of the nominal convertibility of Bank of England promises for gold, it was the notes themselves that increasingly became the object of credit, and the measure for measures of value.

For just as the government debt to the Bank of England became permanent, so also did the notes issued by the Bank against this future security. Allowing the payment of such debts to be perpetually postponed and frequently transferred – as though credit itself, a mere relation, were a commodity – has been described by the monetary historian Marc Bloch as the secret of capitalism:

> Delaying payments or reimbursements and causing such delays to overlap perpetually with one another: this was in short the great secret of the modern capitalist system, which could perhaps be most precisely defined as a system that would perish if all the accounts were settled at the same time. This system is fuelled by an optimism that constantly discounts the profits of the future, its eternal precariousness.[26]

Even today, the primary unit of account, means of exchange and store of value takes the form of credit. Credit has escaped confinement within the intimate sphere of the home to take up residence in the central bank.

The use of bank credit for the purposes of exchange has enabled credit to be understood purely in terms of exchange. For John Locke, considering the need to ensure that the great recoinage was undertaken at full face value, defined credit as debt, '*Credit* being nothing but the expectation of Money within some limited time'.[27] Of course, the notion of credit as creditworthiness was still required, but even this was understood in terms of ability to pay a debt rather than in terms of virtue, diligence and thrift. Abel Boyer, paid to write in support of the new Chancellor of Exchequer Robert Harley in 1710, defined credit as 'The Opinion or Confidence we have in another's Ability, Honour and Punctuality to Discharge or Pay a Debt'.[28] Understood in terms subordinate to market exchange, the notion that economic life was fueled by the creative power of credit rather than human industry alone was buried beneath anticipations of exchange.

Even so, in contemporary economic life, credit in a theological sense as offering has more than a minor, subsidiary role: as we shall see in *Economic Theology*, it is still determining in the last instance by facilitating trust and cooperation.

Conclusion

REFRAMING PHILOSOPHY OF RELIGION

Enlightenment, for Immanuel Kant, involved the courage to make use of one's own understanding without guidance from another, both in the cultivation of one's own mind and in free public discussion.[1] It is an ideal which continues to regulate human culture today. Kant's principal targets were religious authorities: he regarded those who committed themselves and others to certain unalterable doctrines as trampling on the sacred rights of humanity.[2] A mind could become self-sufficient through discovering the reasons for things rather than relying on rules and doctrines given by authorities. Some such reasons took the form, 'if this, then that': rules, laws, models and probabilities offer knowledge of nature as deterministic. Other such reasons took the form, 'if that, then this': the ends of life, its values, aims, objectives and purposes, could be used to regulate the means of life, its instruments, processes, structures and institutions, offering knowledge of history as human freedom. The sciences, including human sciences as diverse as physiology, neuroscience, psychology, economics and sociology, have progressed insofar as they have discovered determinism; the arts and humanities as diverse as law, history, literature and theology have progressed insofar as they have discovered meaning for the sake of guiding human freedom. The ultimate extension of both strands of enlightenment confronts us with a metaphysical dilemma: life seems to be at once fully determined and entirely free. Division and occasional conflict between the faculties of science and arts, like those of knowledge and will, has haunted us ever since the age of Enlightenment.[3] Something is clearly amiss.

Kant endeavoured to resolve the conflict between determinism and freedom by means of three rules. First, one should only apply the categories of the understanding (such as causality, unity, reality and substance) to make judgements about experience; one cannot suppose that such categories represent things in themselves. As a result, metaphysical entities such as God, the self and the world are treated as ideals guiding the progress of reason rather than as representations of what is real. To treat such categories as real in themselves, as representations rather than as ideas, is to fall into an illusion constructed out of one's own mind. Second, one should only apply the categories of practical reason (such as means and ends) to regulate conduct; one should not apply them to things themselves. As a result, one should not think of things such as outcomes, experiences, habits or even virtues as good, for one can only properly say that a will is good – that is, that it is in accordance with the moral law. The third rule, which grounds the preceding two, is that theoretical reasoning (about facts) should be kept entirely distinct from practical reasoning (about values). As a result, the realm of freedom is entirely separate from the realm of nature: one cannot deduce an ought from an is. Nevertheless, for all the theoretical separation, one still has to act in the world, adjusting what is in line with what ought to be. If value cannot be found within nature, it may still be imposed from above by the human will. This assertion of human freedom over nature achieves reconciliation through mastery: science gives us knowledge of the means, while culture and ethics may determine the ends. The shared world becomes a theatre for liberty, reconstructed in practice around ends posited by the will. Should such wills come into conflict, this may be resolved by the projection of a condition of universal agreement based on reason alone. When engaging in moral reasoning, one submits one's particular will to a rational, universal will, by means of a kind of social contract, attaining the true liberty of finding within oneself one's true motive in the form of reason. Enlightenment consists in liberation from one sacred authority in order to submit oneself to another, that of universal reason, by which one is both constrained and set free. Even so, the practical problem remains of returning from the projection of a universal reason to living once more in time: how to decide which reason applies in any given circumstance, how this reason may be applied to change a given circumstance, and how reason enlightens the mind such that it suspends its partial motives. For all the appeal to a universal reason, the courage to employ it is as particular as the occasions and respects in which reason is applied. Following enlightenment, a clash of individual wills remains in practice, each assured by its conscience that its reasoning is in accordance with truth. The Enlightenment may have transformed the world but it has not produced unity; instead, it has removed or depleted many of the conditions for resilience, stability and subsistence, leading to ever new struggles against the oppression of liberty.

Meanwhile, for Kant, the contradiction between determinism and freedom vanishes by legislative decree: Do not think about the metaphysical problem of the human condition, for if you do, you will necessarily fall into contradictions and illusions. Of course, Kant's decree has been widely ignored ever since and the debates between the competing positions which result, such as those between materialism and idealism or naturalism and theism, have been as interminable as Kant's antinomies. When Kant's rules are flouted, philosophical arguments lose dialectical traction: they fail to convince opponents and are condemned to fruitless repetition. On the other hand, if in line with Kant one simply suspends such metaphysical questions for the sake of handling facts and values, then one only sees means and ends: the world can be entirely reconstructed through the exercise of arbitrary power.

Kant's critical turn championed human autonomy in two key respects: humanity itself gives meaning to experience by contributing space, time and the categories by which that experience is interpreted and judged; humanity shapes its own experience by choosing the ends and values which are to be respected in practical conduct. Such Enlightenment assertions of autonomy, with or without Kant's critical turn, have focussed attention on the narrowest bonds of linear causality, 'if this, then that', and simplest maxims of practical conduct, 'if that, then this', at the expense of a wider awareness of life. One may question whether such a focussing of attention is as much an 'endarkenment' as it is an enlightenment; it leaves out so much that is pertinent. Simply stated, Kant's rules appear to be an arbitrary and authoritarian crisis measure rather than an empowering of thought. Moreover, like all crisis measures, they may be suspected of complicity in the arising of further crises. The mindset of linear causality and instrumental reason in the self-assertion of an artificial autonomy is the root cause of the multitude of anthropogenic crises, whether ecological, social or spiritual, which face humankind today. If human civilisation is at risk of collapse under the effects of biodiversity loss and climate change, credit crises and depletion of resources, populist refusals of rational deliberation and war, then the metaphysical dilemma of determinism and freedom should have been an early warning that all is not entirely wholesome with this Enlightenment. Its celebrated reason, autonomy and equality have resulted in irrationality, constraint and oppression.[4] For reality itself shows little respect for any division between facts and values. Like religious authority, a reason claims to be a fact having a normative or justifying force. Likewise, money possessed is a fact which endows its owner with the power of making effective demands. Moreover, between thinking and being, conforming one to the other, are dimensions of life which are neither simply facts nor values: attention, evaluation and trust. Where religions offer a framework for distributing time, care, trust and obligation, such matters which actively bridge thinking and being are comparatively neglected in Enlightenment thought, leaving power and money to determine which particular will may be exercised in fact. For if it is one thing to understand the world as it is and another thing to conform the will to virtue, it is yet another to act in the world in order to produce the outcome of happiness. Where in the age of enlightenment reason, aimed at universal understanding, bridges the gap between what exists and what is understood, a reverse movement is still required. Where a common mind about ends has not yet been achieved it is often money which bridges the gap between what is understood and what is brought into being. The dark side of enlightenment consists in money and power.

Now, one might suggest that, in spite of received interpretations, Kant himself did not really rest content with his rules for separating theoretical and practical reason. He sought to rejoin them in a philosophy of religion. For freedom is not sufficiently achieved through knowledge of the moral law; it also belongs to experience. It is one thing for a will to determine itself in accordance with the moral law; it is quite another for it to act within the world to produce a determinate outcome such as happiness. If moral action endeavours to produce happiness in experience, then it acts as a cause within nature. Lacking the certain knowledge that moral action will effectively produce happiness in experience, one can at least proceed on faith. Practical philosophy is then supplemented by a philosophy of religion: in Kant's formulation, true religion consists in conscientiousness, in treating the moral law as if it were a divine command and so in acting upon it. It consists in acting in the faith that God will ultimately produce some harmonisation between the realm of moral freedom and the realm of determinate nature. Likewise, Kant did not confine theoretical knowledge to interpreting experience alone but supplemented it with speculative judgement. Kant found evidence for attributing purposes to nature as such: in the existence of living organisms, which grow, mature, repair and maintain themselves, acting as if their life were their own end; in the existence of human beings, who are capable of reordering the surrounding world in accordance with their own ends, and who, as such, should be treated morally as ends in themselves and never as means; and in the reproduction of the same principles of organisation in plant life, animal life and human life, as though nature had a purpose as a whole in producing human beings. Such becomes the ground for considering a universal history, willed by nature yet achieved by human freedom, and such becomes the ground for a renewed natural theology.[5] In respect of both freedom and nature, Kant offered a philosophy of religion as that which bridges their gap. Nature and freedom provide a framing for the emergence of the discipline of philosophy of religion.

There are many reasons for dismantling such a framework. Nevertheless, dismantling may also be a reframing. In the first place, the human mind makes sense of experience according to its own categories and point of view. Here, Kant abstracted from experience by seeking the universal and the necessary as marks of the transcendental. Hence, whether it is a matter of intuiting objects in space, thoughts in time or universalisable maxims in morality, the task is to find concepts and principles of universal significance. Now, such a narrowing of attention onto universalisable concepts and principles may obscure the reality of thought, including its motivations, materials and applications. One may learn from a study of Nietzsche's work that there is far more in any actual expression of thinking than in any abstract principle. Philosophy of religion may turn from concepts and principles to investigating actual events of thought. The aim, here, is appropriation: to adopt from such events of thinking those aspects capable of forming categories and perspectives which can then be used to make sense of experience. It may not be a matter of stating them explicitly, which will always be a crude oversimplification, but of using them as tools and lenses with which to think.

In the second place, the attempt to divide reality into the realms of nature and freedom presupposes some underlying reality which participates in both attributes at once. Here, Kant abstracted from this underlying unity in order to postulate a God of practical and purposive reason who accomplished harmonisation of nature and freedom through divine mastery, as though working with the model of means and ends. One may learn from a study of Hegel's work that such mastery offers a very poor model for power, whether human or divine: power consists in participation, in producing and sustaining a common will. Philosophy of religion may turn from postulating self-sufficient entities and concepts to explore the extent to which nature participates in freedom, and freedom participates in nature. The aim, here, is participation: to produce a thought that is at once engaged with necessity and yet free in its judgements.

In the third place, where metaphysical knowledge and moral understanding are lacking, human reasoning has to proceed in the faith that its rational considerations will have the desired outcome in experience. Here, Kant appealed to a Protestant religion restricted to moral conduct alone: only when the moral will had done its duty to reform itself could one hope that grace might work the inner transformation enabling one to have a truly moral will. Nevertheless, the life of faith and grace, manifest in receiving and offering, is far too important to be left to religious traditions alone. One may learn from a study of the works of Kierkegaard and Heidegger that life itself is an offering, lived forwards in the face of possibility within the horizon and course of time. Philosophy of religion may turn from theoretical problems of knowledge to existential problems of how to conduct one's life. The aim, here, is offering a life: to shape one's ideas in such a way that they can be received, appropriated and lived out by others.

Such, then, is the framework within which this inquiry has been carried out. In place of understanding enlightenment in terms of courage or self-assertion, enlightenment may be understood in terms of appropriate trust. Such trust is appropriate to the extent that it is oriented by the value of that which matters under given conditions. The enabling conceptual leap is to reinterpret even knowledge itself, of the form, 'if this, then that', and even morality itself, of the form, 'if that, then this', within an existential project of trust. What is to be trusted? How might I become trustworthy? Knowledge and morality may be understood as instruments, machines, symbols or coins constructed in the service of trust. Knowledge gives an orientation for credit; morality gives an orientation for faith. The metaphysical void between pure knowledge and pure obligation was but a shadow disclosing how such concepts are mere ideals produced by certain strategies of reasoning. In any act of thinking, more fundamental than any will to knowledge, liberation or power is the determination of trust: the allocation of time and attention, care and evaluation, trust and cooperation comes first. For life is only lived insofar as it is spent: it offers itself. The task that results for a reframed philosophy of religion is a reconstruction of metaphysical categories, the forging of new tools and the minting of new coins, adequate for a metaphysics of trust.

A CHRISTIAN MINDSET

In direct contrast with the Cartesian method of doubt, the method of trust experiments by trusting. Instead of withdrawing from the evidence of the senses in search of abstract necessity, it is embodied in engagement with local and finite bodies of thought. The experiment pursued here has adopted economic and religious life as its material for thought. The choice of Christianity is not merely arbitrary: that which, considered hypothetically, offers little grounds for its appeal, may become internally compelling once it is inhabited. Other faiths may share in this compelling character; the Christian mindset is distinctive in the way it draws this character to attention. Only when appropriated and inhabited does this mindset evoke a kind of trust. It is grounded in a strange logic of repetition: only when actually trusted does it start to evoke trust. The Christian mindset evokes trust through a certain kind of fruitfulness or economic productivity: it has a knack of setting aside the logs, machines and coins of one's own making – those means we build to support us which in turn come to dominate us. The fruitfulness of this experiment consists merely in what it gives us to think.

Now, according to a typical Enlightenment critique of religion, religious commitment is indeed submission before an entity of one's own making such that, while one abases oneself before it in one's self-understanding, one secretly participates in its power.[6] This notion provides the template for Marx's account of human alienation before the machine it constructs. This notion may indeed by substantially correct for those who confess, 'Jesus is Lord' while meaning nothing of the kind insofar as they do not endeavour to participate within the mindset of Christ. What saves Christianity from this purely logical form is its very specific content – the ordering it brings to time, care and trust. In this respect, enlightenment – as the courage to make use of one's understanding – demands liberation on multiple fronts. In the first place, it may mean liberation from any authority which draws its legitimacy from an unworldly power. Faith is uncritical if it cannot discern for itself the value of that which it trusts. In the second place, it may mean liberation from any authority which draws its legitimacy from a public, worldly power. Faith is uncritical if it relies on others' estimates of value, submitting its thought for testing and evaluation by the judgements of the crowd. In the third place, it may mean liberation from the instruments and coins of its own making, those short-cuts for assigning extrinsic signs of value or credit for that which matters in itself. By contrast, enlightened understanding is structured by repetition: courageous acts of investment may be tested by whether they offer a rich return.

The circuitous path this book has taken was intended to construct two narratives of trust: one of enrichment, the other of impoverishment; one of credit, the other of debt. The capacity to distinguish between credit and debt is as significant as being able to distinguish between knowledge and illusion or means and end. It is a matter of wealth or poverty, freedom or oppression, existence or nonexistence. A Christian mindset has been appropriated here in order to learn about credit; an economic mindset has been explored in order to learn about debt. What is offered to us by trusting and inhabiting a Christian mindset?

In the first place, what is disclosed is that 'life is more than food, and the body more than clothing'. There is more to life than goods of appropriation; more to existence than appearance before others. The Christian mindset is exposed as one of participation: in the language of both Paul and the Fourth Gospel, this is a matter of mutual indwelling, being in Christ or Christ in us. While people live as separate individuals, they may nevertheless participate in a common mindset. There is an entire dimension of life, wealth and happiness that exists only insofar as it is shared. This dimension may be less a matter of agreement on ideas than a matter of joint attention, shared evaluation, trust and cooperation. It is enabled by institutions as effectively as it is by ideas. This dimension is easily eclipsed, especially by the quest for evidence which appears before the public eye and can be seen by anyone. For the value of what one participates in, a shared mind, is only available to those who participate in it, who share it. Trust, here, is a condition for access to what matters. The preceding discussion, however, has not emphasised this central dimension of Pauline, Johannine, Augustinian, Thomist and subsequent Christian theology because it is so prevalent and well understood. If it is comparatively absent from Jesus's teaching in Synoptic sources, this may have been because its existence depends on a certain freedom of association – one rarely available to the stewards, workers, women and servants who populate these sources except in the form of temporary mass gatherings around healing miracles, in the desert or on pilgrimages. Instead, in a context where everyone was under one authority or another, the mindset of Jesus himself seems to have been one focussed on announcing the power of forgiveness of sin. What is offered, here, is an opportunity to break free from an existing mindset – one that may have been produced as a supporting framework for trust, but one that has come to take hold of and dominate people's minds. Jesus and Paul demonstrated their own capacity to break free from dominating mindsets by means of three strategies. Firstly, one suspends all existing criteria of judgement in the hope that the ultimate judgement and its criteria have yet to be revealed. In doing so, one is set free from all transcendent and unworldly criteria. This gesture holds such a liberating force that one might come to trust that the ultimate criterion of judgement is found within the forgiveness of sins itself. Secondly, therefore, one inverts a hierarchy of values, such that what appeared to be of little account – matters of trust, for example, or the adopting of a mindset, or forgiveness in place of legislation – now starts to assume principal importance. In doing so, one is set free from all immanent and worldly criteria based on the viewpoints of others. This gesture holds such a liberating force that one might come to trust that what holds principal importance is found in this chiasmic inversion itself. Thirdly, then, one holds up a lens to life by means of a parable such that the lens sheds a new light on the meaning of existence, while the meaning of existence changes what is understood in the parable. In doing so, one is set free from extrinsic signs of meaning and significance, for one is able to find significance in a newly created understanding. The liberating force of such a lens is such that one may come to trust that what is worth loving is found in the creation of meaning itself. When stated abstractly, as just done here, these strategies might appear to have little intrinsic appeal. When inhabited as a mindset or practice of thought, they offer their own inner compulsion through what they have to offer to thought.

What is offered is an understanding that life is more than food and the body more than clothing. Life itself is offering: it is the distribution of time and attention, care and evaluation, trust and cooperation. These are matters for the responsibility and stewardship of each individual; they exceed, and give an object for, the life of participation. Any attempt to think the meaning of being, to conform thought to reality, which does not pass through this metaphysical mediation of offering may be suspected of short-circuiting both thinking and reality itself. In place of short-circuits, life as offering engages real existents. Concrete existence is given to each individual by the power of repetition within the flow of time: the time that I live is the time that I spend; the attention that I give to things determines the character of my experience; the trust that I place in things determines whether I am trustworthy. The credit that I offer determines the credit that I am due to receive.

What is it, then, to be trustworthy? It is to direct attention to that which matters. It is to offer the conditions by which life can be created. It is to direct trust to that which is trustworthy. It is to spend one's resources wisely. In each of these respects, it involves handing one's life over to external conditions and dynamics which one cannot control. It involves faith in repetition such that, in spite of the risk and actuality of loss, trusting does indeed make one trustworthy. Expenditure is a source of wealth. For trust, as the basis for human cooperation, is that which exceeds all measure: it is the pearl of great price.

A CAPITALIST MACHINE

Who is to be trusted? The extraordinary creative potential of trust turns creditworthiness, for those who lack the inner necessity of repetition, into an object of desire. In response, creditworthiness is offered for sale. There are those whose words are calculated to produce an effect upon the hearer. One suspects that the substance of such words lies in their effects rather than in their meaning; such are not worthy of trust. By contrast, there are those who endeavour to demonstrate their fidelity by bearing witness to the truth, whether in the form of evidence or idea. Even here, one can deceive others and especially oneself if one overlooks the conditions which have a determining role. Others demonstrate their fidelity by means of their commitment: what they give, offer or sacrifice may be treated as evidence of how much something matters to them. Even here, one can deceive others and oneself if one's evaluations are oriented away from that which matters. The question of who is to be trusted is the most critical of questions. Desires for effects, for pure knowledge, and for commitment may substitute for the faith by which one becomes trustworthy.

The difference between credit and debt is the difference between one who gives, irrespective of any return, entrusting the long circuit of conditions as well as the tight circuit of repetition, and the one who merely seeks to give assurance in the form of a promise, a short-circuit which prescribes a definite return. Such promises may explicitly or implicitly offer a return in three respects: with respect to effects, the return is specified as the content of what is promised; with respect to truth, the return is reputation or credibility of the promiser which increases or decreases in line with fulfilment of the promise; with respect to commitment, the promise can be taken seriously accordingly to the level of collateral or sanctions staked if the promise should fail. Where credit, as issuing trust, multiplies itself by encouraging expectations of further giving, debt, as making a promise, risks impoverishment of the debtor as well as of the creditor should the promise fail. Stated in this way, promises may not appear to be a very effective way of enhancing creditworthiness;

nevertheless, one must not overlook what has actually been achieved through their power. The mechanism of a promise does involve a certain amount of distortion: at the level of effects or goods of appropriation, a promise encloses and directs attention solely to those effects which are specified as its content. At the level of reputation or goods of participation, a promise treats reputation as an object of staking and potential loss, as if it were reconceived as a good of appropriation. At the level of commitment or goods of offering, a promise substitutes its explicit or implied collateral for the trust that it is willing to offer. Such distortions may give grounds for supposing that all will not run smoothly with the issuing of promises.

Credit is the issuing of some mark of the value, significance, reliability and response of things; its issue transmits wisdom, authority, confidence and friendship. Such marks may be replete with meaning in the context in which they are issued; nevertheless, the passage of time and the transfer of such marks into new contexts erode their meaning. It is the nature of credit to be handed over, to lose the fullness of appropriate context and meaning which it once bore. Indeed, credit only transmits value on the condition of losing control over the meaning of its marks. In this way, it is a good of offering rather than just a good of participation. It is exposed to external dynamics, including the dynamics of promise and debt. Moreover, credit, while it may be transmitted in the form of marks, coins or goods of appropriation, is not reducible to these like 'charity' because in addition one offers capital: a seed, a 'seminal reason', an intention that the resources offered may become the conditions of possibility of new creation. The intention is one of investment rather than mere consumption. At the level of effects, credit hands over resources as conditions of production. At the level of reputation, credit hands over trust as a sign that the recipient is to be trusted. At the level of commitment, credit gives attention and value to that which matters. In these respects, the Christian economy of giving to the poor also participates in other, spiritual economies.

Nevertheless, if the Christian economy of giving sparked into life the medieval merchant economy, it was perhaps less through care of the poor than through the supply of money. For the circulation of coinage had collapsed in Western Europe after the fall of the Roman Empire, much of it being offered to the churches and, lacking other uses, was melted down into plates, vessels and decorations. With new technologies permitting the building of Gothic churches and cathedrals, the growth of towns was stimulated by reminting such precious metals back into coins in order to pay for their construction. By offering service in deference to the image of a sovereign stamped on a coin, one demonstrates one's creditworthiness as one who is willing to work. The coin one receives through such acts of deference is a demonstration of that creditworthiness, enabling one to be trusted and served oneself in the name of that same sovereign when one comes to spend that coin. Coins may be at once signs of distributed trust as well as signs of sovereign power. The paradox, here, is that if one seeks to possess that power by hoarding coin, one cannot access the value signified by the coin itself. In addition to being goods of appropriation, capable of being hoarded, and goods of participation whose value is the object of collective recognition, coins are also goods of offering: one only realises the value signified by spending that coin. Trust, cooperation and the creation of wealth are achieved when coins start to circulate: the condition for the creation of wealth is the passing on of trust. The crucial point which demonstrates that the seed of productive power, or capital, consists in offered credit rather than desire for the precious metal value of coin is this condition of liquidity: a coin hoarded is worthless, whereas a coin spent realises its value. A coin possessed is sterile, whereas a coin invested may yield a return. Desire becomes productive in offering investment, not in possession of its object.

A promise may also be a sign of credit in this way. Yet it also participates in other economies. In the form of deferred payment, a promise may substitute for coin to elicit trust and cooperation. If those who issue such promises stake their reputation and their business on their ability to pay, then their promises may be transferred to others as far as reputation allows. Now, whereas coins issued by sovereign authorities are ultimately underwritten by the power of the sovereign, in its power to demand taxes and in the exercise of legislative authority backed up by force, a promise issued by a merchant is ultimately underwritten by their creditworthiness, their ability to pay. A merchant may have the ability to pay if their business is indeed profitable and they are in receipt of goods, services and coin; a merchant may also have the ability to pay if their creditworthiness, perhaps based on their honesty, diligence and thrift, is sufficient to attract advances from associates and creditors. The conditions for credit, here, are at once material, in the form of the accumulation of possessions, social, in the form of the reputation for creditworthiness, and spiritual, based on the way the individual does indeed conduct themselves.

There is, however, a key economic difference between a coin and a promise: where coins circulate in one direction, promises effect a similar distribution only at the cost of anticipating a further circulation to come. A promise is an advance on the payment. Its collateral, the ground upon which it is believed, is the future payment itself – and should this not be forthcoming, then the value of promises evaporates. Likewise, in the case of a debt, an advance is received on the condition of a reverse circulation to come in the form of repayment. Here, credit is offered in exchange for a promise: the condition for offering credit, where distrust seems more appropriate, is in exchange for a debt or obligation. While the advance of credit offers the seed of trust and cooperation, what is promised in return is merely a good of appropriation, like the precious metal value of the coin. While credit flows outward, what returns is merely a coin.

The decisive factor which elicits production and cooperation, the creation and distribution of wealth, is the passing on of credit as capital, as a seed of productive power. Of course, this effect only operates within the limits of the productive capacity of an economy; beyond a certain threshold, vicious circles of inflation and divestment of savings set in. Nevertheless, for much of economic history, credit has been scarce relative to potential productive power. The key to wealth, as William Potter saw, lay in eliciting this productive potential by more effectively distributing trust – one could not simply rely on the haphazard distribution of coins. What was required was a change from treating effective demand or credit as a good of appropriation or coin to treating it as good of participation, a shared mindset. The innovation required involved a form of collective promise, a kind of social contract which does not depend on universal consent. The collective wager was as follows: promises could be advanced, circulate, and be used as money if their aggregate effect was to elicit an increase in the production of wealth. Since, in the future, one could expect one's debtors to be wealthier, one could trust their ability to pay – the collateral offered for individual debts consisted, in part, of collective future wealth. Collective trust is placed, here, in an alchemical machine for converting promises into gold. If few understood the theoretical significance of Potter's proposal, many could recognise from experience how promises did function, up to a point, as a helpful substitute for coins. Even if the eventual granting of the right to print such promises by the Bank of England was a crisis measure, its success proved indispensable once commerce began to depend upon this currency. The collective promise involved in treating such notes as bearing value was an advance on the future wealth to be enjoyed once production was reordered for the sake of profit.

This collective promise, eliciting a virtuous circle of dynamic economic growth, was however rather fragile. Since payments were in fact made with promises of further future payments, the prosperous future, when it arrived, could not simply pay off its debts with payments in kind. Money that was borrowed against future prosperity had to be paid in the form of more money. This imposed a constraint: either money must circulate faster and faster or else more money had to be created as debt. In practice, the rate of circulation – when people actually spent paper money – was determined by specific acts of production, trade and consumption, rather than by any collective demand on the system. Any shortfall had to be compensated by a further increase in debt in the system, grounded in the collateral of further future prosperity. Under the constraints of such debt, activities had to be redirected from their primary focus on production and consumption towards the making of profit. The material significance of such constraints, especially when operating beyond the aggregate threshold by which an increase in debt contributes much less to an increase in production, will be explored in subsequent volumes.

For now, it is simply sufficient to note the change in perceptions which arrived with such constraint. In line with the Puritan principle that those who demonstrated honesty, diligence and thrift were the most creditworthy, in an age of paper money it was those who generated profit who appeared to contribute the most to the collective creation of wealth. Just as the oppressed earn liberty with the currency of being constrained by reason, the indebted earn liberty with the currency of being constrained by earning. Those who paid in paper money, rather than promising deferred payment, paid with the reputation of the central bank rather than with their own. Those whose activities accumulated paper money appeared to be those whose activities enhanced at once their own individual property, the common wealth of all, as well as their individual reputation and creditworthiness. Pursuit of gain became identified with pursuit of the common good. Given this presupposition, attention was directed primarily towards goods of appropriation. The network of mutual credit which enabled economic cooperation could be increasingly taken for granted by those who interacted with each other primarily in terms of exchange. Its ongoing presence in the institutional forms of the mutual indebtedness of sovereign states, central banks and commercial banks could be neglected as something extrinsic to free market exchange. Even debts themselves could be reconsidered as incomplete exchanges taking place over time.

In sum, we can observe the components of the capitalist machine and its ordering of credit. Credit is invested through a mark, sign or note of value. This note is then detached from the original meaning and valuations which it bore in order to circulate as a token of trustworthiness. Those notes which were most liquid, which circulated most easily, freely and widely, were those which functioned effectively to distribute credit and increase wealth. Moreover, in the transition from credit to debt, such notes came to signify no longer a past offering but now a future payment. Finally, such promises of future payment came to be appropriated in turn. By means of detachment, liquidity, debt and appropriation, the capitalist machine was able to give order to a collective distribution of trust. Ultimately, capitalism is a collective investment of trust in the creative power of this machine itself: capitalism is trust in capitalism, a religion which worships itself. In practice, such trust is expressed through the appropriation of assets valued in terms of such notes as the measure for measure. Since capitalism only counts what it measures, the entire history of capitalism is simply a long-term bubble.

There are, however, some rather fatal flaws in this machine of credit. Asset prices may fluctuate wildly in response to the moods and dynamics of market forces. The machine can make profits from appropriation of the wealth of others as easily as it can through productive cooperation. The

wealth appropriated as the power of effective demand may be entirely detached from any attribution of value to that which matters. The network of
debts and obligations which composes the present economic order foreshad-
ows a future order which must be realised for such debts and obligations to
be fulfilled. Liquid notes, as mobile capital, may escape the control of any
sovereign territory. Tokens of trust are transmitted to those who satisfy preferences irrespective of whether such preferences matter. Nominal equality is
replaced by oppression; nominal freedom is replaced by constraint; nominal
rationality, now understood as the pursuit of self-interest, becomes wildly
irrational in its detachment from giving value to that which matters. Finally,
the capitalist machine, concerned only with itself, finishes by consuming the
conditions of human existence.

These, then, are the contrasting narratives of credit and debt: a Christian
mindset and a capitalist machine. Money in capitalism, as a basis for trust,
has numerous advantages over God: where God promises eternal life, money
promises the world; where God appears to offer a deferred payment, money
is offered as an advance; where God requires conversion from self-interest,
money serves any interest. Where a Christian mindset requires a common
mind, capitalism serves any ulterior goals. Where the benefits of a Christian
mindset are the spiritual ones of repetition, the benefits of the capitalist
machine are the tangible goods and services bought with money. With such
advantages of immediacy, universality, tangibility and utility, money easily
replaces God as a vehicle for trust. It does, however, have considerable
drawbacks: by short-circuiting truth, value and justice it undermines its conditions of existence and heads towards self-destruction. Even more urgent
than stopping this machine in its tracks is the discovery of an appropriate
way for ordering trust. For in a time of crisis, appropriate trust is more
precious than ever.

Notes

PREFACE

1. John Macmurray, *Persons in Relation* (London: Faber and Faber, 1961), 211.
2. Akkineni Nagarjuna, *Sunyatasaptati*, verse 66, in Christian Lindtner, *Nagarjuniana* (Copenhagen: Ak. Forlag, 1982), 65.
3. Friedrich Nietzsche, *Thus Spoke Zarathustra*, trans. R. J. Hollingdale (London: Penguin, 1961), 161.

INTRODUCTION

1. Pankaj Mishra describes the history of modernisation, with a considerable weight of evidence, as one of carnage and bedlam rather than peaceful convergence, one characterised by a politics of violence, hysteria and despair. *The Age of Anger* (London: Penguin, 2017), 21. Likewise, Wolfgang Streeck understands capitalism in terms of crisis giving rise to crisis. *Buying Time: The Delayed Crisis of Democratic Capitalism* (London: Verso, 2017).
2. Kathryn Tanner suggests as much, at least in respect of discourse: *Economy of Grace* (Minneapolis, MN: Fortress, 2005), x–xi.
3. The aim will be to work towards conceptions of faith and redemption that are entirely worldly and secular, a 'religion without religion' accessible without acceptance of a particular deposit of revelation or a living tradition. If such a task were successful, then, for that very reason, such conceptions would be entirely incarnational, Christian and revelatory. There would no longer be any distinction between the secular and the religious – precisely the object of Christian hope: 'thy kingdom come'. This does not, of course, preclude other faiths from achieving their own consummation in worldliness, yet it does continue a trajectory implicit within a distinctively Anglican rationality.
4. There is no aim here to continue the dialogue between the disciplines of theology and economics from one side or the other. I write as a participant in distinctive and contemporary forms of religious and economic life.
5. Søren Kierkegaard, *Journals and Papers*, trans. Howard V. Hong and Edna H. Hong (Bloomington, IN: Indiana University Press, 1967), I. 1025. G. W. F. Hegel had argued that the reason for things only appears with hindsight, such that philosophy comes on the scene too late to offer advice. *Philosophy of Right*, trans. T. M. Knox (Oxford: Clarendon, 1942), 12–13.

6. It does, however, have roots in speculative naturalism: see Arran Gare and Wayne Hudson (eds.), *For a New Naturalism* (New York: Telos, 2017).

7. Franz Rosenzweig, 'The New Thinking', in Nahum H. Glatzer (ed.), *Franz Rosenzweig: His Life and Thought* (New York: Schocken, 1961), 200.

8. Immanuel Kant, *Religion within the Boundaries of Mere Reason*, trans. Allen Wood and George di Giovanni (Cambridge: Cambridge University Press, 1998), 164–66.

9. Kant, *Critique of Practical Reason*, trans. Lewis White Beck (New York: Garland, 1976), 232.

10. Jürgen Habermas points out that a unity between facticity and validity is found in background assumptions of the lifeworld as well as in sacred authorities. Habermas, *Between Facts and Norms*, trans. William Rehg (Cambridge: Polity, 1997), 23. In this respect, the reconstruction of this unity through rational deliberation and agreement replaces the function of theology. The hypothesis explored here is that this unity between fact and value also occurs, beyond agreement, in economic interactions of credit.

11. As Rosenzweig put it: 'The unlimited cannot be attained by organization. That which is distant can be attained only through that which is nearest at the moment. Any "plan" is wrong to begin with – simply because it is a plan. The highest things cannot be planned; for them readiness is everything'. Rosenzweig, 'On Being a Jewish Person', *Franz Rosenzweig*, 222.

12. Jean-Jacques Rousseau, 'A Discourse on the Arts and Sciences', in *The Social Contract and Discourses*, trans. G. D. H. Cole (London: J. M. Dent, 1913), 122.

13. Hannah Arendt, *The Human Condition* (Chicago, IL: Chicago University Press, 1998), 5.

14. Arendt, *The Origins of Totalitarianism* (New York: Shocken, 2004), 604–5.

15. This conception of philosophy exploded in the 1840s, catalysed by the suggestive yet unsatisfactory originality of F. W. J. Schelling's lectures on 'positive philosophy', in the diverse endeavours of Ludwig Feuerbach, Søren Kierkegaard, Friedrich Engels, and Karl Marx. Later iterations of a nontheoretical philosophy were based on a fresh engagement with the temporality of being, beyond Hegel's historical reflection, in the projects of Henri Bergson, Friedrich Nietzsche and Martin Heidegger. While Marx and Nietzsche proceeded to view thinking itself as a political act, Arendt implicitly raised the question of whether trust constitutes the essence of the political in her own reworking of Jesus's forgiveness and Nietzsche's thought on promising. What follows here is a further outworking of the implications of such considerations.

16. The mainstream of Western philosophy has taken a semantic turn here during the twentieth century following Frege, Russell, Moore and Husserl, distinguishing a thought, a specific propositional or semantic content, from a representation, holding an idea before the mind. It has almost become a defining gesture of philosophy to bracket out one's subjective impressions in order to enter a shared world of the discussion of timeless meanings. This leaves three issues unexplained: how such sentence meanings reflect events in the world, enter into minds and convey rational necessity. The approach adopted here is instead rooted in such nineteenth-century philosophers as Schelling, Feuerbach, Kierkegaard, Nietzsche, Lagneau and Bergson, some of whom offered a critique of any oncoming linguistic turn. For contemporary considerations against restricting philosophy to the shared world of meanings, see Philip Goodchild (ed.), *On Philosophy as a Spiritual Exercise: A Symposium* (Basingstoke: Palgrave Macmillan, 2013).

17. Rosenzweig, 'The New Thinking', 201.

1. THROUGH THE EYE OF A NEEDLE

1. Martin Heidegger, *Off the Beaten Track*, trans. Julian Young and Kenneth Haynes (Cambridge: Cambridge University Press, 2002), 199.

2. As pointed out by Giorgio Agamben, *The Kingdom and the Glory: For a Theological Genealogy of Economy and Government*, trans. Lorenzo Chiesa (Stanford, CA: Stanford University Press, 2011), 38.

3. Also noted by Harvey Cox in claiming Adam Smith as an heir to this prophetic tradition: 'One of the most overlooked features of Jesus as a prophet is that in his principal teaching, the parables, he focuses almost entirely on "worldly" (including economic) issues and the moral challenges they present'. *The Market as God* (Cambridge, MA: Harvard University Press, 2016), 163.

4. Although I am persuaded that Jesus was probably recalling his community to an economic regime prior to imperial taxation and the market: see Richard Horsley, *Covenant Economics: A Biblical Vision of Justice for All* (Louisville, KY: Westminster John Knox, 2009). Such an economic order is largely incompatible with contemporary tastes and technologies.

5. Søren Kierkegaard, *Works of Love*, trans. Howard V. Hong and Edna H. Hong (New York: Harper Perennial, 2009), 352.

6. Indeed, it is only by suspending concern with the explicit contents and judgements of thought, inverting values such that the attention which gives value is itself valued more highly than the attention attracted by prior valuations, and repetition of these operations of suspension, inversion and repetition within the work of thought itself that the significance of such operations can come to light.

2. ECONOMY IN THE NEW TESTAMENT

1. Dotan Leshem, *The Origins of Neoliberalism: Modeling the Economy from Jesus to Foucault* (New York: Columbia University Press, 2017), 12.

2. Aristotle, *Politics*, 1253a.

3. Xenophon, *Oekonomikos*, trans. Sarah B. Pomeroy (Oxford: Clarendon Press, 1994).

4. Aristotle, *Nicomachean Ethics*, 1134b.

5. Aristotle, *Politics*, 1257b.

6. Hannah Arendt, *The Human Condition* (Chicago, IL: University of Chicago Press, 1998).

7. Weil, *Oppression and Liberty*, trans. Arthur Wills (London: Routledge & Kegan Paul, 1958), 69; note that Arendt restricted means and ends to the life of work. See 'Labor, Work, Action', in Peter Baehr (ed.), *The Portable Hannah Arendt* (London: Penguin, 2003), 176–78.

8. Agamben, *The Kingdom and the Glory*; Dotan Leshem, *The Origins of Neoliberalism.*

9. Richard A. Horsley and Asher B. Silberman, *The Message and the Kingdom: How Jesus and Paul Ignited a Revolution and Transformed the Ancient World* (Minneapolis, MN: Fortress, 2002).

10. Arendt reports evidence that in the Roman Empire no one was free and everyone had a master. *The Human Condition*, 130n81.

11. As in the Septuagint: see Isaiah 22.15, 20; to suppose, by contrast, that *oikonomia* is primary, as John Reumann does despite it only appearing twice in the Septuagint in contrast to twelve appearances of *oikonomos*, is already to accept the primacy of Greek metaphysical thinking over Jewish relational thinking. Reumann, *Stewardship and the Economy of God* (Grand Rapids, MI: Eerdmans, 1992).

12. John Goodrich, *Paul as an Administrator of God in 1 Corinthians* (Cambridge: Cambridge University Press, 2012), 27–102.

13. See further Goodrich, *Paul as an Administrator of Christ in 1 Corinthians*, 143.

14. Goodrich, *Paul as an Administrator of Christ in 1 Corinthians*, 145.

15. There is little consensus amongst commentators on this point. Goodrich has Paul both administering the mysteries and subordinate to them, but overall decides that the genitive is objective and Paul dispenses the mysteries. *Paul as an Administrator of Christ in 1 Corinthians*, 144.

16. Note that the Pauline notion of grace as a gift or resource to be managed is taken up in the Petrine usage of *oikonomos*, which seems to allude to a division of labour in the body of Christ: 'Be hospitable to one another without complaining. Like good stewards of the manifold grace of God, serve one another with whatever gift each of you has received' (1 Pet. 4.10).

17. An alternative interpretation would be that the mystery and fullness of time are both commissioned, rather than planned; I have not found a commentator who adopts such an alternative.

18. M. Douglas Meeks explicitly welcomes the scandal of calling God an appointed servant in order to bring out the emphasis on servanthood in Christ's divinity in contrast to ruler, king or judge. This does not really deal with the issue of to whom God might be accountable. See Meeks, *God the Economist: The Doctrine of God and Political Economy* (Minneapolis, MN: Fortress, 1989), 76.

19. The preeminent reformulation of *oikonomia* as plan was offered by Irenaeus in *Against Heresies*, 5.13.1.

20. Simone Weil suggests that there is 'a great difference between a truth recognized as such and introduced and received into the mind as such, and a truth which is active in the soul and endowed with the power to destroy within the soul those errors that are clearly incompatible with it'. *First and Last Notebooks*, trans. Richard Rees (London: Oxford University Press, 1970), 352.

21. Keiji Nishitani drew attention to this dimension of necessity in writing about the need for religion: 'We become aware of religion as a need, as a must for life, only at the level of life at which everything else loses its necessity and utility. Why do we exist at all? Is not our very existence and human life ultimately meaningless? Or, if there is a meaning or significance to it all, where do we find it? When we come to doubt the meaning of our existence in this way, when we have become a question to ourselves, the religious quest awakens within us. These questions and the quest they give rise to show up when the mode of looking at and thinking about everything in terms of how it relates to *us* is broken through, where the mode of living that puts us at the center of everything is overturned'. *Religion and Nothingness*, trans. Jan Van Bragt (Berkeley, CA: University of California Press, 1982), 3.

22. See Justo L. González, *Faith and Wealth: A History of Early Christian Ideas on the Origin, Significance and Use of Money* (San Francisco, CA: Harper and Row, 1990), 71–88.

23. Elettra Stimilli notes that this ascetic practice is the primary meaning of 'economy', in contrast to Agamben who concentrates on Tertullian's development of the divine economy. Elettra Stimilli, *The Debt of the Living: Ascesis and Capitalism*, trans. Arianna Bove (Albany, NY: SUNY Press, 2017). In a similar vein, Devin Singh explores how economic life remains the source for the formulation of doctrines of atonement in the fourth century. Singh, *Divine Currency: The Theological Power of Money in the West* (Stanford, CA: Stanford University Press, 2018).

24. In gathering such a case, L. William Countryman cites Clement of Alexandria's sermon, 'Who Is the Rich Man That Is Saved'? on redemptive sacrifice: 'What splendid trading! What divine business! You buy incorruption with money. You give the perishing things of the world and receive in exchange for them an eternal abode in heaven'. *The Rich Christian in the Church of the Early Empire: Contradictions and Accommodations* (New York: Edward Mellen, 1980), 54.

25. Max Weber, *The Protestant Ethics and the Spirit of Capitalism*, trans. Talcott Parsons (London: Allen & Unwin, 1965); for a critical assessment, see Charles Y. Glock and Philip Hammond (eds.), *Beyond the Classics? Essays in the Scientific Study of Religion* (London: Harper & Row, 1973), chapter 2; Susan Budd, *Sociologists and Religion* (London: Collier-Macmillan, 1973), 57–67.

26. For such accounts of neoliberalism, see, for example, Franco 'Bifo' Berardi, *The Soul at Work: From Alienation to Autonomy*, trans. Francesca Cadel and Giuseppina Mecchia (New York: Semiotext(e), 2009) and Wendy Brown, *Undoing the Demos: Neoliberalism's Stealth Revolution* (New York: Zone, 2015).

3. IMPERTINENT GUESTS

1. For the significance of patronage as part of economic life, see Bruce J. Malina, *The Social World of Jesus and the Gospels* (London: Routledge, 1996).

2. François Bovon, *Luke 1: A Commentary on the Gospel of Luke 1 – 9.50*, trans. Christine M. Thomas (Minneapolis, MN: Fortress Press, 2002), 291; E. J. Tinsley, *The Gospel According to Luke* (Cambridge: Cambridge University Press, 1965).

3. Eduard Schweizer, *The Good News According to Luke*, trans. David E. Green (London: SPCK 1984).

4. Robert J. Karris, *Bonaventure Texts in Translation Series, Volume XII: Part I: Commentary of the Gospel of Luke: Chapters 1–8* (New York: Fransciscan Institute, 2011), 630, 632.

5. G. W. H. Lampe, 'The Atonement: Law and Love', in Alec R. Vidler, *Soundings* (Cambridge: Cambridge University Press, 1962), 186–87.

6. Karl Marx and Friedrich Engels, *The Communist Manifesto*, ed. David MacLellan (Oxford: Oxford University Press, 1993), 6.

7. This famous remark of Hegel on Schelling's philosophy is counteracted by Gilles Deleuze and Félix Guattari, who observed that this is a ruse of power: either you accept given differentiations, or fall into the undifferentiated, thus excluding the possibility of self-differentiation: *Anti-Oedipus*, trans Mark Seem, Helen R. Lane and Robert Hurley (London: Athlone, 1984), 78.

8. This is one difficulty of Paul Tillich's invocation of this characteristic inversion as the 'Protestant principle' that overturns any fixed religious claims: it aims at the removal of fixed status, a theoretical approach to understanding existence, without establishing a new ground for the value of values. *The Protestant Era*, trans. James Luther Adams (London: Nisbet, 191), chapter 11.

9. Daniel Boyarin attributes such a Hellenistic prioritisation of spiritual life over the Jewish rituals of physical life to Paul. *A Radical Jew: Paul and the Politics of Identity* (Berkeley, CA: University of California Press, 1994).

4. THE ECONOMY OF SALVATION

1. At times, Pauline scholarship goes so far as to eliminate the possibility of an original gospel as a methodological principle, as does Troels Engberg-Pedersen, *Cosmology and Self in the Apostle Paul* (Oxford: Oxford University Press, 2010), 9. While this discussion has in fact benefited from historical critical as well as theological scholarship I have encountered over the decades, it aims to offer its own abstraction from Paul rather than an interpretation. Likewise, while familiar with the philosophical appropriations of Paul inspired by Jacob Taubes, Stanislas Breton, Alain Badiou, Slavoj Žižek and Giorgio Agamben, my own appropriation remains rooted in both historical scholarship and Christian theology.

2. See, for example, the approach of Michael J. Gorman, *Cruciformity: Paul's Narrative Spirituality of the Cross* (Grand Rapids, MI: Eerdmans, 2001).

3. Clear exceptions, such as the teaching on divorce (1 Cor. 7.10–11), are made so obvious as 'a command from the Lord' as to prove the rule.

5. CREDIT OR GRACE

1. Jacques Derrida famously interpreted this in terms of an economy of sacrifice. *The Gift of Death*, trans. David Wills (Chicago, IL: University of Chicago Press, 1995), 99–103.

2. The established practice in early Christianity was that giving alms effectively atoned for sins. For Augustine, alms provided the wings that brought the daily prayer 'forgive us our sins' up to heaven, as though they were the evidence of sincerity of faith. This conception does not quite reduce the grace of forgiveness to an exchange transaction. For further discussion of this as the context for the Pelagian controversy, see Peter Brown, *Through the Eye of a Needle* (Princeton, NJ: Princeton University Press, 2012), 363.

3. Weil suggested that contradictions show that a subject is being approached on the wrong level. The discovery of contradictions to reach an impasse, then, is an opportunity for a change in level, for transcending one's current understanding. Conversely, 'All errors in level produce false opinions which are contrary and equivalent to each other'. *Notebooks* volume 1, trans. Arthur Wills (London: Routledge & Kegan Paul), 152.

4. Pascal interpreted these as the lust to feel, to know and to dominate. Blaise Pascal, *Pensées*, trans. W. F. Trotter (Grand Rapids, MI: Christian Classics Ethereal Library, 2002), section 458.

5. Augustine, *On Free Will*, II.7.17.

6. Economists follow Fred Hirsch in referring to these as 'positional goods'.

7. For example, William Temple: 'All such self-centred value judgements are non-social in essence and anti-social in effect; for they bring men into rivalry and enmity with one another'. Temple, *Nature, Man and God* (London: Macmillan & Co., 1953), 518. Basil of Caesarea and Augustine of Hippo made similar observations.

8. Adam Smith, *Theory of Moral Sentiments* (Cambridge: Cambridge University Press, 2001), 61; emphasis added.

9. According to Smith, people desire not only to be praised but also to be praiseworthy, to be what they approve of in others. For to desire or accept praise without its being due can only be the effect of 'the most contemptible vanity', *Theory of Moral Sentiments*, 136. 'When a man has bribed all the judges, the most unanimous decision of the court, though it may give him his law-suit, may not give him the assurance that he was in the right; and had he carried on his law-suit merely to satisfy himself that he was in the right, he never would have bribed the judges', 147.

10. See further Kierkegaard, *Works of Love*, 112–13.

11. St Augustine, *Concerning the City of God Against the Pagans*, trans. Henry Bettenson (London: Penguin, 2003), XV.5 600; Alasdair MacIntyre, *Dependent Rational Animals: Why Human Beings Need the Virtues* (Chicago, IL: Open Court, 1999), 119.

12. Temple, *Nature, Man and God*, 518; Augustine said much the same of wisdom: 'From that common store you can convert nothing into your private possession. What you take remains unharmed for me to take also', *On Free Will*, II.14.37.

13. Whatever minimal degree of Greek philosophical thought filtered through into Jesus's teaching, Aristotelianism was not part of it.

14. Temple, *Nature, Man and God*, 518.

15. As David E. Jenkins phrased it: 'to give all is to receive all and to be all'. *The Contradiction of Christianity* (London: SCM, 1976), 24.

16. Insofar as modern political philosophy is founded upon such notions of ownership of one's self or body, whether explicit as in John Locke, or implicit as in conceptions of social contract, then it is founded upon a category error.

17. Note how close this is to Weil's insight: 'All sins are an attempt to escape from time. Virtue is to submit to time, to press it to the heart until the heart breaks'. *First and Last Notebooks*, trans. Richard Reed (Oxford: Oxford University Press, 1970), 102.

18. For repetition as a metaphysical category, see Catherine Pickstock, *Repetition and Identity* (Oxford: Oxford University Press, 2013).

19. Kierkegaard, *Works of Love*, 351–52.

20. Weil, *Notebooks*, 403.

21. In respect of action, Maurice Blondel referred to 'a commerce between the agent and something other than the agent, a new synthesis of the individual life and the milieu in which it unfolds'. *Action (1893): Essay on a Critique of Life and a Science of Practice*, trans. Oliva Blanchette (Notre Dame, IN: University of Notre Dame Press, 2003), 201.

22. As the internal rational ordering principle of a kind of religious life, this is a philosophy of religion in a sense close to that of Hegel's original coinage of the term in his eponymous lectures. G. W. F. Hegel, *Lectures on the Philosophy of Religion*, trans. E. B Speirs and J. Burdon Sanderson (London: Routledge & Kegan Paul, 1974).

6. REDEMPTION

1. Yves Citton, *The Ecology of Attention*, trans. Barnaby Norman (Cambridge: Polity, 2017).

2. Hannah Arendt, *The Human Condition* (Chicago, IL: University of Chicago Press, 1998), 5; see further her distinction between cognition and thinking, *The Human Condition*, 170.

3. Georg Simmel, *The Philosophy of Money*, ed. David Frisby (London: Routledge, 1990), 77–78.

4. Jürgen Habermas, *Between Facts and Norms*, trans. William Rehg (Cambridge: Polity, 1996), 35.

5. This critique of pleasures was one of the founding gestures of philosophy: see Plato's *Philebus*, to be discussed further in *Metaphysics of Trust*.

6. Pierre Klossowski, 'Sade and Fourier', in *Living Currency*, ed. Vernon W. Cisney, Nicolae Morar and Daniel W. Smith (London: Bloomsbury, 2017), 87 (emphasis in the original).

7. VALUE

1. Spinoza, *Ethics*, trans. G. H. R. Parkinson (London: J. M. Dent, 1989), Book II, Proposition 32: 64.

2. Spinoza, *Ethics*, Book 1, Definition 3.

3. Plato, *Phaedo*, in John M. Cooper (ed.), *Plato: Complete Works* (Indianapolis, IN: Hackett, 1997), 97c. All subsequent references to Plato are to translations taken from this volume.

4. *Phaedo* 97c–d, in *Plato: Complete Works*, 84.

5. *Theaetetus* 174a, in *Plato: Complete Works*, 193.

6. *Greater Hippias* 304c–e, in *Plato: Complete Works*, 921.

7. Plato, *Republic* VI 493a–c, in *Plato: Complete Works*, 1115.

8. Plato, *Republic* VI 492b–c, in *Plato: Complete Works*, 1114.

9. Plato, *Republic* VI 492e, in *Plato: Complete Works*, 1115.

10. Weil, *Science, Necessity and the Love of God*, trans. Richard Rees (London: Oxford University Press, 1968), 98.

11. Weil, *Oppression and Liberty*, trans. Arthur Wills and John Petrie (London: Routledge & Kegan Paul, 1958), 165, 180.

12. Weil, *Formative Writings 1929–1941*, trans. Dorothy Tuck MacFarland and Wilhelmina Ness (London: Routledge & Kegan Paul, 1987), 62.

13. Weil, *Lectures on Philosophy*, trans. Hugh Price (Cambridge: Cambridge University Press, 1978), 75–76.

14. Weil, *Lectures on Philosophy*, 139.

15. Note the comparable judgement of Aquinas on this point: it is a far greater evil to be insensible to the presence of sin and disorder than to suffer ill consequences from them. *Summa Theologiae* I.2 39.1.

16. Weil, *Science, Necessity and the Love of God*, 12.

17. Weil, *Lectures on Philosophy*, 196, refers to 'the ontological point of view' as absurd.

18. Weil, *First and Last Notebooks*, 364.

19. The influence of Maine de Biran is also clear here.

20. Weil, *Lectures on Philosophy*, 89.

21. Immanuel Kant, *Critique of Pure Reason*, trans. Norman Kemp Smith (Basingstoke: Macmillan, 1929), 47.

22. Ludwig Feuerbach, *Principles of the Philosophy of the Future*, trans. Manfred H. Vogel (Indianapolis, IN: Bobbs Merrill, 1966), 3.

23. Feuerbach, *Principles of the Philosophy of the Future*, 23.

24. Feuerbach, *Principles of the Philosophy of the Future*, 44.

25. Feuerbach, *Principles of the Philosophy of the Future*, 50.

26. Feuerbach, *Principles of the Philosophy of the Future*, 52.

27. Feuerbach, *Principles of the Philosophy of the Future*, 60.

28. Feuerbach, *Principles of the Philosophy of the Future*, 60.

29. Feuerbach, *Principles of the Philosophy of the Future*, 68. For Feuerbach, the Christian religion, unlike philosophy, is founded on the sensuous perception of God through Christ.

30. Simone Weil, 'Some Reflections on the Concept of Value', in Eric O. Springsted (ed.), *Simone Weil: Late Philosophical Writings* (Notre Dame, IN: University of Notre Dame Press, 2015), 30–31.

31. Weil, 'Some Reflections on the Concept of Value', 32–33.

32. Weil draws her usage of 'supernatural grace' in this context directly from Lagneau. See further below.

33. Jules Lagneau, *De l'existence de Dieu* (Paris: Félix Alcan, 1925). For the influence of Lagneau on Weil, both via Alain and through this publication, see Simone Pétrement, *Simone Weil: A Life*, trans. Raymond Rosenthal (New York: Pantheon Books, 1976).

34. The nineteenth-century use of the term *value* in philosophy is somewhat unfortunate if it is taken to mean the public comparison of relative values, as in Arendt, *The Human Condition*, 164. Lagneau's sense of 'value' is of a worth prior to any distinction of public and private.

35. Harry Frankfurt, *The Importance of What We Care About* (Cambridge: Cambridge University Press, 1988), 80.

36. Lagneau, *De l'existence de Dieu*, 9; all translations from this work are my own.

37. Lagneau, *De l'existence de Dieu*, 45–48.

38. Lagneau, *De l'existence de Dieu*, 49.

39. Lagneau, *De l'existence de Dieu*, 57.

40. Lagneau, *De l'existence de Dieu*, 36.

41. Simmel wrote much the same about the objectivity of value, which can be neither proven nor explained: 'The value that attaches to any object, person, relationship or happening demands recognition'. *Philosophy of Money*, 68.

42. Lagneau, *De l'existence de Dieu*, 142.

43. Lagneau, *De l'existence de Dieu*, 68.

44. Lagneau, *De l'existence de Dieu*, 67.

45. Lagneau, *De l'existence de Dieu*, 76.

46. Lagneau, *De l'existence de Dieu*, 92.

47. Lagneau, *De l'existence de Dieu*, 130.

48. Lagneau, *De l'existence de Dieu*, 87.

49. Lagneau, *De l'existence de Dieu*, 136.

50. Lagneau, *De l'existence de Dieu*, 137.

51. Lagneau, *De l'existence de Dieu*, 144.

52. Lagneau, *De l'existence de Dieu*, 152.

53. It is worth remarking how much Christian trinitarian and incarnational theology has been formulated specifically to loosen such knots by introducing some mediation.

54. F. W. J. Schelling, *The Grounding of Positive Philosophy: The Berlin Lectures*, trans. Bruce Matthews (Albany, NY: SUNY Press, 2007).

55. This is the relation of thinking and being proposed by Deleuze and Guattari, *What Is Philosophy?* trans. Hugh Tomlinson and Graham Burchell (London: Verso, 1994), 38.

56. Kant, *Religion within the Boundaries of Mere Reason*, trans. Allen Wood and George Di Giovanni (Cambridge: Cambridge University Press, 1998), 166–70.

8. NECESSITY AND FREEDOM

1. On this distinction of ethics from economics, see R. G. Collingwood, 'Economics as a Philosophical Science', *International Journal of Ethics* 26, no. 2 (1926): 162–85.

2. Immanuel Kant, *Prolegomena to Any Future Metaphysics*, ed. Beryl Logan (London: Routledge, 1996), 54.

3. Kant, *Prolegomena*, 102.

4. Kant, *Critique of Pure Reason*, 32.

5. Even Simmel, who operated within a sharp Kantian dualism between Reality and Value, recognised the need for their underlying metaphysical unity, 'for which there is no linguistic term unless it be religious symbols', *The Philosophy of Money*, 62. Indeed, he went so far as to explain the increasing concurrent significance of the objective determination of things and the subjective freedom of the individual as a consequence of the replacement of personal obligation with exchange relations facilitated by money. *The Philosophy of Money*, 303.

6. Kant, *Critique of Pure Reason*, 29.

7. Weil describes this as Marx's truly great idea 'that in human society as well as in nature nothing takes place otherwise than through material transformations. . . . To desire is nothing; we have got to know the material conditions which determine our possibilities of action; and in the social sphere these conditions are defined by the way in which man obeys material necessities in supplying his own needs', *Oppression and Liberty*, 45. This approach offers a different system of categorisation of goods from those based on human capabilities, such as those of Martha Nussbaum and Amartya Sen (eds.), *The Quality of Life: A Capabilities Approach* (Oxford: Clarendon, 1993), as well as those based on human goods, such as that of Robert Skidelsky and Edward Skidelsky, *How Much Is Enough?: Money and the Good Life* (London: Penguin, 2013). The concept of 'cultivation' of cultural values is intended to combine notions of agent-centred capability with an objective sense of the good, drawing from both approaches.

8. David Wiggins expresses the point thus: 'What I need depends not on thought or the workings of my mind (or not only on these) but on the way the world is'. *Needs, Values, Truth* (Oxford: Clarendon Press, 1998), 6.

9. Adam Smith: 'By necessities I understand not only the commodities which are indispensably necessary for the support of life, but whatever the custom of the country renders it indecent for creditable people even of the lowest rank to be without'. *An Inquiry into the Nature and Causes of the Wealth of Nations* (Oxford: Clarendon Press, 1976), V.2.2.

10. As the Chicago economist Frank Knight put it: 'Life is not fundamentally a striving for ends, for satisfactions, but rather for bases for further striving; desire is more fundamental for conduct than achievement, or perhaps better, the true achievement is the refinement and elevation of the plane of desire, the cultivation of taste'. *Selected Essays by Frank Knight*, Volume 1 (Chicago, IL: University of Chicago Press, 1999), 43.

11. Joan Robinson points out how deeply integrated basic needs and social relations produced by a surplus are: 'All the same, in any society there is some notion of a distinction between daily bread and something extra – for a guest, for a feast, or for tribute to whom tribute is due. The imperative requirement to produce a surplus is useful for mere survival. It provides a margin that can be forgone in times of dearth. Enough is too little. Just as the incentive of hunger is needed to make us eat, so the incentive of good name and proper behaviour is necessary to keep an economy going'. *Freedom and Necessity* (London: George Allen & Unwin, 1970), 25.

12. Of course, it is debateable whether such inclusion and exclusion takes place in truly 'cultured' societies. 'When claims of need go unheeded, that which is disappointed is the expectation that it would be taken into account that the claimant's actual survival or most minimal well-being was at issue'. Wiggins, *Needs, Values, Truth*, 29.

13. According to Kierkegaard, the lily in the field declares: 'I myself, of course, have not been able to determine the place and the conditions; this is not in the remotest way my affair'. Human freedom may be differentiated from plant life to the extent that it can determine place and conditions. *Without Authority*, trans. Howard V. Hong and Edna H. Hong (Princeton, NJ: Princeton University Press, 1997), 27. See further Arendt, *The Human Condition*, 9.

14. Weil emphasised the significance of the economists' turn towards the value of labour, one that she encountered in Marx: 'The idea of labour considered as a human value is doubtless the one and only spiritual conquest achieved by the human mind since the miracle of Greece'. *Oppression and Liberty*, 106.

15. Weil put it like this: 'By work, man creates the universe around him. Remember the way you looked at the fields after a day's harvesting. . . . How differently from a person going for a walk, for whom the fields are only a scenic background! In precisely *this* consists the power of a true monument of work over the universe that surrounds it'. *First and Last Notebooks*, 18.

9. ESTRANGEMENT

1. Marx, *Economic and Philosophic Manuscripts of 1844*, trans. Progress Publishers (London: Lawrence & Wishart, 1977), 66.

2. Marx, *Economic and Philosophical Manuscripts*, 20.

3. Louis Dumont interprets Marx in this way as an individualist, inheriting the primacy of the relation between people and things over the relation between people established by Locke, Mandeville and Smith: Marx is not saying that each particular person is a social being, but that the human totality is found in each particular person. Dumont, *From Mandeville to Marx: The Genesis and Triumph of Economic Ideology* (Chicago: University of Chicago Press, 1977), 131. By contrast, to interpret this relation as social and historical, see John Bellamy Foster, *Marx's Ecology* (New York: Monthly Review Books, 2000), 116.

4. Marx is, of course, working from within the assumptions of political economy to effect an immanent critique: the labourer 'must constantly look upon his labour-power as his own property, his own commodity, and this he can only do by placing it at the disposal of the buyer temporarily, for a definite period of time'. Marx, *Capital* I.2.6, ed. David MacClellan (Oxford: Oxford World's Classics, 1999), 109.

5. Moishe Postone argues that both individual labour and abstract, social labour in Marx's theory are specific to capitalism itself. See Postone, *Time, Labor and Social Domination: A Reinterpretation of Marx's Critical Theory* (Cambridge: Cambridge University Press, 1996), 48.

6. Marx, *Economic and Philosophic Manuscripts*, 72.

7. Yet note that in the subsequent 'Theses on Feuerbach' the human essence, while practical, is the 'ensemble of the social relations' (thesis 6); it is best fulfiled in the 'revolutionary practice' of at once changing self and circumstances (thesis 3). Marx, *Early Writings*, trans. Rodney Livingstone and Gregor Benton (London: Penguin, 1975), 422–23.

8. Marx, *Economic and Philosophic Manuscripts*, 74.

9. Marx, *Economic and Philosophic Manuscripts*, 92.

10. Marx, *Economic and Philosophic Manuscripts*, 96.

11. Marx, *Economic and Philosophic Manuscripts*, 94.

12. Marx, *Economic and Philosophic Manuscripts*, 75.

13. Marx, *Economic and Philosophic Manuscripts*, 77.

14. In claiming that 'the political economist postulates the original unity of capital and labour as the unity of the capitalist and worker', Marx anticipates many recent accounts of 'neoliberalism' as the ideology that requires the worker becomes an entrepreneur of the self. *Economic and Philosophic Manuscripts*, 108.

15. Marx, *Economic and Philosophic Manuscripts*, 104.

16. Marx, *Economic and Philosophic Manuscripts*, 63.

17. Feuerbach, *Essence of Christianity*, trans. George Eliot (Amherst, NY: Prometheus, 1989), 26.

18. William Temple, *Christianity and Social Order* (London: Macmillan, 1942), 60.

10. FIDELITY

1. David Hume, *A Treatise of Human Nature*, ed. L. A. Selby-Bigge (Oxford: Clarendon Press, 1896), 266–67.

2. See the discussion in Martin Hollis, *Trust within Reason* (Cambridge: Cambridge University Press, 1998), 41.

3. Friedrich Nietzsche, *On the Genealogy of Morality*, ed. Keith Ansell Pearson (Cambridge: Cambridge University Press, 1994), 38.

4. Nietzsche, *Genealogy*, 39.

5. Nietzsche, *Genealogy*, 41.

6. Nietzsche, *Genealogy*, 44.

7. Nietzsche, *Genealogy*, 61.

8. Nietzsche, *Genealogy*, 49. Maurizio Lazzarato bases his account of the economy on this claim (*The Making of Indebted Man* [New York: Semiotext(e), 2012], 39–40). But this is the precise point which David Graeber disputes in Nietzsche, arguing that relations of communism and hierarchy are at least equiprimordial with relations of exchange, if not primary. *Debt: The First 5,000 Years* (New York: Melville, 2011). Lazzarato, in his retort, seems to have missed Graeber's wider argument about the multiple bases for society; he finds Nietzsche's theory uniquely valuable for explaining contemporary capitalism as making debt infinite and unpayable. *Governing by Debt*, trans. Joshua David Jordan (New York: Semiotext(e), 2015), 84–87. Lazzarato's reading of Nietzsche draws out the important dimensions of power, interiority and temporality in the debt relationship, yet neither Graeber nor Lazzarato pose the crucial philosophical question of the basis on which trust is appropriate.

9. Marx, *Economic and Philosophic Manuscripts*, 89.

10. Nietzsche, *Genealogy*, 49.

11. Nietzsche, *Genealogy*, 49.

12. Nietzsche, *Genealogy*, 44.

13. Nietzsche, *Genealogy*, 53.

14. Nietzsche, *Genealogy*, 39.

15. Nietzsche, *Genealogy*, 44–45.

16. Nietzsche, *Beyond Good and Evil*, section 259.

17. Weil, *Oppression and Liberty*, 65.

18. The point, here, is not that animals do not anticipate or fear; they clearly do. In this respect, animals, and perhaps even plants, are free. Carl Safina, *Beyond Words: What Animals Think and Feel* (New York: Souvenir Press, 2016). The point is that natural necessity is understood according to a metaphysics of presence, while temporal acts of labour, desire, investment, care, attention and devotion can only be understood in terms of recollection and anticipation.

19. Weil, *Oppression and Liberty*, 67–68.

20. Weil proposed an improvement of Marxism inspired by Darwin's improvement on Lamarck: to inquire into the conditions of existence of societies, rather than invoking a dialectical account of the progress of history. See *Oppression and Liberty*, 56–61.

21. Weil, *Intimations of Christianity among the Ancient Greeks* (London: Routledge, 1957), 135.

11. LIGHT AND REPOSE

1. Jacques Le Goff, *Your Money or Your Life* (New York: Zone, 1990), 40–41.

2. David Graeber, *Debt: The First 5,000 Years* (New York: Melville, 2011), 85.

3. Graeber, *Debt*, 350.

4. Weil, *First and Last Notebooks*, 19.

5. Weil, *Gravity and Grace*, trans. Emma Crawford and Mario von der Ruhr (London: Routledge, 2002), 164.

6. Weil, *Gravity and Grace*, 165.

7. *La condition ouvrière* (Paris: Gallimard, 2002), 186–87; cited from translation in Chenavier, *Simone Weil: Attention to the Real*, trans. Bernard E. Doering (Notre Dame, IN: University of Notre Dame Press, 2012), 33.

8. Weil, *Notebooks*, volume 1, 111.

9. Weil, *Notebooks*, volume 2, 334.
10. Weil, *First and Last Notebooks*, 342.
11. Weil, *Waiting for God*, 173.

CREDIT AND CREATION:
ECONOMIC ROOTS

1. W. H. Vanstone saw being 'handed over' as the central category of the Christology of the Synoptic Gospels. *The Stature of Waiting* (London: DLT, 1982).

12. CREDIT AS OFFERING

1. It is arguable that Vanstone's phenomenology is actually grounded in Augustine's ontology of desire, while also being shaped by notions of divine vulnerability to creation probably drawn from Whitehead and/or Weil.
2. Vanstone, *Love's Endeavour, Love's Expense* (London: DLT, 1977), 43.
3. Vanstone refers specifically to Christ's teaching that forgiveness should be more than seven times. *Love's Endeavour*, 43.
4. *Love's Endeavour*, 45–46.
5. The widespread modern rejection of the concept of God as a *paterfamilias* having complete dominion or ownership over creation is exemplified in M. Douglas Meeks, *God the Economist*, 66–68. As a translator of Jürgen Moltmann's theology, Meeks is heavily dependent on Moltmann's formulation of a social Trinity in opposition to the dominant God of classical metaphysics.
6. The classical statement of this theology is in Charles Gore (ed.), *Lux Mundi* (London: John Murray, 1891); a more recent collection, John Polkinghorne (ed.), *The Work of Love: Creation as Kenosis* (London: SPCK, 2001) is dedicated in memory of Vanstone. A classic critical appropriation of kenosis is offered by John A. T. Robinson, *Thou Who Art: The Concept of the Personality of God* (London: Continuum, 2006), chapter 10.
7. Vanstone, *Love's Endeavour*, 52–53.
8. Vanstone, like some of his contemporaries, diverges here from the classical notion of divine impassibility. The metaphysical problems of a passible God may be solved if one understands divine power in creation, redemption and judgement as the active power to grant credit instead of in terms of substance or will.
9. Vanstone, *Love's Endeavour, Love's Expense*, 119.
10. Vanstone, *Love's Endeavour*, 57–76.
11. This conception of Christian freedom, based on freedom of attention, was first developed by Peter of John Olivi, a contemporary of Aquinas, prior to Scotus and Ockham, in an introspective phenomenology of attention that anticipated and made possible the distinctively French tradition of Descartes, Maine de Biran, Lagneau, Bergson and Merleau-Ponty. See Juhana Toivanen, *Perception and the Internal Senses: Peter of John Olivi on the Cognitive Functions of the Sensitive Soul* (Leiden: Brill, 2014), 12.

13. CREDIT AND PARTICIPATION

1. Aquinas, *Summa Theologiae* II.2.118.1.

2. See the discussion in Peter Brown, *Through the Eye of a Needle: Wealth, the Fall of Rome, and the Making of Christianity in the West 350–550 AD* (Princeton, NJ: Princeton University Press, 2012), chapter 19.

3. Brown, *Through the Eye of a Needle*, 349.

4. Brown, *Through the Eye of a Needle*, 377.

5. *Summa Theologiae* II.2.66.2.

6. *Summa Theologiae* II.2.32.5.

7. Jacques Le Goff, *Money and the Middle Ages*, trans. Jean Birrell (Cambridge: Polity, 2012), 7.

8. Le Goff, *Money and the Middle Ages*, 16.

9. It may even be suggested that Gregory of Nyssa offered the first theory of economic growth in the fourth century based on the unlimited progress enabled by the infinitely creative God. See Dotan Leshem, *The Origins of Neoliberalism* (New York: Columbia University Press, 2017), 94.

10. Aristotle, *Politics* I.10.

11. Cited in Diana Wood, *Medieval Economic Thought* (Cambridge: Cambridge University Press, 2002), 163.

12. Aquinas, *Commentary on the Sentences*, III.1.6.

13. Aquinas, *Summa Theologiae*, II.2.78.1.

14. Peter of John Olivi, *A Treatise on Contracts*, ed. Sylvain Piron (St Bonaventure, NY: Franciscan Institute Publications, 2016), II.8.42, 32.

15. Olivi, *A Treatise on Contracts*, II.8.34–37, 31.

16. Olivi, *A Treatise on Contracts*, II.8.44–48, 33.

17. Olivi, *A Treatise on Contracts*, II.8.43, 33.

18. Olivi, *A Treatise on Contracts*, II.8.59, 36.

19. Olivi, *A Treatise on Contracts*, III.3.24, 46.

20. Olivi, *A Treatise on Contracts*, III.2.16, 44.

21. Olivi, *A Treatise on Contracts*, I.1.12, 4.

22. Olivi, *A Treatise on Contracts*, I.2.24, 7.

23. Olivi, *A Treatise on Contracts*, III.4.45, 51.

24. As Georg Simmel would later explain the power of wealth from its diverse possibilities of usage: 'A great fortune is encircled by innumerable possibilities of use, as though by an astral body'. *The Philosophy of Money*, ed. David Frisby (London: Routledge, 1990), 218.

25. For capital as essentially the ability to manufacture a financial asset based on the present value of something that does not yet exist, a derivative, see Robert Meister, 'Liquidity', in Benjamin Lee and Randy Martin (eds.), *Derivatives and the Wealth of Societies* (Chicago, IL: University of Chicago Press, 2016), 154.

26. Cited in O'Donovan, *Bonds of Imperfection*, 114n66.

27. Juhana Toivanen, *Perception and the Internal Senses*, 119.

28. Toivanen interprets Olivi's notion of a terminative cause in perception as a decisive break with Aristotle's four causes. *Perception and the Internal Sense*, 150.

29. Cited in Joan Lockwood O'Donovan, 'The Theological Economics of Medieval Usury Theory', *Bonds of Imperfection* (Grand Rapids, MI: Eerdmans, 2004), 106. O'Donovan notes that this is grounded in a more Neoplatonic or Augustinian metaphysics.

30. Cited in O'Donovan, *Bonds of Imperfection*, 106n22.

31. Christopher A. Franks, *He Became Poor: The Poverty of Christ and Aquinas's Economic Teachings* (Grand Rapids, MI: Eerdmans, 2009), 81.

32. Aristotle, *Nicomachean Ethics*, 3.1 1110a.

33. Olivi, *A Treatise on Contracts*, III.4.41, 51.

34. For a brief account of how Franciscan thought and practice offered the conditions for the development of capitalism, see Stefano Zamagni, 'Catholic Social Thought, Civil Economy and the Spirit of Capitalism', in Daniel K. Finn (ed.), *The True Wealth of Nations: Catholic Social Thought and Economic Life* (Oxford: Oxford University Press, 2010).

14. APPROPRIATING CREDIT

1. David Graeber, *Debt: The First 5000 Years* (Brooklyn: Melville House, 2014), 208.
2. Graeber, *Debt*, 104.
3. Cited in Graeber, *Debt*, 29.
4. Graeber, *Debt*, 34.
5. Rabelais's *Gargantua and Pantagruel* is cited by Graeber, *Debt*, 126.
6. Graeber, *Debt*, 126.
7. Graeber, *Debt*, 146.
8. Graeber, *Debt*, 386.
9. Richard Seaford, *Money and the Early Greek Mind* (Cambridge: Cambridge University Press, 2004); the implications of such considerations, first put forward by Alfred Sohn-Rethel, were explored in my *Capitalism and Religion: The Price of Piety* (London: Routledge, 2002).
10. Bernard Stiegler, *For a New Critique of Political Economy* (Cambridge: Polity Press, 2010), 53, 65–66.
11. Martin Luther, '95 Theses', *Reformation Writings of Martin Luther*, trans. Bertram Lee Woolf (London: Lutterworth, 1952), 79th thesis.
12. Stiegler, *New Critique*, 29–33. At first sight, it would seem that Stiegler, as well as Graeber, are neglecting Derrida's arguments about the 'supplement of writing at the origin' which show the necessary role of grammatisation in all memory and social bonds. Nevertheless, their discussions, like this one, are not concerned with a pure origin or an absence of mediation, but with the loss of bonds concomitant upon taking a relation out of context.
13. Stiegler, *New Critique*, 57–59.
14. Pierre Hadot, *What Is Ancient Philosophy?* trans. Michael Chase (Cambridge, MA: Harvard University Press, 2001).
15. Richard Seaford, *Money and the Early Greek Mind* (Cambridge: Cambridge University Press, 2004), 209.
16. Kant gives this dual role to the ideas of pure reason. See Kant, *Critique of Pure Reason*, 309–22.
17. 'The last, thinnest, emptiest is placed as the first, as cause in itself, as *ens realissimum*'. Nietzsche, *Twilight of the Idols*, trans. R. J. Hollingdale (London: Penguin, 1990), 47.

15. A CULTURE OF CREDIT

1. Cited in Craig Muldrew, *The Economy of Obligation: The Culture of Credit and Social Relations in Early Modern England* (Basingstoke: Palgrave, 1998), 311.
2. Erik S. Reinert, *How Rich Countries Got Rich and Why Poor Countries Stay Poor* (London: Constable, 2007), 77–83.
3. Carl Wennerlind, *Casualties of Credit: The English Financial Revolution 1620–1720* (Cambridge, MA: Harvard University Press, 2011), 18.
4. Some estimates of the ratio of credit to coin transactions at the time were as high as 11:1. Wennerlind, *Casualties of Credit*, 19.
5. Muldrew, *The Economy of Obligation*, 100–2.
6. An anonymous pamphleteer is cited by Wennerlind, *Casualties of Credit*, 97.
7. Daniel Defoe, *The Complete English Tradesman* (London: 1725), 406.
8. Muldrew, *The Economy of Obligation*, 273.
9. Defoe, *The Complete English Tradesman*, 235.
10. Defoe, *The Complete English Tradesman*, 225.
11. Muldrew, *The Economy of Obligation*, 148.
12. Muldrew, *The Economy of Obligation*, 130.
13. This was indeed a source of political division: while the Whigs and merchant classes were broadly in favour of toleration, the Tories and landowners regarded the national fate as

intimately tied up with the Church of England. It is difficult to appreciate today why such political divisions were so heated. An excellent illustration of this is the outcome of a fiery but paranoid sermon preached on 5 November 1709 by high churchman Dr Sacheverell, warning of the threat of dissenters within the church seeking to undermine it – when Sacheverell was threatened with legal redress for stirring up conflict, some 250,000 copies of his sermon were printed, as large as the total electorate, and riots ensued destroying dissenting chapels, with Sacheverell hailed as a hero. Religious unity was clearly seen as the condition for national unity and mutual trust, just as it had been in relation to the 'Roman threat' of the previous century and a half.

14. Muldrew, *The Economy of Obligation*, 304, 309.

15. Muldrew, *The Economy of Obligation*, 311.

16. Muldrew, *The Economy of Obligation*, 234.

17. Muldrew, *The Economy of Obligation*, 255.

18. David Graeber discusses the striking case of Margaret Sharples, who was hanged in 1660 for an unpaid debt of 'stealing cloth' from Richard Bennett's shop, even though she had paid a deposit and agreed a future payment. His conclusion is that 'the criminalization of debt, then, was the criminalization of the very basis of human society. It cannot be overemphasized that in a small community, everyone normally was both lender and borrower'. Graeber, *Debt*, 333–34. Whatever the abuses in this particular case – and one can only imagine that few customers were willing to enter Bennett's shop thereafter – this cannot be regarded as a sudden accessibility of violence transforming society; the economy of obligation had always relied on the courts. Not only did court action peak much earlier in the 1580s, but it was even widely used in the fourteenth century. A recourse to litigation is a necessary part of any economy that agrees exchanges as quid pro quo; and perhaps only those cultures that do so can easily increase the range and quantity of mutually beneficial interactions.

19. Muldrew, *The Economy of Obligation*, 286–87.

16. MEASURE FOR MEASURE

1. An allusion to such arts of persuasion is present in Adam Smith's famous remarks about obtaining his dinner from the butcher, the brewer and the baker. *Wealth of Nations*, I.2.2: 26–27.

2. William Potter, *The Key of Wealth* (London: Printed by R. A., 1650), 7.

3. Potter was a member of the circle around Samuel Hartlib, which advocated progress through Baconian science and alchemy, accelerating nature's own progress towards perfection. Wennerlind, *Casualties of Credit*, 54.

4. Wennerlind, *Casualties of Credit*, 41.

5. John Briscoe, *A Discourse of Money* (London, 1695).

6. John Locke, *Locke on Money*, volume 2, ed. Patrick Hyde Kelly (Oxford: Clarendon 1991), 360–98.

7. Briscoe, *A Discourse of Money*, 136. Briscoe was actually an opponent of the Bank of England on the political grounds that a monied interest would put their own deposits first before the interests of state, but he was one of the promoters of the Land Bank of 1697 that completely failed to attract any significant subscriptions.

8. Thomas Hobbes, *Leviathan* (Cambridge: Cambridge University Press, 1996), 28–29; emphasis in original.

9. Hobbes, *Leviathan*, 32; emphasis in original.

10. Tony Aspromourgos, *On the Origins of Classical Economics: Distribution and Value from William Petty to Adam Smith* (London: Routledge, 2013), 11.

11. Aspromourgos, *On the Origins of Classical Economics*, 47.

12. Petty is quoted in Aspromourgos, *On the Origins of Classical Economics*, 30.

13. Mary Poovey argues that, in contrast to the Royal Society's emphasis upon observation, Petty used estimates since he appealed primarily to the authority of computation as opposed to

experience. *The History of the Modern Fact: Problems of Knowledge in the Sciences of Wealth and Society* (Chicago, IL: University of Chicago Press, 1998), 129–31.

14. Such principles, we may note, because of their reduction of quality to quantity, had eliminated methodologically all need for metaphysics.

15. Aspromourgos, *On the Origins of Classical Economics*, 39.

16. Petty, *Quantulumcunque*, question 23.

17. Petty, *Quantulumcunque*, question 26.

18. Philip Mirowski has articulated clearly why Petty failed to find a measure for intrinsic value: there was no fixed ratio between land and labour as basic commodities, and thus no measure for all other exchanges. Thus, 'If everything – the whole of social existence – may be indifferently bought and sold as commodities, where is the Archimedean point from which one might posit a value index other than money'? *More Heat Than Light: Economics as Social Physics, Physics as Nature's Economics* (Cambridge: Cambridge University Press, 1989), 153.

19. Massimo Amato and Luca Fantacci, *The End of Finance* (Cambridge: Polity, 2012), 195.

20. Wennerlind argues, to the contrary, that the recoinage became urgent in order to offer security for the new credit money. *Casualties of Credit*, 124.

21. Robinson comments that it is the exaltation of making money for its own sake to respectability and dominance that distinguishes the capitalist system from all former civilizations. *Freedom and Necessity*, 67.

22. The way in which gold and silver might increase the wealth of the nation by replacing insecure credit agreements is missed in Adam Smith's critique of mercantilism for ignoring productive resources in favour of stocks of gold. Smith's view presupposes that money is not in fact a productive resource, but a mere means of circulation. Smith, *Wealth of Nations*, I.5.6: 49; on the mercantile system, see chapter 4: 429ff.

23. A pamphleteer signed simply as L. R. argued that paper notes, which could only be redeemed if the government survived, would create a vested interest in the prosperity of the nation as a whole. Wennerlind, *Casualties of Credit*, 138.

24. J. K. Galbraith, *Money: Whence It Came, Where It Went* (London: André Deutsch, 1975), 21.

25. Andréadès, *History of the Bank of England 1640–1903*, fourth edition (London: Frank Cass, 1966), 135.

26. Cited in Amato and Fantacci, *The End of Finance*, 59.

27. Locke, 'Further Considerations', in Patrick Hyde Kelly (ed.), *Locke on Money* (Oxford: Clarendon, 1991).

28. Cited in Wennerlind, *Casualties of Credit*, 179.

CONCLUSION

1. Immanuel Kant, 'Answer to the Question: What Is Enlightenment'?, in Allen W. Wood (ed.), *Basic Writings of Kant* (New York: The Modern Library, 2001), 135; for a profound commentary, see Michel Foucault, *The Government of Self and Others: Lectures at the Collège de France 1982–3*, trans. Graham Burchell (Basingstoke: Palgrave Macmillan, 2010), 1–40.

2. Kant, 'What Is Enlightenment'? 138–39.

3. It is, indeed, a rather older conflict, having further roots in medieval debates between Dominicans and Franciscans over the metaphysical priority of understanding or will.

4. See Pankaj Mishra, *Age of Anger: A History of the Present* (London: Penguin, 2017).

5. See Kant, 'Idea for a Universal History', *Perpetual Peace and Other Essays on Politics, History and Morals*, trans. Ted Humphrey (Indianapolis, IN: Hackett, 1983); Kant, *Critique of Judgement*, trans. James Creed Meredith (Oxford: Oxford University Press, 2007), §§83–91.

6. Ludwig Feuerbach, *The Essence of Christianity*, trans. George Eliot (New York: Harper, 1957).

Index

About the Author

Philip Goodchild is Professor of Religion and Philosophy at the University of Nottingham, UK. His main expertise is in philosophy of religion, continental philosophy and the philosophy of political economy. His most influential books include *Deleuze and Guattari: An Introduction to the Politics of Desire* (1996), *Capitalism and Religion: The Price of Piety* (2002), *Theology of Money* (2007/2009), and *Philosophy as a Spiritual Exercise: A Symposium* (2013). This work is part of a trilogy consisting of *Credit and Faith*, *Economic Theology*, and *Metaphysics of Trust*.
ORCID ID: 000-002-8326-6721